0

And
these
signs
shall
follow

Serpent-
Handling
Believers

And these signs shall follow them that believe; In my name shall they cast out devils; they shall speak with new tongues; They shall take up serpents; and if they drink any deadly thing, it shall not hurt them; they shall lay hands on the sick, and they shall recover.

Mark 16:17-18

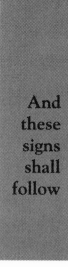

And
these
signs
shall
follow

Serpent-
Handling
Believers

Thomas Burton

The University of Tennessee Press / Knoxville

Frontispiece. Services at Dolley Pond Church of God with Signs
Following, Birchwood, Tennessee, 1947. Photograph courtesy of
J. C. Collins.

The paper in this book meets the minimum requirements of the
American National Standard for Permanence of Paper for Printed
Library Materials. ∞ The binding materials have been chosen for
strength and durability.

Library of Congress Cataloging in Publication Data

Burton, Thomas G.
      Serpent-handling believers / Thomas Burton.— 1st ed.
            p.   cm.
      Includes bibliographical references and index.
      ISBN 0-87049-787-1 (cloth: alk. paper).
      ISBN 0-87049-788-X (pbk.:alk. paper)
      1. Snake cults (Holiness churches)—Tennessee.
      2. Tennessee—Church history.
      I. Title.
BX7990.H6B87   1993
289.9—dc20

                                                    92-30409
                                                          CIP

And these signs shall follow

Contents

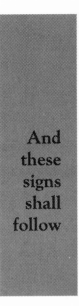

And these signs shall follow

Illustrations

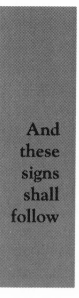

And these signs shall follow

Acknowledgments

It is not possible for me to recognize by name all those who have significantly contributed to this work or to express adequately my appreciation for the assistance of those whose names are listed. I can but indicate a few names and categories.

First are the serpent handlers themselves and the congregations to which they belong. Liston Pack has spent the most time with me, traveling, talking, explaining, introducing; Dewey Chafin next, who even taught me how to catch rattlesnakes. After these have been many, especially Jimmy Williams, Charles Prince, Allen Williams, Bob and Barbara Elkins, Lydia Elkins Hollins, Ray McAllister, Arnold Saylor, Bud Gregg, Carl Porter, Jimmy Morrow, Andrew Click, Perry Bettis, Henry Swiney, Bill Pelfrey, James Wade, Gerald Fleenor, Harvey Grant, Jack Young, Bradley Shell, Joe Short, Joe Laws, Kermit Creech, Pete and Charles Rowe, Gregg and Jamie Coots, Wayne Ray, Sherman Ward, Ulysses Prince, and Byron Crawford. And there are those associated with serpent handlers who have contributed significantly, particularly Geneva Chafin, Joyce Williams, Anna Prince, Linda Prince, and Flora Bettis.

Vital to this study also have been the family members of George Hensley who generously provided facts, anecdotes, family gossip, photographs, newspaper clippings, documents, telephone calls, and their time: J. R. and Anna Lee Hensley, J. C. and Juanita Lamb, Gene and Margaret Brown, Grace Cook, Dorothy Piotter, Raymond Piotter, Hannah Ruth Bettis, Winifred and Helen Harden, Loyal Hensley, LaCreta Simmons, Lloyd Stokes, Jean Potts, Janette Painting, LaVerne Dalton, Thelma Dean Hartman, and William Hutchinson.

East Tennessee State University provided physical support in various ways. The principal assistance was provided through the ETSU Center for Appalachian Studies and Services and its director Dr. Richard

Blaustein. A fifteen-hundred-dollar travel grant was given by the Research Development Committee; computer and secretarial assistance by Ruth Hausman, Ruth Tapp, and especially Deanna Bryant and Patti Patterson; important bibliographical research by Priscilla Wise, complemented by Ray Sybert; research assistance by my son Lewis, Todd Tipton, and Dona Addington; a carrel by Sherrod Library Director Dr. Fred Borchuck; and special considerations by the English Department through its chair, Dr. Styron Harris.

Various librarians, archivists, and individuals in records have played a vital role in securing information. Some have patiently given much time: Beth Hogan, particularly, Dr. Marie Tedesco, Norma Myers, Rick LaRue, Sherrod Library, East Tennessee State University; Lourdes Morales, Yvette Ashe, Hal Bernard Dixon, Jr., Pentecostal Research Center. Others too have been very helpful: Gayla L. Cassidy, Norman Fontana, Tomlinson College Library; Carol Norris, Rita Scher, Stephen Patrick, Sherrod Library; Betsy Williams, Quillen College of Medicine Library; Ned Irwin, Chattanooga-Hamilton County Bicentennial Library; the Department of Business and Records, Church of God (Cleveland); Gwen in the Hamilton County Criminal Court Clerk's office; Janie Sealey, Asheville Citizen-Times; file clerk, Chattanooga News-Free Press; Andrea Kalas, UCLA Film and Television Archive; Carol Vandevender, West Virginia Office of Vital Statistics.

Mike DuBose granted permission to use his engaging photographs, as did Bill Snead; J. B. Collins, Chattanooga News-Free Press, graciously offered his historic photos of the Dolley Pond Church of God. Larry Smith and Jim Slemp, ETSU Public Relations, provided multiple photographic prints. Dr. Harold Hunter, Church of God of Prophecy, gave significant information, as did Dr. Charles W. Conn of the Church of God (Cleveland). Lou Crabtree kindly permitted use of one of her poems.

Others who should be mentioned include Judge Oris Hyder, District Attorneys Al Schmutzer and C. Burkley Bell, Sheriffs Gail Colyer and Jack Arrington, Elmer Gist (State of Virginia Division of Forensic Science), Charles and Ola White, Julia Brumlow, Minnie Harden, and both Barbara Robinson and her mother, who are responsible for my first visit to a serpent-handling service.

Those who read the manuscript and encouraged its completion are vital to the work: especially Marie Graves from the first, John Taylor, Ambrose Manning, Anna Lee Gibson (who also provided videos and other materials), Peggy Henry (who gratuitously proofread), and David Hatcher, whose suggestions were extremely valuable in the final draft.

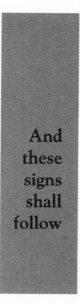

And these signs shall follow

Introduction

It was one thing to acknowledge the existence of a God, of powers and forces beyond your intellectual grasp. After all, something had been going on. Clem's leg had regenerated itself, and the copperheads hadn't struck, the flame hadn't singed. But it was quite another thing to play hot potato with copperheads yourself.

—*Lisa Alther, Kinflicks*

One Saturday evening in November 1972 I attended for the first time the Carson Springs Holiness Church of God in Jesus Name. The congregation was meeting, as it still does, in a converted hunting cabin near Newport in the mountains of East Tennessee. The worship service was much like that witnessed in many churches throughout the area—preaching, singing, and praying. What made this service different was a practice that is referred to as "following the signs" as set forth in the sixteenth chapter of the Gospel according to Saint Mark, a practice that includes handling deadly serpents.

I had never seen anything like it before. I must confess that my sensory responses were somewhat overloaded and my intellectual reactions were suspended, as if I were observing some strange ancient ritual. What was really going on here? What did it all mean?

The proposal to visit a serpent-handling church had emerged the previous year during a graduate class I was teaching in the techniques of collecting regional traditions. No one in the class knew of a church where the ritual was being practiced, but later one of the students informed me that her mother had taught a serpent handler in Newport and could arrange an invitation to visit his congregation. Not only was the invitation extended,

Facing page: Dewey Chafin, of Jolo, West Virginia, probably the most publicized of all religious serpent handlers. Photograph 1985 by Mike DuBose.

Serpent boxes at foot of pulpit in Jolo, 1988. Photograph by the author.

but another professor, several students, and I were permitted to film the service. In fact we were even allowed to film what occurred inside the home of the assistant pastor, where one of the members was taken after being bitten by a rattlesnake. Six months later at one of the church's meetings that same assistant pastor, along with the pastor's brother, died in another act of following the signs—drinking poison. Ten years after that event a colleague and I produced a documentary on the Carson Springs church exploring the effects of these two deaths, the litigation that followed, and the influx of the mass media.

My interest continued over the years and resulted in close associations with different serpent handlers, as well as another documentary on the conflict between the legal restrictions on serpent handling and religious freedom. It was not, however, until Fred Brown, a newspaper feature writer, requested that I introduce him to the church in Carson Springs and later proposed collaborating in some way on a book that the present work was ini-

*Barbara Elkins,
dominant force in the
Church of the Lord
Jesus in Jolo, who has
handled serpents in
religious services for
some fifty years.
Photograph by the
author.*

tiated. Fred and I, therefore, continued to attend various serpent-handling churches together and separately, sometimes accompanied by a newspaper associate, photographer Mike DuBose. From the first what was proposed was not a highly theoretical study, as might be the case in a theological, anthropological, or sociological treatise. We were interested rather in presenting a descriptive, analytical, partly oral-historical insight into the belief and the believers of the taking up of serpents as an act of Christian obedience. What we wished to provide was a perspective for understanding the people as well as the practice.

That perspective, however, is not easily attained. Since most of us tend to seek simple, concrete explanations for phenomena, it is easy to view one aspect of serpent handling rather than the whole and, consequently, either to romanticize or brutalize the people and the practice. One can feel after attend-ing a service that it is completely irrational, wild—people running around, falling down, quivering, uttering strange sounds; drinking deadly poisons; taking venomous serpents (giant and tiny ones, coiled, extended, limp, knotted together, rattlers, cottonmouths, copperheads, cobras) and staring at them nose to nose, wrapping them around their necks, wearing them on their heads, pitching them, carrying armloads of them, shaking them, petting them; displaying arms tattooed with snakes, hands atrophied by bites, fingers missing, clothing embroidered and etched with snakes—or feel the same sense of the bizarre after going into homes and seeing live deadly snakes in closets and adjoining rooms, pictures framed on the wall of people with handfuls of rattlers, photo albums of disfigured bodies from venom poisoning, or a huge frozen rattlesnake taken out of a freezer by a relative of a person whom the serpent killed during a funeral service for yet another snakebit victim. All of this can seem as abnormal as an episode from "The Twilight Zone."

On the other hand, one can leave a service or a home and feel completely awed by the faith, sincerity, and mysterious power manifested by these people—sensing that somehow they know, feel, have something in their lives that is redeeming amidst a lost world. As Lou Crabtree's persona in her poem "salvation" says, "jesus jesus this old body aint so important / i got holiness flirtin with death." The integrity of serpent handlers strikes one as something real in the omnipresence of appearances, an inspiring breath in the mists of "mouth honor." Moreover, their commitment to the "word of God" is clearly metamorphic, like that of Tennyson's knights to the vows of King Arthur:

> . . . for every knight
> Believed himself a greater than himself . . .
> Till he, being lifted up beyond himself,
> Did mightier deeds than elsewise he had done.

What then is bizarre from one perspective may be profound from another, or humorous at the same time. Even serpent handlers sometimes laugh about a brother's good time in the Lord, or smile and say: "Yeah, he's something now." Anna Prince, the daughter of a serpent handler, recounts sign followers "in the Spirit" being completely uninhibited as though they were preschoolers, instances like that of one believer who poured drinking water over his head while others got up and danced in the water and laughed at him, yet loving him and having fun. There is in fact a childlike innocence about the whole religious approach of these believers.

It is difficult to get at the reality or essential nature of the ritual of serpent handling. Serpents have been associated with religion in some form

Lydia Elkins Hollins, organist, singer, and serpent handler, entering the Church of the Lord Jesus (her mother, Columbia Gay, died at twenty-two of serpent bite). Photograph 1988 by the author.

since ancient, perhaps prehistoric, times. Some of the earliest artistic images—from twenty to thirty thousand years ago—are serpentine, and serpents were significant in the religions of the ancient world of the Fertile Crescent, from Egypt to India, the region "thought by some experts to be the primary source of snake worship and symbolism" (Morris and Morris 10, 41). Serpents have continued to be prominent in religious rituals up to and including modern times in various parts of the world. Even though what the serpent specifically represented to the prehistoric cave dweller is unknown, it clearly has always inspired the creative imagination: "On the one hand, it has been a symbol of procreation, health, longevity, immortality and wisdom; on the other, it has represented death, disease, sin, lechery, duplicity, and temptation" (Morris and Morris vii).

Serpent handling by Christians in modern times, however, has been evidenced for less than a hundred years, although contemporary adherents trace their belief to the words of Jesus to his disciples immediately prior to the ascension as recorded in Mark: "And these signs shall follow them that believe; In my name shall they cast out devils; they shall speak with new tongues; They shall take up serpents; and if they drink any deadly thing, it shall not hurt them; they shall lay hands on the sick, and they shall recover" (16:17-18). Because of the initial words of this text, serpent handlers are often referred to as "sign followers." They consider themselves simply Christians who are following the will of God.

Sign followers believe that at some point they are baptized by the Holy Ghost. They trace this baptism to the description of the Day of Pentecost found in the second book of the Acts of the Apostles, where the followers of Jesus "were all filled with the Holy Ghost, and began to speak with other tongues, as the Spirit gave them utterance" (verse 4) and where "many wonders and signs were done by the apostles" (verse 43). Serpent handlers as a group are considered by church historians to be part of what is referred to as the Pentecostal movement in America. From a historical point of view, this movement may be said to have evolved around the turn of the twentieth century from the closely preceding Holiness movement, which was rooted in the eighteenth-century Wesleyan emphasis on experiencing Christian perfection after redemption. During the close of the nineteenth century and the early part of the twentieth, many individuals and groups separated themselves from established religious organizations in order to avoid what they perceived as liberalism, modernism, and worldliness. Some of these groups remained independent; some joined fellowships and created new religious organizations, which in some cases splintered and formed other church bodies or again became independent. Church historian Charles Conn says that between "1880 and 1926 a total of twenty-five Holiness and Pentecostal churches were formed" (11).

The Church of God, which early in this century claimed exclusively for itself serpent handling—among other signs—as a manifestation of its authenticity, was among the earliest Holiness separatist groups that became Pentecostal bodies (Conn xxvi). This church, with headquarters in Cleveland, Tennessee, but organized in Monroe County, Tennessee, in 1886 with eight members as the Christian Union, changed its name to the Holiness Church in 1902 and to the Church of God in 1907 (xxix). It may be easily confused with others since its name is used in one form or another by some "200 independent religious bodies in the United States" (Mead 74).

The Pentecostal experience as set forth by the Church of God occurs in three stages (M. Crews 8). First comes *regeneration*, or new birth, when one experiences salvation from sin. Second is *sanctification*, when one experiences instantaneously the eradication of one's sinful nature, which effects Christian perfection or the "way of Holiness," the pursuit of a strict moral, self-denying, ascetic lifestyle. The third stage is *baptism of the Holy Ghost*. The manifestation of the Holy Ghost in the speaking in tongues first occurred in the Church of God in 1898, according to Conn, "ten years before the outpouring of the Holy Ghost in California in 1906 which is popularly regarded as the beginning of the modern Pentecostal movement" (25). There is, however, considerable debate as to "when the full blown Pentecostal doctrine of Spirit-baptism emerged" (Hunter, *Spirit-Baptism* 5).

The Church of God has disassociated itself from the practice of serpent handling as it is presently known, but Pentecostal serpent handlers share with other Church of God members and other Pentecostals a belief in salvation and sanctification (though diversely interpreted): in the baptism of the Holy Ghost, the manifestation of the Holy Ghost in the speaking in tongues, and in the other eight spiritual gifts listed in 1 Corinthians 12:1-10. They do not share with all Pentecostals their interpretations of the other "signs," which include the taking up of serpents.

Apparently serpent handling sprang up during the first ten years or so of the twentieth century in East Tennessee, and certainly from this state it was widely disseminated. I have paid particular attention, therefore, to serpent handling in Tennessee, although a complete historical investigation of the practice in the state was not attempted. Such an examination would be valuable for each of the states where serpent handling is evidenced, yet only a few have received such treatment and only in unpublished theses (Ambrose, Kimbrough, Vance).

We asked ourselves why this ritual got started in Tennessee, if in fact it did, instead of somewhere else. The necessary elements were certainly present, but what exactly those elements were and whether they were present in other places are difficult matters to explain, perhaps ultimately inexplicable. Certainly vital was the presence of a fervent fundamentalist religious community with a traditional approach to biblical interpretation and with traditional values that would evoke and reinforce the practice. Ministers were most certainly preaching on the key biblical text in some manner as a part of Jesus' final words; and no doubt the situation in many places was as Henry Swiney describes it up on Newman's Ridge in Tennessee, where serpent handling had long been preached by those who did not practice it. To sign-following believers, baptism of the Holy Ghost had been manifested for decades by the speaking in tongues; taking up serpents was a phenomenon just waiting to happen.

Once the ritual started, that it spread quickly and widely indicates the presence of the vital elements elsewhere, particularly in the southern Appalachians and other parts of the South. But one crucial factor necessary was there being the right person to take up a serpent first and to convince others to do the same. That person in East Tennessee was George Went Hensley. About the same time in northern Alabama, according to Paul Vance (36), the individual was James Miller. Miller was a Baptist preacher in DeKalb County whose knowledge of Holiness belief was apparently from hearsay rather than direct contact, and it was from his personal reading and religious experience that he independently took up serpents in 1912. He then experienced what many sign followers were to undergo, being forced out of conventional churches for handling serpents. Miller was turned out of the Baptist church that he served, yet he continued to preach in homes and brush arbors. Miller was responsible for the introduction of the belief of serpent handling not only to the Sand Mountain region in 1912 but ultimately to the southern Georgian counties of Berrien and Cook (5, 55), vital since 1920. Also linked to Miller's influence may be the many experiences that Church of God evangelist J. B. Ellis had with serpent handling at religious meetings during 1912 in Straight Creek, Alabama (M. Crews 84; *Evangel* 9 May 1914: 8). Then again, the instances observed by Ellis—who was not a

Facing page: "Sign follower" Jimmy Larr in Baxter, Kentucky, belying any special technique in taking up serpents. Photograph 1985 by Mike DuBose.

Lydia Elkins Hollins handling a rattlesnake. Family members looking on are her uncle Dewey; grandmother Barbara, who raised her; and step-grandfather Pastor Bill Elkins. Photograph 1991 by Bill Snead.

practitioner and who preferred that handling not occur at his meetings (Ellis 49)—may be independent of both Miller and Hensley.

Since, however, George Hensley is the person generally credited with the founding of contemporary serpent handling, and probably justly so, it was imperative to present as much information as possible about him. There is relatively little specific published data pertaining to Hensley, but to know that which is reported in oral historical accounts as well as in public record is to know in large measure not only the man himself but also the story of sign followers in general. The itinerant ministry, the themes of sermons, the preaching style, the unyielding adherence to belief in the face of social and legal opposition, the ebb and flow of public impact, and the complexity of personal involvement—all are features of George Hensley's life

that are simultaneously highly individual and representative.

When Hensley began serpent handling, he was associated with the Church of God, although later he resigned his ministry with that organization. Other Independents, such as Miller in Alabama, introduced serpent handling in their areas; but the evangelists of the Church of God, particularly at first, were responsible for the spread throughout the missionary fields. A graphic picture of those early days of sign followers as they went forth is provided by their reports from what they considered the "Battlefield" to the official church paper, the *Evangel*.

Serpent handlers immediately came into conflict with those who did not believe as they did, both the rabble and the religious. Later they confronted legal restrictions on the practice of their belief. George Hensley himself was faced with a city ordinance in Bartow, Florida, as early as 1936 "forbidding the transportation, exhibition of or the handling in public of any venomous reptile within the city limits unless the snake is confined in a suitable container or pen." Violations of the ordinance were "punishable by a fine of $100.00 or 60 days at hard labor" ("Fatal Snake Bite" 1). This particular legal action was taken, as was to be the common circumstance, in response to a person's being injured by a serpent bite; the Florida ordinance was passed the day Alfred Weaver died after being bitten the previous evening in a revival service of a Pentecostal church. Within a few years a number of southern states began to legislate against the practice. Kentucky was first in 1940; Georgia, Virginia, Tennessee, North Carolina, and Alabama were to follow. Of particular interest is the litigation in Tennessee; it provides the means of examining the principal legal issues involving serpent handling, including the subtle constitutional balance between maintaining both a healthy society and the religious freedom of its members.

One purpose of our visits with sign followers was to refine our sensitivity toward these people, not to delineate all their highly idiosyncratic beliefs or to ferret out all the people involved in the practice. Since each person is viewed as responsible for his or her own interpretation according to one's own light, there is a wide variety and fluidity of explications of scriptural texts. Even relative to the statement regarding the signs in Mark 16, there are great differences in particulars, such as the meaning and significance of the words *shall* and *if* in "They *shall* take up serpents; and *if* they drink any deadly thing."

The differences in scriptural interpretation are the bases of numerous divisions and are important in a number of ways, but these are beyond the intended focus upon the sign of serpent handling. Whereas an in-depth analysis of the other four signs, the nine spiritual gifts, the handling of fire, the trinity, and any number of other beliefs would be helpful in providing theological perspective, many of these doctrines have received considerable examination by other writers and are not distinctive to serpent handlers. Consequently, rather than producing a demographic study of the faith or a comprehensive religious treatise analyzing systematically all the tenets of the belief, I have attempted to emphasize the quality and nature of that belief.

There are drawbacks, though, in focusing on the single sign of taking up serpents. For one thing, it reinforces a distortion represented by expressions such as "snake religion" or "snake cult." I have tried to offset this impression by emphasizing that these folks are normal people; they are not members of an esoteric, unorthodox religion; they are Christian fundamentalists who view the taking up of serpents as only one teaching of the Bible. Toward conveying a proper perception of sign followers, sketches are presented of the lives of some individual serpent handlers. The choice could have included any number of persons, but perhaps none better. Still, as clear as our insights might be, they are from the point of view of outsiders, even though we often allow serpent handlers to speak for themselves. The inside perspective we lack is provided by an autobiographical account of Anna Prince, who grew up in a family in which the father and a brother were serpent handlers. Implicit in her narrative is the whole story of serpent handling—its faith, sincerity, simplicity, joy, suffering, light, and darkness.

Other paths could have been taken, but the one I have chosen is to provide both by exposition and illustration a sensitive, general, but scholarly perspective on the people and the practice of sign-following serpent handling. An interviewer for National Public Radio asked recently what had caused me to maintain contact over the years with a number of serpent handlers. My answer was that they are good friends. They are strong, courageous, ethical people. Some have remarkably gentle spirits, and some, I believe, would stand by me in the face of any opposition. I am proud of their friendship.

An especially compelling quality of most serpent handlers is that they are willing to die for their beliefs. Not only are they willing, they repeatedly verify that commitment directly and concretely. Like Matthew Arnold's Scholar Gypsy, they seek "the spark from heaven" whereas most of the people of the world are "Light half-believers of our casual creeds."

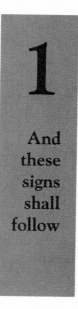

1

And these signs shall follow

Believers

Serpent handlers are believers—believers in God, in God's power, in the Bible as God's word, in God's direction through the Holy Ghost. Many of them have great faith, and they will often quote the passage: "Now faith is the substance of things hoped for, the evidence of things not seen" (Heb. 11:1); but their faith in large part is based not on "things hoped for" and "not seen," but on personal experience. And that experience goes beyond the handling of serpents. For example, in the case of Marvin "Bud" Gregg from Morristown, Tennessee, snakes had nothing to do with his becoming a believer. Rather, as he relates, it had to do with something that happened in his life one Saturday afternoon when a group of people were gathering for evening worship:

> Some of them began to come in at one, two o'clock in the afternoon for services at seven thirty. I never would go to church. That day, my uncle was working on a car down here and had some cleaning fluid; and my daughter at that time was a real small child, she got out there and drunk some of the cleaning fluid and she died. And a lot of people say, well, how do I know she died? Well, her breath left her body and her jaws locked; she turned black, and blood was coming from her mouth. And people began to pray, began to get around her and pray; and when they did—I guess they prayed for five minutes—anyway, the Lord moved and brought her back, put breath back in her body. And that night, I repented.

This claim of the dead being raised is not uncommon among those who handle serpents. It is an experience that Charles Prince from Canton, North Carolina, witnessed in his family:

Peter [the apostle] even went far enough as to raise the dead, and that's something we shouldn't flinch at a bit because I have seen the dead raised. Now I was raised up in a Christian home. I never have had a reason to doubt, because they was a girl—she was about maybe ten years old at the time. She had died, and her daddy was standing in the road, and it a-raining, and flagged down my daddy—knowing that my daddy and some other people coming from church were believers. He flagged them down, and they stopped there in the rain—and they's a mill right near it—and took the girl inside this mill where they grind corn and laid her on the table there. And I don't know how many people, examined her there carefully, said she was done getting stiff and that she was cold; she wasn't breathing, no heartbeat, no pulse. Just plain dead. But this brother was crying and said, "Pray for her." And they prayed, seemed like over and over for maybe forty-five minutes. Directly, that girl sat up. And then she's alive today and has got children. And she was brought back from the dead.

Besides this incident, Charles experienced other wonders manifested by his family.

Now my mother, she had real good victory in handling fire for years. I hadn't seen her do it recently, but back when I was just a child, it was common then to have coal, be burning coal in heaters. And she'd open the front of the heater and dip her arms plumb down—I mean, plumb down into those coals—and come out with both hands full and put them against her clothes and hold it like this [*cupped in her arms*] and shout around through the church. And they'd be coals fall off, and my dad would come along and pick them up, them still red. Now he never did really

get the victory that good himself; but seeing her, he could come along and pick those coals up, and they wasn't even hot—they's red, but they wasn't even hot.

Harvey Grant, from Sweetwater, Tennessee, also experienced his mother's "miraculous" powers— gifts of prophecy and healing. He recalls her at different times starting to shout, then getting down on the floor and praying that God reveal to her if somebody were sick so she could go heal them:

I seen the power of God knock her down, where she got the Holy Ghost, in the kitchen and her head hangin' out the back door. I went over to her. I said, "Mother, you hurt?" She just raised up and went to speakin' in tongues, and so she was done prayin' and she said to my Daddy, said, "John, I'm gonna go up here and tell ——— to set his house in order, he's gonna die. Daddy said, "You're crazy." She said, "I'm goin'." Said, "His blood's not gonna be on my hands on the Day of Judgment." She went up there and said, "How are you, Mr. ——— ?" He said, "Oh, I feel good"; said, "Feel like I'm gonna be here about twenty years." Mother said, "Mr. ——— , God sent me up here to warn you. Set your house in order; you just got three weeks to live." He said, "You're crazy, Mrs. Grant." She said, "I may be, but your blood's not held by my hand." Next day he stepped on a nail, set up blood poisoning, and about three days after that he had to have his leg took off at the knee. And about two days before three weeks was up, they took his leg off up here in Charlotte. He died. He went unprepared to meet God.

And Mother went to pray for a woman that got syphilis. And Dr. Roberts had a sign on, "Quarantine," and said to mother, said, "You can't be goin' in there all by yourself." She said, "I'm not"; said,

Services at the Church of Jesus Christ, Baxter (strychnine, anointing oil, and fire-handling torch on the pulpit). Photograph 1983 by Mike DuBose.

Visitors William Hollins (with serpent to face) and Bruce Helton at Baxter. Photograph 1983 by Mike DuBose.

Jenette Kennedy, who regularly handles serpents at Jolo. Photograph 1988 by the author.

"I'm takin' God in there with me." Said, "He sent me down here to pray for ———. He's gonna heal her." He said, "All right." God healed that woman. She went and got married after that in Detroit and had three or four children. That's what kind of a God it is.

Charles Rowe from Baxter, Kentucky, recounts miraculous events of a different nature in his family. His sister was apparently possessed with a demon. Rowe was on the floor beside her in the church, praying, and she started to strangle as if she were about to choke to death. Then she spit up a glob that he assumed to be the evil spirit. After this, she wanted to be rebaptized by her father. She was then taken to the river, but it was so cold that, before she and her father could enter the water, ice had to be chipped away. As she emerged, Charles wrapped a blanket around her but noticed that her body was warm. She refused the blanket, saying she did not need it. Others there testified that she walked to the house several hundred yards away in clothing dripping wet without feeling any cold.

Bud Gregg has had similar experiences of con-

fronting evil spirits. During church services, demons have talked to Pastor Gregg, even growled. Sometimes angels are seen. Pastor Gregg has seen the Holy Ghost in the form of a mist inside the building. When he has had a full measure of that Spirit, he has been able to cast out demons, handle any serpent, drink the "deadly thing," and handle fire (even a propane torch) without being burned.

These individuals, along with many others, accept all the signs—speaking in tongues, casting out demons, handling serpents, drinking deadly things, healing the sick—because "It's Bible." Their belief, however, transcends simple acceptance of the validity of the Scripture since they have personal experience to substantiate it. Relative to serpent handling in particular, as Pastor Carl Porter of Kingston, Georgia, strongly affirms, "I do know that it's right. I've had it move on me too many times for me to ever say that it wasn't right, for it's right. There ain't no way around it."

In explaining the purpose of the signs, serpent handlers emphasize Mark 16:19-20. These verses provide the context in which the signs were ini-

Tim McCoy testifying before the church at Jolo. Photograph 1991 by Bill Snead.

Visitors and members handling serpents at Jolo Homecoming: Barbara Elkins (behind pulpit); Verlin Short, Mayking, Kentucky (center); Larry Muncy, Logan County, West Virginia (behind him); recent member Jeff Hagerman (to the right); and thirty-year member Ray McCallister (extreme right). Photograph 1991 by Bill Snead.

tially given as well as their relationship to the preaching of the gospel.

> So then after the Lord had spoken unto them [Jesus' disciples], he was received up into heaven, and sat on the right hand of God.
>
> And they went forth, and preached every where, the Lord working with them, and confirming the word with signs following.

The argument by contemporary serpent handlers is that they are believers and that the signs follow them exactly as Jesus promised. The purpose, they say, is the same as for the disciples of the first century, that is, to confirm the word preached

to unbelievers. Their experience in the signs, however, goes beyond confirming the gospel to unbelievers; it confirms their own belief that the power of God is available to them. Moreover, that power is unlimited, but it takes repentance, remission of sins, and a godly life for them to receive it fully. As the late Perry Bettis of Birchwood, Tennessee, forcefully expressed in one of his sermons:

> Jesus Christ come, brother, and he granted them a mission to go out. He sent them out, brother, two by two. And he give them power, hallelu, to cleanse the leprosy and raise the dead and give sight to the blind, heal the lame, heal

Lydia Elkins Hollins at the organ in the Church of the Lord Jesus, Jolo. Photograph 1985 by Mike DuBose.

every kind of disease there was. Jesus give them the power to do it. Why, there ain't no power like God's power.

Have you got the Holy Ghost? Huh? Yeah. You got the greatest power in you that's in the whole world. Right inside that body is the greatest power that's ever been known to man and ever will be known to man, is God Himself. You that's got the Holy Ghost has got it in you. It's your fault for not usin' it. It's not God's fault. God give it to you to use, and if you don't want to get in shape to use it—hey listen, hold it, hold, let me tell your mind, listen to me. God give me the gift of ministry, the preachin' the word. I can't read, I know that; but, wait, when God moves on me, I can preach. God

give me that gift. It's in me. I'll preach on the street corner, I'll preach on top of this building, I'll preach anywhere that God—hallelujah, I'll preach it right in the Devil's face. I don't care. But God expects me, me, me, myself to live the life to be proud of there to do that job.

God expects you, brother, and you, sister, to live their life to where God can work through ye. Why, God's not goin' to work through that den of Babylon. They is things that we do that God absolutely hates—six and sixteen, brother, Proverbs.

Tonight, children, we need to learn how to worship God worser than anything in the world. We learn how to repent a little bit, but some of us ain't learned how to fully repent. Repentance is to

Church of the Lord Jesus at Jolo. Photograph 1985 by Mike DuBose.

quit doin' anything and not go back to it. Change your walk of life, change your way of thinkin', change your way of talkin', change everything in you—Jesus can make a new creature in God out of you.

Still, a question that always rears its head, even to serpent handlers, is: "What if someone gets hurt or dies?" As in almost every other aspect of the beliefs of serpent handlers, it is inappropriate to begin an analysis of this question with the preface, "Serpent handlers believe . . . ," as though there were a consensus of opinion or an authorized position. One of the few instances in which such a

statement would be appropriate is: "Serpent handlers believe in autonomy regarding their interpretation of the Bible and their perception of the direction of the Holy Ghost."

Serpent handlers do, however, often divide themselves into two groups according to their interpretation of the Godhead and, subsequently, according to the name in which they are baptized. That difference centers upon two concepts, often referred to as "Trinity" and "Jesus Name": (1) The Godhead is made up of three entities. From this tenet a person is baptized "in the name of the Father, and of the Son, and of the Holy Ghost" according to Matthew 28:19. (2) There is "One God

Members of the Church of the Lord Jesus healing the sick by prayer and laying on of hands, one of the five "signs" cited in St. Mark 16:18. Photograph 1991 by Bill Snead.

and Father of all" (Heb. 4:6), Jesus and the Holy Ghost being human and spiritual manifestations of God respectively. A person from this perspective is baptized "in the name of Jesus Christ" according to Acts 2:38; *Father, Son,* and *Holy Ghost* are not considered to be names, unlike "Jesus." Variations on the second concept for the name employed in baptism are "Jesus" (omitting "Christ") and "the Lord Jesus."

Other differences revolve around foot washing, the Lord's Supper, divorce and remarriage (called "double marriages"), and various other practices and interpretations of Scripture. Some of these differences occur within congregations as well as between churches. Some serpent-handling churches describe themselves as Pentecostal Holiness, but they are not members of any formal organization— they are independent. The term *Holiness people* is sometimes defined simply as "people living godly, holy lives," and *Pentecostal* as "anything that speaks in tongues and claims the Holy Ghost."

Serpent handlers might attend religious services where they would be allowed to handle serpents but be excluded from preaching and even be considered as "going to hell" unless they changed their beliefs. On the other hand, preachers who are known as serpent handlers might be allowed to preach to non-serpent-handling congregations. The late Perry Bettis's personal circumstance is a good illustration of the complexity in matters of fellowship that exists among the various churches. Bettis was baptized in the name of the Father, the Son, and the Holy Ghost at the Dolley Pond Church of God with Signs Following, but some years after he changed from "Trinity" and was baptized "in the name of Jesus Christ." (Dolley Pond, in Grasshopper Valley, Tennessee, was originally serpent

JESUS MADE THE WORLD.
St. John 1:10

Tommy Coots (deceased) former pastor at Middlesboro, Kentucky, following a common practice of placing serpent on the pulpit. Photograph 1955 by Mike DuBose.

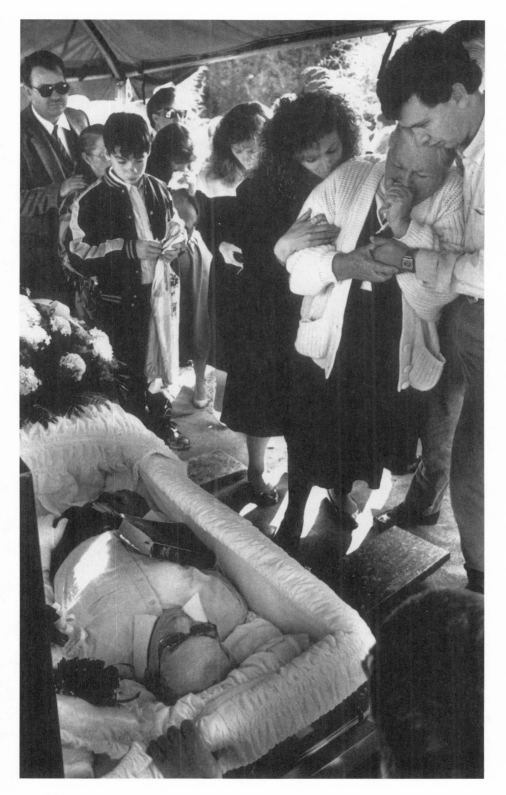

Lue Blankenship, mother of Ray Johnson, who died of serpent bite, being comforted by her daughter and son-in-law. Photograph 1991 by Bill Snead.

handling and non-denominational, but later the building was sold to a group of non-serpent handlers who are members of the Church of God of Prophecy.) He worshipped with different groups, and his participation in their services varied according to the particular church he attended: "Well, I went to the 'Free Holiness,' but they wouldn't let me preach, but I handled the snakes. And I preached, mostly when I preach, I preach in the Jesus Name movement, and that's saying whether they be 'Lord Jesus' people or whether they be 'Jesus Christ' people or 'Jesus'; and, you know, I preach mostly in them churches. But a lot of the 'Jesus Name' people will not have serpent handling no way you can fix it." The comments of Liston Pack, of Newport, Tennessee, give further insight into the complexity of the divisions:

> This "Free Holiness" don't accept the Church of God. They will not, yet they handle serpents. They won't accept. And the "Jesus Name," what they call the "Single Name" or the "Jesus Name," will not accept the "Lord Jesus" people. And some of them believes in foot washing and the communion, and some don't. And those of them that do won't participate with the others. However, you've got different groups in different areas that handle serpents, but they won't communicate with one another because "you wash feet and I don't," and "I'm a 'Free Holiness' and you're a 'Church of God'"; "he's a 'Jesus Name,' but he handles."

All these people from Grasshopper Valley, Tennessee, to the Appalachian Mountains in West Virginia and the state of Florida ([years] back) in the eastern half of the United States—there'd probably be four to five thousand people

handling serpents at one time. But maybe out of five thousand, they wouldn't be over fifty or sixty in joining in believing accurate the same thing. There'd be "Free Holiness," "Elders" Church of God [the Church of God with headquarters in Cleveland, Tennessee], Pentecostal, different types of religion, "Jesus Name," and "Lord Jesus." And everybody says that they are right in what they were doing, but they won't communicate with one another.

As one would expect, the answer given by serpent handlers to the question "What if someone gets hurt or dies?" is varied. The responses to the death of Charles Prince from serpent bite and strychnine poisoning during a religious service is a case in point. Those who spoke and prayed at Charles's funeral, including Charles's father, Ulysses G. Prince, repeatedly stated that it was the Lord's will that a servant of God (who was obediently following the signs) had been taken "home" according to a divine purpose not necessarily clear to those who remained behind on earth. The fatal result for them did not reflect anything negative toward the participant or the practice itself.

There are other views. Bud Gregg, who felt especially close to Charles both as an individual and as a member of the congregation he pastors, thinks there were several factors involved: "I believe he tried to help the lost people, help anyone, anywhere, that he saw in need—I believe Charles Prince tried to help him. The Devil didn't like that and so, therefore, I believe that he was fighting Charles with all he had. The Bible says we war 'not against flesh and blood, but against powers and principalities and spiritual wickedness in high places.'"

Besides this war with the powers of darkness,

according to Pastor Bud, there was opposition from the church where Charles was bitten. Gregg says, "I talked to Charles about the difference in the belief, you know, how some people just absolutely got a spirit against Jesus Christ people. They definitely got a spirit against it, and it's not so much the word *Jesus*; it's the word *Christ* that a lot of people don't like. He knew that they were against him because we talked about it many times; and he said, 'I believe that I can help those people if I keep going up there.'" Charles, though, was not able to change their attitudes; instead, they felt that Charles was bound for hell. Gregg thinks that this "spirit" of opposition was detrimental to Charles's safety: "I was not there at that service. I don't know what really happened, but a person working the signs of the Gospel needs to be careful about what's going on in the congregation around him. When you're taking up serpents, I do believe that there needs to be love and unity in the church in order to do it for complete safety."

Of utmost importance, however, as Gregg explains, is the spiritual state of the handler himself.

> We shouldn't walk after the flesh, and the flesh is contrary to the spirit, and the spirit contrary to the flesh. It's a warfare there. The Bible says it's a warfare, and it's continuously fighting; and if there's something in our flesh that fights against our spirit, which is the Holy Ghost, then I believe we should do away with that completely before we should try to work the works of God. I believe everything should be right in the sight of God in your life before you started to work in the works of God.

Although Pastor Bud does not "judge" Charles,

he does not think "everything was right in the sight of God." He even "prophesied" a warning to Charles the evening before he was bitten:

> I won't say all that the Lord had showed me; but anyway, the Lord showed me that the serpent bite was coming, and I talked to Brother Charles immediately after the service on Friday night, and I told Brother Charles, I said, "Brother Charles, the bite is coming." I said, "Now, I don't know what the consequences of the bite is going to be." But I knew that it was going to be a bad bite, and I told my brother, I said, "Whatever you do, you need to be careful." Now, Brother Charles had this saying—someone asked him to be careful one time, and he said, "How can you be careful with a rattlesnake in your hand? The anointment of God is the safety."

Pastor Gregg's warning included the admonition that Charles was "exalting" himself rather than God in the signs. Charles, nevertheless, said that he would have to go on and accept whatever God's will was. After he was bitten, he confessed to the congregation of being guilty of self-exaltation.

Charles's sister Anna also says that God spoke to her regarding Charles's death. The revelation, she says, was a single word, "attitude." Unlike her father, who would fast and pray prior to handling serpents, Charles would go to services at different churches, two, three, four times a week—week after week—carrying boxes full of serpents that he had predetermined to handle. She felt that Charles had gotten things out of perspective and that his death was divine retribution, as well as a forewarning to those who were following Charles's example. Her feeling was reinforced by a vision of another individual who in viewing her brother's body in the casket saw a cobra in Charles's bosom, which was interpreted as a sign of evil.

Years before his death Charles himself talked about some of the circumstances that would cause one to be hurt in the signs. (The word *hurt* is used by sign followers specifically to signify suffering serious effects from taking poison or being bitten.) He, in agreement with Bud Gregg, was aware of the effect that those who attend the service can have on the serpents: "I mean, if they's a lot of unbelief, and a lot of fear, then the serpent—you can see it—acts different too, some of them swinging, moving real fast and struggling; but fear in the church can cause that. But if the church is united in faith, in just a good strong, steady faith all over the church, then just about anything can be done." Also along with Brother Bud, Charles felt that of supreme importance was the state of the individual—a fearless state produced by God's Spirit. "If we know that His Spirit is dwelling in us and His hand has made that serpent, He's able to control it and He does control it. But when we do get hurt by them, it's when we get fear." At one time in Charles life that fear was dispelled only by the anointing of the Holy Ghost, but later another element became increasingly important—his faith in the assurances of the Bible.

> I used to only take the serpents up in the anointing. I mean, the Spirit of God would come over me so strong that that fear would temporarily be gone. Then when that started wearing off, then I'd realize I was there maybe looking a rattlesnake in the eye; and they'd be a sudden fear come over me. And, boy, it'd feel so good when I got it out of my hand. But now, that was just only with anointing without

the faith, without the faith that backs it up. But the anointing still comes, but I've got a faith that when the anointing starts to wear off, still the faith is in that written word that backs it up. But with anointing alone, then the fear has a tendency to come back. But that faith is in that written word, and it's solid like a rock. It just don't give way, it don't, don't leave.

But unwavering faith was not always the circumstance with Charles. He described an instance of handling fire in which his faith wavered and he was burned:

> And that was along about the time when I got serpent-bit those three times. And my faith wavered at that time. But now we've had copperheads that would actually, you could put your hands—it's double screened—and you could put your hand on top of the wire, and they would hit this bottom wire so much that it'd wet your hand and make it sticky with venom. But then when the Lord moves, you can reach in there and get them, and no harm. I mean, there ain't no wire in between, but they become harmless.

Charles also said that, if he were bitten, he believed it would be from a lack of faith: "I definitely believe it would be my faith wavering if I did get bit; but then, if I could get a-hold of my faith, then after I'm bitten, then they'd still be no harm."

Charles suggested that some sign followers who are bitten are simply having their prayers answered:

> There's some that'll get up and preach and say, "When the Lord takes me, I hope he takes me by serpent bite or in the signs." Then if they make that request to the Lord, then it might be that

He'll go ahead and give them what they requested. And that's the way they go. They's one brother up in West Virginia—I've not really met him—but I've heard of him a lot. I've heard of him that he's been bitten up near a hundred time. But the way he bases his faith is that they will bite him, but they won't hurt him. And so it's a miracle that he's lived through that many bites. But he says that he wants to be bit by all different kinds of serpents including the cobra and the serpents he has imported from other countries; and yet he says he wants to die by a copperhead bite, which is the least likely to kill you.

Charles, on the other hand, did not want to die by any of the signs, and for a selfless reason: "I'd rather believe that I won't be hurt by the signs. I'd rather believe that I won't, and if the Lord calls me out—well, it would be all right if I died by someone that hates the word, some man would kill me, or some government was to kill me because of serving the Lord. Now that would be all right, but I wouldn't want to die by a serpent or by any of the signs. I don't really want to be hurt by them because it don't really edify."

Jimmy Williams, who also died in the signs (in his case, drinking strychnine) took a somewhat different stance. He pointed out that the verse in Mark said "they shall take up serpents," not "they shall not bite." He also felt that, if one died in following God's Word, one would be doing just what the apostles did: "If you can keep your mind right on the Lord, well, God will move for you every time regardless of what it is. If a serpent bites you, you have to keep your mind right on the Lord; if you get your mind off the Lord, you'll swell up. Well, there have been people that died from ser-

pent bites, but if you keep your mind right on the Lord, well, God will recover you. You won't have to suffer too much. But there's always been people who suffered for the gospel's sake. Just glad to be counted worthy."

Another explanation offered by some believers for being bitten is that it is a proof to unbelievers of the imminent danger. Byron Crawford, former assistant pastor of the Church of the Lord Jesus Christ in Kingston, Georgia, holds that opinion: "I'm not trying to justify serpent bites and people getting hurt, but if I'd handled serpents, and all the serpent handling churches handled them all the time, and nobody ever got bit, and nobody ever suffered—the world out here would say, 'Hey, we can do that 'cause they ain't getting hurt by them,' you know, 'big deal.'"

This perspective is rejected by Pastor Henry Swiney of Sneedville, Tennessee, who has handled serpents for some fifty years without getting hurt, although he has been bitten on some seven or eight occasions: "There come a man through Kentucky, said that if they didn't bite you and people didn't get hurt, they'd say that they didn't have no teeth. I say they don't know what they say; God knows about that." Pastor Swiney says that he always waits on the anointing: "Every time you feel good, you don't shout; and every time you feel good, you don't take up serpents. If you do, you're going to get bit one of these times when you're not anointed to do that job." But if he were bitten when he was anointed to handle a serpent, he confidently states: "I don't believe that I would die or I don't think it would hurt me."

Many serpent handlers would agree. One of the members of Swiney's congregation, however, was hurt by a serpent in a service in Kentucky.

Gerald Fleenor, the young minister who was bitten, feels he knows what went wrong:

> Well, I preached and I've been preached to that there's something to get a-hold of you and will take care of you, and no harm will come to you when you're handling serpents. And I've experienced that and I know that it's true. Now Brother Swiney was preaching that day that I got bit and he was preaching—and I never will forget it; as a matter of fact, I guess it was the next day in ICU [*his family had put him in the hospital*] when I thought about it—he was preaching on James 1, on patience, having a perfect gift. Brother Swiney was handling them and maybe a few others, and I believe it was Brother Swiney who said pour them out over where he was at. And I went over to the box, and instead of pouring them out (like he told me to), I wanted to handle them so bad 'cause it's a good feeling to get to handle them. And I guess I moved a little bit quick and got them out instead of waiting for that anointing to take care of me. And when I did, I knew what I had done (and shouldn't've done it) but before I could get them back up and get rid of it or give to someone who did have anointing in handling them, one bit me.

As far as Gerald Fleenor is concerned, the experience taught him patience, but his belief is unchanged: "I still believe that a man can take them up and handle them, always will. I mean, I know that people miss at times and people get bit, people dies, and one thing or another, but it still doesn't change the word of God. I don't care who dies or whatever; it's still right."

Byron Crawford believes in a "perfect" anointment, that is, as he explains, "You can get in the power of God so strong that they ain't nothing can

hurt you." He also believes that there is purpose in getting hurt other than proving the danger to unbelievers; there is a reason relative to the believer as well: "It's a test of faith. God tries you sometimes to see whether you're really gonna stand for him, and hold the faith or not. 'He that has suffered in the flesh has ceased from sin.' Now they is some suffering that we have to do, you know. I don't believe that that's all the suffering that you have to do; but sometimes it happens that way, and sometimes it don't." But dying in the signs is quite another matter to Crawford. Regarding the "deadly thing," he says, "I believe this much, that if you get hurt on the strychnine and you die, I believe that you miss God, you know. I really believe that you missed him because it's not supposed to hurt you. And I've been hurt on the strychnine—I mean, I've had it to work on me; and it's not because God let me down. It's 'cause I just didn't hold the faith like I should have."

Bud Gregg talks about a condition similar to that mentioned by Crawford, in which the serpents cannot bite, when one is in the "perfect will of God." He tells of having serpents strike him numerous times, from one hand to the palm of the other, without being able to bite. He, however, has been bitten seven times, and one time he was hurt; but he also believes that if one is hurt, then something is wrong. In his own situation, he had been told by God not to go to a particular place, but he went anyway: "I knew that I wasn't going to die. I knew that I was going to hurt some. I knew that I was going to suffer some, but it was for disobedience to the Spirit of God. And the Bible says, 'When the hedge is broken, the serpent will bite.' Disobedience is sin. What breaks the hedge? Sin breaks the hedge." Gregg also believes in the handling of serpents by

Dewey Chafin, elder of the Church of the Lord Jesus, Jolo (bitten over one hundred times). Photograph 1991 by Bill Snead.

faith, as well as handling them by anointment, though his position is somewhat different from that of Charles: "Faith is good, and it's all right to work the works of God by faith, but we have something much greater than faith. We have the anointing of God. We have the Spirit of God. I believe we need to use it."

To some believers in the signs, however, even being anointed is not foolproof. One must be sure of being "led by the Spirit" and not misinterpreting the anointment, lest mishap occur. Liston Pack, for example, says that it was his misinterpreting the anointment that caused him on one occasion to be bitten:

> I know when I got bit, I was under the influence that one [a serpent] couldn't bite you under the anointing, but I misunderstood the Scripture. They was a woman possessed of the devil. This woman, she was screaming out like she was a Christian, dancing in the aisle—I knew better because God had showed me. But, see, I was hung up on serpent handling; I was wanting to handle that old black rattlesnake. Well, I got anointed really to cast the devil out. Well, on a Wednesday night, here I would go get him [the serpent] and I come out with him—I'm bad to play with him, you know; I want to play with him, just toss him around, pitch him up and catch him. Well, he whopped around, and he hit me in the left hand behind the thumb. Whenever he bit me, I just pitched him, and he hit directly in that box. And I wrapped a handkerchief around my hand. And that Saturday night, I fasted and prayed; and God, he opened it up to me what I was supposed to have done. Well, believe it or not, I got anointed the same way Saturday

> night, and the same timber rattler was there, and I had the anointing come on me again. My hands drawed back, and I went in and pulled him out; and when I done that, the Lord spoke to me, said, "Put him up."
>
> Well, I just laid him back, and here that woman come down the aisle screaming. I just tapped her on the forehead, didn't have to pray all day because she went out like a light [*i.e., she became unconscious when the evil spirit left her*]. But if I'd did that the first time, I could have ignored that first bite—I sure could. But I was wanting to handle the snake. I wasn't wanting to help somebody else.

Although some serpent handlers would disagree with Pack and say that the anointment is the same for all the signs, Dewey Chafin of Jolo, West Virginia, talks about the differences as well as the feeling he has if he fails to obey any anointing of the Spirit:

> And then if you don't really obey it, like following the Spirit of God—if you don't obey that, then you feel like you're spiritually dead. It ain't just takin' up serpents like that. Anything, like praying for people, or anything that God wants you to do—it's a different anointin', but you get the same aftereffects, the feeling that you don't obey God. It's a little different feeling [the anointment to handle serpents]; it mostly works on my arms and my hands. The strychnine always works just in my stomach and my throat. When I get a taste in my mouth [*if he doesn't get a bitter taste like strychnine, he doesn't feel he is totally anointed*], it's alright.

He adds, "I can drink strychnine by faith just like I can handle serpents," that is, without the anointment. Chafin, who has been bitten over one hundred times, believes that, when he is hurt by a serpent bite, it is a victory of the Devil, since the serpent to him is a visible part of the Devil. If, however, he were to die—and there have been times when he thought he might—it would not be a victory for the Devil because only God determines when a person dies. Chafin's conclusion about dying in the signs is: "The Lord giveth, and the Lord taketh away; blessed be the name of the Lord."

Serpent handlers are, first of all, believers—believers in God and His word as presented in the Bible and through direct revelation. They are sign followers secondarily because of that belief, as well as recipients of spiritual gifts, witnesses of miracles, and acceptors of what they perceive as God's will.

2

And these signs shall follow

Where and When It All Started

George Went Hensley is generally recognized as the founder of Christian serpent handling in modern times and as the source of its wide dissemination. Hensley may or may not have been the first person in the twentieth century to handle deadly serpents in obedience to a literal interpretation of the biblical text "they shall take up serpents," but he did lay claim to being the first. His first wife denied that claim, saying that George had seen someone else take up serpents prior to handling them himself. The whole matter is something of a mystery.

George's account of his initially taking up a poisonous serpent circulates widely. The general outline of the incident is that he went up into White Oak Mountain near Ooltewah, Tennessee, to a spot called Rainbow Rock. There he prayed for a divine sign to direct him how he should respond to the verse in St. Mark relative to serpents. Then indeed before him appeared a rattlesnake, which he picked up without being bitten. He descended the mountain and went to the Grasshopper Church of God. He entered with the serpent, and members of the congregation, following his example, took it up.

He must have enjoyed telling about how it all happened, for his grandson Winifred Harden recalls:

> He'd always tell us his tales and stories of what he experienced through prayin' and God giving him the courage to take it [the serpent] up, and he believed that in the Bible, that verse in Mark— when he got to that and he read it, the tale was he went out in the mountains and prayed and there was a rattlesnake and he handled it. I've heard him say this, "If you go to believe the Bible you gotta believe it from the front to the back. You can't cut out some pages and skip it."

George Went Hensley, generally credited with introducing serpent handling in the twentieth century. Photograph c. 1927 courtesy of La Creta Simmons.

Homer Tomlinson, the son of A. J. Tomlinson, the first general overseer of the Church of God, gives other accounts of the initiation of serpent handling—apparently but not necessarily contradictory in the main. In *The Shout of a King* Homer Tomlinson says: "The accounts which we will give will show that miracles of healing, and all the other signs in St. Mark 16-18, started right with me, or rather I should say I was present. This included the taking up of serpents, of raising the dead, of drinking deadly things, without hurt" (5). The account of serpent handling to which he obviously refers is given later in the description of events surrounding the con-

version of Hensley: "We saw the wonder of the taking up of serpents in 1908. . . . Some of the people twelve miles south of Cleveland, in a community called Owl Holler, having received the Holy Ghost, built a church, set a day to dedicate it. My father being away they asked me to come, preach the sermon of dedication" (39). At the conclusion of the afternoon service, Homer gave his "first call for sinners to come to the altar, kneel there and be saved, sanctified, and filled with the Holy Ghost" (39-40). He says that five young men responded; then he goes on to single out one of them:

It is of a third one of the five from Owl Holler I would speak more particularly, whose name was George Hensley. Stirred in his soul to serve the Lord as fully as he had served with moonshine and outlaw gangs in those mountain scenes, shortly after his conversion went over in the next "Holler," set up a brush arbor, lighted it with gasoline torches of those days, and began to preach. As in all our churches, he was preaching of the signs that would follow, and this, the third sign, of Mark 16:17-20, "They shall take up serpents."

Possibly more in sport and rowdiness than in any sense of making a mockery of Hensley's religion, his moonshine and gambling cronies, some of whom were known to have taken part in actual killings, gathered a box full of deadly snakes of those parts, copperheads, water moccasins, rattlesnakes, turned them loose right in front of him where he was preaching. The audience scattered in terror, but George Hensley, in pure faith, the power of the Holy Ghost upon him, just stepped from the platform and began to gather the serpents up in his arms, like a boy would gather stovewood in his arms to carry into the house. Continuing his preaching, and calling upon his old cronies to forsake their evil ways, turn to the Lord and be saved from sin, he walked out toward them in the shadows outside the brush arbor, and they now

Family homecoming for George Hensley's first wife, Amanda, in 1946. Photograph courtesy of La Creta Simmons.

fled in terror before him. He returned to his pulpit, the whole crowd came back, and before this amazing miracle a revival broke out that brought thousands from everywhere. (39-42)

The year given, 1908, and the circumstances described at the Owl Holler dedication may be accurate in most details. Homer Tomlinson in his later writings was seemingly given to exaggeration and self-aggrandizement. This propensity would make suspect such details as "brought thousands from everywhere" and "all the other signs . . . I was present." But in the main, as Charles W. Conn, author of an authoritative history of the Church of God, suggests, there is no ostensible reason to doubt Tomlinson's veracity in this report, especially considering the circumstance of its being

Tomlinson's second sermon. The year 1908 is the one Hensley himself gives for his conversion, and the role Tomlinson played in that conversion is at least suggested by a letter from Hensley's wife Amanda written to the church paper about her sanctification and reception of the Holy Ghost: "I began to pray for God to save my life and my soul. . . . I asked Him to spare my life till I found out what was the matter. Then I heard Bro. Homer Tomlinson preach and saw they had more of the Lord than I did. I began to trust the Lord from that time, and he has healed me, sanctified me and given me the Holy Ghost" (*Church of God Evangel* 4 April 1914: 7). When these incidents occurred, or whether they occurred in conjunction with George's conversion, is not stated. Amanda apparently had been converted earlier, as had George, while attending a Baptist church, but she did not choose to be baptized at that time.

Even if the description of the Owl Holler service is basically accurate, that George Hensley first took up serpents as Tomlinson describes is another matter. Tomlinson says that shortly after the Owl Holler dedication Hensley set up a temporary brush arbor in the next hollow. J. C. Lamb, a resident of the Owl Holler area and a relative of George by marriage, says this site could be the brush arbor that George had set up in Scroggins Holler on the land owned by George's sister Jane and her husband. Even if the events at the brush arbor were nearby and "shortly after" the dedication service, the bringing in of serpents would strongly suggest that it was known that George already handled serpents. The incident could have been preceded by the traditionally reported experience at White Oak Mountain. Tomlinson does not say that he himself was at the brush arbor; it is likely that the account is an anecdote he was told and did in fact occur, but not in the sequence Tomlinson gives. In that case, Hensley could have first handled a serpent at White Oak Mountain soon after his conversion in 1908 and the brush arbor story might be a fusion of the Grasshopper church incident with one of any number of situations that occurred later, perhaps years later.

There are other details in Tomlinson's account that are difficult to reconcile. Some seem inexplicable. Following the description of Hensley at the brush arbor, Tomlinson says, "I did not hesitate to publish this in our church paper" (*Shout of a King* 42). If he means these particular incidents were published in 1908 or soon thereafter, he would be referring to their being in the church's evangelistic paper *The Way*. Unfortunately, relevant issues

of *The Way* are not available, but reports of George may have been included in it. If he means simply that he did print references to Hensley's serpent handling, he could be referring to later editorials in the *Evangel*, which he published while serving as his father's assistant. Since Hensley had been converted but had not become a member of the Church of God in 1908, Tomlinson may not have known much about his activities until 1914 when George held a meeting at the South Tabernacle in Cleveland. Tomlinson, therefore, may be generally correct about the circumstances in which he himself was involved but inaccurate in regard to those activities of his convert where he was not personally present.

One would expect that the diary of his father, which Homer Tomlinson edited, would clarify these questions about the initiation of serpent handling. Instead, although there are relevant entries, they do not resolve the problems:

[13 Jan. 1908]. Also the 16th of Mark came up, these signs shall follow, dwelling on casting out devils, speaking in tongues and taking up serpents. [*What brought up the subject of the signs? Was it initiated because of the actions of some individual, specifically Hensley?*]

[4 Aug. 1908.] God wonderfully confirmed the word with signs following. [*Although there is no mention of serpents, was the confirmation by speaking in tongues only or by other signs as well, including the taking up of serpents?*]

[26 Nov. 1908.] During my sermon I broke down and went to crying, and the Holy Ghost caught up Homer, my own son, and he went to preaching in tongues. [*How does this relate to the date of Homer's second sermon, which "shortly" anteceded George's handling serpents? Would there be a distinction be-*

Amanda Mertila Wininger, George Hensley's first wife. Photograph courtesy of J. R. Hensley.

tween "preaching in tongues" and standing before a congregation and preaching a "complete" sermon?]

[4 Jan. 1909.] Homer is wonderfully used by the Holy Ghost. Preached one sermon. [*Did Homer or A. J. preach the sermon?*] (*Journal of Happenings,* unnumbered)

Other considerations regarding the date that Hensley first took up serpents revolve more around his religious status. At the time of his conversion he may or may not have received the Holy Ghost as Tomlinson said he did; but the handling of serpents, as Charles Conn agrees, could have come

immediately after conversion in 1908 as a result of his believing that Mark 16:18 applied to him as a believer. He may well have handled serpents prior to 1910 when he was starting to preach, abstaining from tobacco, and "resorting to the Bible way for healing" or before becoming a member of the Church of God in 1912 or being baptized by the Church of God in 1913. As Conn suggests, the baptism of the Holy Spirit would almost certainly have been confirmed by the speaking in tongues, but the handling of serpents at that time could have preceded or followed sanctification, Holy Spirit baptism, or coming "to see the light" in matters of personal conduct. As an example, Harvey Grant, who was a convert of Hensley and who handled serpents before he was baptized, says: "I took them up when I just repented, didn't even have the Holy Ghost." Being a preacher would also not necessarily have been associated with whether one took up serpents, nor would becoming a member of the Church of God. As Conn states: "There was very little pressure about becoming a member of the Church of God at that time. It is most believable that he [Hensley] would want to keep himself apart from an organization, to keep associated with the Independent churches. That was not uncommon."

Family stories also provide important information in establishing where and when George's serpent handling began. J. C. Lamb remembers George's sister Jane saying that the serpent handling got started "right over here," meaning near her house, which would have included Rainbow Rock, Owl Holler, and Scroggins Holler. All these were on or adjacent to her land. Her statement might also apply only to her brother's first picking up a serpent, or it might include his introducing the belief to a group of worshipers. Lamb also remembers Jane's daughter, his mother-in-law, saying specifically that George handled serpents before she was born, which would have been prior to January 1912. (There is a record in the 18 September 1915 *Evangel* of a Jane Hensley of Loudon, Tennessee, likely George's mother, receiving the Holy Ghost in 1912, a date which may or may not have relevancy to George's religious experiences.)

There is additional support from interviews with George that the initial act of his taking up a serpent did indeed occur at White Oak Mountain "shortly after" his 1908 conversion. Chattanooga newspaperman J. B. Collins, for example, talked with George and gives the following account.

> This strange cult originated one summer day in 1909 atop White Oak Mountain. This cradle of the snake-handling sect forms the eastern rim of Grasshopper valley, and its slopes the banks of winding Tennessee River.
>
> On this particular day, George Hensley, a small but powerfully-built man in his early thirties, decided to settle once and for all a matter of great importance to him. . . . The first phrase in St. Mark 16:18 had caused him much spiritual unrest. . . . this, he felt, was a command spoken by Jesus after resurrection and just before His ascension.
>
> Hensley had never taken up serpents, yet he believed that if he was to receive eternal life after death he must do so. His decision was to risk his life in order to have rest from his spiritual burden. . . .
>
> In a great rocky gap in the mountainside he found what he sought, a large rattlesnake. He approached the reptile, and . . . knelt a few feet away from it and prayed loudly into the sky for God to remove his fear and to anoint him with "the power." Then suddenly with a shout he leaped forward and grasped the reptile and held it in trembling hands. . . .

His first evangelistic endeavor was in Grasshopper valley, which he entered within a few days after his encounter with the mountain rattlesnake. (*Tennessee Snake Handlers* 1-2)

Harvey Grant, Hensley's serpent-handling associate during the 1940s, gives a similar account but in a different time of year:

> And Uncle George when he first took up the serpent, he was up there in Owl Holler, Tennessee. And his wife was readin' that "They shall take up serpents," and he said, "Wait a minute, honey," said, "I'll be back directly." And he went up in the hollow a little ways, and they's about a three-four-inch snow on the ground. And he reached back [made] an altar; and he said he went to prayin' and askin' God, said, "Now, this must mean I can handle serpents, you let one come a-crawlin' out of that snow." Uncle George said he didn't know how long it'd been, but he looked up and there's one comin' out of that snow. He said, "It's just as pure and white as snow."

Both of these retellings, with the exception of the season, agree almost verbatim with one given by Perry Bettis, the last active serpent handler in Grasshopper Valley. A somewhat later date is given in another personal account by reporter K. Kerman. In a 1938 story for the *St. Louis Post-Dispatch* Kerman states that Hensley "says he started the snake handling rite 28 years ago in Sale Creek, Tennessee" (11)—that is, in 1910, near Birchwood and the Grasshopper Church of God.

Although there is strong evidence that Hensley's serpent handling began during the period 1908-10, there is good reason to think that it occurred three or four years later. The earliest record, for example, of serpent handling in the official Church of God paper the *Evangel* (which began in 1910) appears in an editorial on 24 January 1914. The editor, A. J. Tomlinson, implies that it was during 1913 that this sign had been "slightly demonstrated." He makes no reference to any experiences with serpent handlers of fellow gospel preacher J. B. Ellis in 1912 (M. Crews 84), although he does include a report in 1914 from Ellis, who attested to "considerable experience with those who take up serpents" (9 May: 8). In a 1916 editorial (August 26: 1) Tomlinson says that he supposed hundreds had taken up serpents "in the last two or three years," i.e., 1913 or 1914. His calculation refers solely to the activity of "our people," the Church of God, although he consistently considers the sign of handling serpents as following only members of the Church of God. Hensley would have been included in these figures since he became a member in 1912. It would appear at first that Tomlinson's editorial would set the origin of serpent handling in 1913, but the emphasis of Tomlinson's statement is not on the date serpent handling was initiated. Rather, his focus is on the prevalence of the practice without harm among the members of the Church of God. In fact there is no direct reference in the *Evangel* to the first time a sign-following believer took up a serpent.

There is additional support, however, in several newspaper accounts for 1913 being the year Hensley initiated serpent handling. Reported personal interviews in 1936 state: "'I've been handling serpents for 23 years,' he said"; and "Hensley said in his 23 years of snake-handling demonstrations . . ." ("Preacher Juggles Snake" 1; Abbott 1).

On the other hand, there are newspaper stories that infer other dates. An eyewitness to Hensley's death in 1955 writes in an article published in 1973: "His followers said Hensley, 56 years ago [*i.e., in 1899 if this means prior to his death*], picked up a rattler in Tennessee's Grasshopper Valley and it didn't bite him" (Kimsey D9). Another report states: "George W. Hensley, 70 years old, started the snake rites when he was 14," i.e., in 1899 if calculated on his being "70 years old" in 1955 ("Snake Kills Cultist" 12).

Apparently there is no contemporary document that directly establishes the time of Hensley's first taking up a serpent. (Homer Tomlinson's book was not written until 1967.) What seems to be the first contemporary citation of Hensley's handling serpents is one that records the Cleveland revival of August 1914 (*Evangel* 12 Sept. 1914: 6; 19 Sept.: 2-3). It is likely that this revival is the one Homer Tomlinson describes immediately following his account of the brush arbor incident, although he does not date the occasion:

> Enemies, however, took this occasion to bring in deadly serpents, seeking to discredit The Church of God in Cleveland. Only a single serpent was brought in, tempting Hensley, when of a sudden the power of the Holy Ghost came upon him, and he reached into the box and took up the viscious [*sic*] rattlesnake, and it became docile in his hand. Others, including my sister, Iris, in some amazing testimony that this sign would also follow them which believed, anointed by the Holy Ghost, and acting beyond their own volition, one by one took the serpent, and from hand to hand. The serpent remained docile, and before hundreds of witnesses, all without hurt, the four-foot rattler was then returned to the box, and was later taken out and destroyed. (*Shout of a King* 42)

The juxtaposition in Homer's mind of the brush arbor incident and the Cleveland revival may sug-

George Hensley, center, seemingly around thirty years old with an unidentified man and woman (perhaps his sister Bertha). Photograph courtesy of La Creta Simmons.

gest that the former event, where he says serpent handling began, occurred in 1913 or 1914.

There are other references to Hensley's handling serpents in 1914. Articles in the Chattanooga *Daily Times* of that year report his conducting a tent meeting at Ooltewah in which a serpent was handled by "fifteen or twenty 'believers'" ("Reptile in the Meetin'" 3). But George could have been handling serpents much earlier. These articles follow the Cleveland, Tennessee, meeting, which would have drawn the attention of city papers to the sign followers, who otherwise might have escaped notice. Af-

ter all, these were farmers in a remote area where travel was basically still by foot or horse-drawn vehicle. (Even when serpent-handling was re-established in that area thirty years later, the Chattanooga press did not pick it up for several years, and then only by chance [Collins, *Tennessee Snake Handlers* 17].)

As rewarding as it would be to know exactly where and when George Hensley first took up a serpent—or whether in fact he initiated the practice—the solution to the mystery remains elusive. If one were writing a novel, one could choose any of several plots. As good a scenario as any might be that George, a relatively young married man of mountain stock who had not remained completely faithful to his strong religious background, hears during the late summer or early fall of 1908 another even younger man speaking in strange tongues and preaching about miraculous signs that would follow believers, such as taking up serpents without harm. He hears and believes. He feels that the preacher has "more of the Lord" than anyone he has ever heard, and he answers the altar call. But he goes away puzzled though fascinated by the words of Jesus in St. Mark about handling serpents. He has seen some of his drinking buddies do anything on a dare, even pick up a snake; and he resolves that if it is meant for him to take up serpents, the Lord will somehow direct him.

To continue this scenario: time passes—perhaps that fall or the next summer or fall, he goes up into the mountain to pray, still puzzled about the verse in St. Mark. He feels the power of God upon him, sees a rattlesnake, takes it up, and is not bitten. The Lord has spoken to him. Later he goes several miles down the road to a church that belongs to the same organization that the inspiring young preacher belonged to. There George testifies of his personal experience and manifests God's revelation to him by handling a serpent. Others believe, and some follow his example. Periodically during the summer months, serpents are handled.

Then, in the summer of 1910, he is called to preach; in 1912 he joins the Church of God, which was responsible for showing him the way. He finds that he has no trouble drawing an audience—even in brush arbors on his sister's land—when he preaches on the text, "They shall take up serpents." Crowds of hecklers and others come to see him prove his belief. In 1914, news finally gets to the headquarters of the Church of God, whose general overseer—the father of the very same young man whose altar call he had answered only a few years earlier—invites George to come and preach in Cleveland. He goes. His reputation as a snake handler precedes him. He is again tested by unbelievers and has "victory" over death. Even the overseer's own daughter takes up serpents. Others, who have already been filled with the Holy Ghost and spoken in tongues, see handling serpents as another sign of the Spirit confirming the word and the church. The papers hear about what is going on and eat it up—the best show in town. The believers go forth, the signs following them. And it all started with George Hensley.

3

And these signs shall follow

George Hensley

If George Went Hensley had been as dedicated to other areas of experience, particularly domestic life, as to his religious practices, his influence on the ritual of serpent handling would no doubt have been entirely different.

It is not certain when Hensley first came into the Owl Holler area near Ooltewah, Tennessee, where he apparently took up his first serpent. In 1880 his family, according to the United States Census, was living further east in the Watterson community of Hawkins County. George told his son Loyal that he was originally from West Virginia (corroborated by Loyal's birth certificate but invalidated by another certificate that lists Scott County, Virginia; perhaps George's spotted career had something to do with the discrepancies). George's grandparents were from Tennessee as well, and his statement to Loyal that the Hensleys further back had come from Pennsylvania may very well be true since settlers commonly migrated from that state down the Shenandoah Valley.

George's family probably moved by the time he was ten years old from Hawkins County to Loudon County. His sister Jane married James Brown of Loudon County around 1890, and it was there that George married Amanda Wininger in 1901 (the year after he had given up his membership in the Baptist church), and apparently it was his mother who was writing from there to the *Evangel* in 1915.

George's sister and her husband moved to Ooltewah near Chattanooga, where they purchased some four hundred acres of land, mainly for the timber. Brown made good money as a molder in a Chattanooga foundry during the week and as a saw-mill man weekends on his land in Ooltewah. George and his wife moved to the Browns' farm and lived there in a shack where George could work in the

George Hensley with his sister Bertha Weaver when she was a minister of the Church of God in Cleveland, Ohio, c. 1931. Photograph courtesy of Grace Cook.

lumbering business with his brother-in-law, as well as in the local mines digging ore for use in paint. George's small stature contributed to his efficiency as a miner and was not detrimental to his other occupation, which was common to the area—moonshining.

Whether his mother, Susan Jane, was living with his father, Emanual, at the time is unknown. The mother was ill and apparently living with her daughter Jane in 1919 when another daughter, Bertha, returned to Ooltewah to visit her (*Evangel* 1 Feb.: 2). Jane Brown's daughter Grace Cook recalls as a child seeing her grandfather Hensley, but he and her grandmother had apparently already separated. George's mother moved to Ohio (perhaps after her illness) to live with Bertha, whose daugh-

ter Dorothy says about her grandfather Emanual, "He chased women"—an interesting comment as one thinks about George's life.

George's sister Jane was a devoutly religious person who knew her Bible, and her son was later a song leader and singing-school master. His sister Bertha was a Church of God preacher. The strong religious influence on the family must have come from their mother, a woman who is cited as sending five dollars to the Church of God tabernacle building fund late in her life during a time when money was hard to come by (*Evangel* 1 Jan. 1916: 3).

Some ten years after George's marriage to Amanda he was preaching, later pastoring in Cleveland and in Birchwood; then in another ten years he had "backslid." Fourteen years after his Owl Holler conversion, Hensley had slipped from his godly life and fallen into some of his former activities, including drinking, and abandoned his family. He resigned his ministry in the Church of God and left the Ooltewah and Birchwood area. The reason as stated on a Revocation of Ministry form by Tennessee Overseer M. W. Litzinger is: "resigned—has much trouble in the home."

There are several versions of the immediate cause of his leaving, but the account by his son Roscoe, who was seven years old at the time, places the blame on George. Roscoe's mother Amanda, the other children, and Roscoe were returning from church one evening and saw George sitting on the bank at the side of the road, drunk. George made certain accusations that culminated in a fight with another man. Later that evening George said that Amanda could have the children. She left for Chattanooga the next day, where she found work with a hosiery mill, which provided housing and other necessities for her and the six children. George left for parts unknown, but a mailing address for him that year was at his sister's home in Walbridge, Ohio.

Even before he left, George was a poor provider for his family. His son Roscoe remembers that he held revivals locally, as well as all up and down the Tennessee River valley. He apparently never really owned a house, except a shack he and one of his sons built later on to live in for a short period of time. Sometimes, as his daughter Jean remembers, they lived in the church buildings. Once they lived upstairs in the back of the church, another time in a space separated from the worship area by quilts. In 1918, when he was the first pastor of the East Chattanooga Church of God, he may have lived in a parsonage, as he did later in the Birchwood area. But when the weather allowed, he was out evangelizing.

Soon after Amanda's move to Chattanooga, according to Roscoe, she became bedridden and incapable of supporting the family. She and the children were assisted for a while by George's sister and husband from Birchwood who came to live with them. Later Amanda and her children were to return and live in the Birchwood area. As Roscoe remembers, George made only one visit to the family in Chattanooga; he came by and gave the children a ride in a car. George wrote Amanda for a divorce; but he was, for all practical purposes, out of touch with the family for about twenty years.

A short part of that time George spent in a county jail. He had gone back to moonshining with a black man, was caught for selling liquor, convicted, and on 27 March 1923 was fined one hundred dollars and sentenced to four months in jail. According to Roscoe, his father had served most

George Hensley with his second wife, Irene Klunzinger, on her father's farm in Ohio. Photograph c. 1927 courtesy of La Creta Simmons.

of his time in the workhouse at Silverdale near Chattanooga when one day, being sent off for a bucket of water, he did not return. He hid out in the mountains above his sister's farm in Ooltewah where he had grown up; and although law officers looked for him there, he was not captured.

There is a curious entry in the Hamilton Criminal Court docket noting that a George Hensley was found *not* guilty of selling liquor on 8 May 1923, a month after George's incarceration. There are some questions about the entry; but apparently it would not be at all impossible, considering court procedures of that time and place, that George could have been charged a second time without being detected as a fugitive.

George turns up next in Ohio, where he probably went to visit his sister Bertha Weaver and his brother. It was not too long until he was back to preaching, holding revivals, and faith healing. He may have been preaching at the Salvation Army in Cleveland where he met one of the workers, an attractive young woman, Irene Klunzinger. She believed she bore a curse placed on her while in her mother's womb by a Gypsy her mother had caught stealing. Irene thought Hensley could cure her, and apparently the family did too at first. He did not, but he did marry her. Irene was twenty-two, George almost forty-seven. Irene's family were very religious, staunch German Lutherans originally, living on a well-managed, prosperous hundred-acre farm. It seems that George was instrumental in their becoming Pentecostals themselves for a while, hoping that their daughter's problems would be miraculously removed.

Irene and George went to live in Washingtonville, Ohio, where George's brother was and where George could get a job in the coal mines. Faith, their first daughter, was born while they were living there. Several years later when their second child, Loyal, was born, they were living in Malvern, Ohio. Irene and George began to have trouble off and on; and according to her sister, seven or so years after they were married, Irene returned home for an extended period of time. According to family members, George would always "sweet talk" her into returning. It is not difficult to imagine what the Klunzingers later felt about their daughter's marriage to a southern Holiness serpent-handling faith healer who did not take to keeping a job. Irene's sister Lavern remembers her parents saying that George would find some way to make money so he would not have to work. She also re-

members her mother continually making clothes and sending them for Irene's needy children.

Through correspondence with Irene, however, Mrs. Klunzinger received a worse impression of George than simply of a person who did not want to work. As a result of that correspondence some members of the Klunzinger family have come to think of George as a charismatic but evil, perverted, hypocritical man. Lavern states directly, "My sister went through living hell." Even Loyal's impression of his father is that George was not a very religious person. Loyal considers that his mother Irene was a genuinely devout person devoted to Christian living and who tried to convince George to be the same. She would read the Bible to George, assist in the services by reading the scriptures for him, and encourage him in living the Christian life; but to Loyal's thinking as a boy, George was not devout. He did not spend a lot of time praying, fasting, or doing good works, nor did he seem particularly interested in helping others. When the deacons came, Loyal says, it was a different story. Then he would put on an extremely religious appearance, but when they left, he "would take it off like a coat."

What particularly caused family problems seems to be his not working to support the family. Although he did apparently have several jobs while living in the northeastern area of Ohio, this problem continued to be a bone of contention. It is interesting that on Loyal's birth certificate George is listed, not as a minister, but as a laborer. Loyal thinks his father worked at the brickyard. One of his jobs, according to an incident recounted to Loyal, resulted in George's being electrocuted by high-voltage lines but being brought back to life by prayer.

George continued his evangelism, even holding a meeting near Toledo at the Church of God his sister Bertha pastored in Walbridge. That meeting included the handling of serpents. Bertha herself did not personally take up serpents, although she did assist George in his preaching. She would read a scripture and George would expound upon it, the same method he employed with Irene and earlier with Amanda. Apparently George could not read anything, even road maps. Some of the family are not sure whether he could write his name. Loyal remembers his father saying that he had gone to school three days but had been kicked out and had never returned. George preached in an oral tradition in which the preacher calls for a particular scripture, sometimes interrupting the reader in order to repeat it, then expounding on the word, phrase, or passage before proceeding.

George's wanderlust, however, never subsided for long. In 1932 he returned to his home ground in the Southern Appalachians, across the Tennessee border in Kentucky. "With the help of Jim Jackson, a local Holiness man, he built a 'free Pentecostal' house of worship, the 'East Pineville Church of God,' and installed himself as pastor" (Kane, "Snake Handlers of Southern Appalachia" 60). Three years later, in July, a daughter, Jean, was born at nearby Pennington Gap, Virginia. In August, George reportedly lived not far away in St. Charles and was going out from there preaching and handling serpents. One of these expeditions found him along the highway near Norton, Virginia, before some five hundred "followers," where a rather bizarre incident occurred. A serpent as it was passed among various handlers was seized by a twelve-year-old boy who tore its head off, and a "near riot" ensued ("Wave Rattler in Frenzy" 17). It was in the year following this incident, according to an implica-

tion by a 1944 article in *Newsweek*, that Hensley was responsible for the institution of serpent handling in Stone Creek, Virginia (near St. Charles), as well as in the adjoining area: "It was in 1936 that George Hensley of Harlan County, Ky., established the weird cult among the miners and farmers of southwestern Virginia on the Tennessee border" ("They Shall Take Up Serpents," *Newsweek* 88).

Soon afterward, Hensley constructed a house trailer and left with the family for Georgia and Florida. His son Loyal tells the story of their crossing the Tampa Bay Bridge and having the side of the trailer torn off by an oncoming truck. On 1 March 1936 the family was in Tampa with George preaching and handling a rattlesnake during a mission service before a group of some 125 persons in a vacant store. The themes of his sermons included abstaining from lipstick, gambling, drunkenness—and even baseball games. He also answered a common charge against serpent handlers: "They say it's tempting the Lord. Well, don't you know the Bible says the Lord can't be tempted, and don't it say for the servants of God to handle serpents?" He talked about faith: "The first chapter of James tells what it takes to handle serpents. It just takes faith without wavering. Listen, the Bible says he who wavers is like a wave of the sea." Hensley, however, did not handle serpents solely by faith: "When they brought that snake in here a few minutes ago . . . the spirit was working. I'd have handled it then but the box was closed. I'll handle it when the spirit works again." It did and he handled it, as did three others, but the snake got loose and caused quite an excitement before being caught. In his sermon Hensley also implied that the reason for handling serpents is that it is a modern manifestation of Old Testament deliverance by the Lord, such as Daniel from the lion's den, the three Hebrew children from the fiery furnace, and Jonah from the belly of the whale: "But you don't know that," he said. "That was before your time. I'll show you something in your time. I'll show you how to handle a rattlesnake, and you all know the result of rattlesnakes." The newspaper description of Hensley is noteworthy as well: "a quiet little man with gray hair, wiped the perspiration from his forehead and went about the congregation to shake hand [*sic*]" ("Pastor Here Whirls Snake" 1, 12).

Hensley moved on about twenty miles southeast of Tampa to a trailer camp in Bloomingdale. At a county church nearby he held services before a congregation so large that he had to move outside the building to a roped-off area with a makeshift pulpit ("Preacher Juggles Snake" 1, 8). In the course of handling a rattlesnake purchased by an individual from a local cannery, Hensley was bitten twice. He showed the bites to the crowd, explaining that he would not seek medical attention. The man at the cannery who sold the rattlesnake was reported as regretting that he sold the serpent, but he also indicated a personal response that must have been common: "Hensley is extremely fervent in his religious belief to the degree that I personally believe he sincerely believes that his faith protects him from the effects of the snake venom" ("Snake Expert Warns People" 7).

Hensley's plan was to go west into Georgia before returning to Tampa. The next report of his evangelistic efforts, however, finds him conducting a tent revival east of Tampa at Bartow the last of April and early May. For the first time, George witnessed death by serpent bite. At a Sunday evening service, Alfred D. Weaver, a thirty-five-year-old itin-

erant strawberry picker and shoe peddler, was bitten by a rattlesnake and died the following day. Hensley believed the man would recover: "'He was bitten because he was not quite ready for the demonstration of the power. . . . He will get all right. I have seen people bitten twice as worse'" (Abbott 1). Hensley said that he himself had been bitten two hundred times and as a result had only been slightly ill once. The day of Weaver's death, the Bartow city commission passed an ordinance against anyone's transporting, exhibiting, or handling in public an unpenned poisonous serpent ("Fatal Snake Bite" 1). After Hensley conducted the funeral service, he and the family likely went as reportedly planned to the western part of the state before returning to Ohio ("County Buries Snake Victim" 7).

Once they arrived in Ohio, they left Loyal with Irene's sister in Cleveland so that he could go to school, and then they returned to Pineville, Kentucky, to which they would move back and forth several times. In 1938 George was reported as a railroad conductor and again pastor of the East Pineville Church of God. He was also arrested and "charged with breach of the peace in handling snakes" along with two other men at the Pine Mountain Church of God in Harlan County (Kerman, "Rattlesnake Religion," *Post* 10). The following year he was holding revivals and handling serpents in Knoxville, Tennessee. In a few more years Hensley moved his family to Duff, Tennessee, where according to Loyal he bought a farm. Loyal remembers they were living there when Pearl Harbor was bombed, but George was soon on the move again—this time to Evansville, Indiana. Here he was separated from Irene. According to Loyal he did something "real bad," bad enough for Irene to threaten him with

George Hensley's granddaughter La Creta, on the left, and his children by Irene (Loyal, Faith, Jean, Vinette), who were reared together by George and Amanda's daughter Esther Lee. Photograph courtesy of La Creta Simmons.

being arrested—"a prison offense." One problem they had was the old one of George's failure to keep a job. Loyal says his mother permitted George to return when he promised to get work but soon realized that she had made a mistake.

The work was apparently back in Pineville because that's where George, Irene, and all four of their children moved, but the marriage was not to last much longer. Loyal says that a significant factor in the breakup was George's wanting to put the children in an orphanage so that he and Irene would be free to evangelize. And the evangelizing always went on.

One of the houses in Pineville where the Hensleys lived had a high porch with banisters from which George fell and broke both arms while reaching

out to pick some apples. It was about the time of this accident that Irene wrote about her marital problems to one of George's daughters of his first marriage, Esther Lee. Esther Lee and a sister visited their father and saw for themselves that things were not going well.

In 1943, shortly after that visit, George again left Irene and his second family, which by now had lasted sixteen years. Irene with two of the older children went to stay, not back at home in Ohio, but in Chattanooga with Esther Lee. One of the children, Vinette, was retrieved from Kentucky by two other daughters of George's first marriage. Jean, the youngest of the four, was also left in Kentucky until she was taken to the home of Franklin, a son of the first marriage, before rejoining her mother at

Lewis Ford's funeral service at the Dolley Pond Church of God with Signs Following; co-founders of the church, George Hensley (to the left of "Boots" Parker, handling a serpent) and Raymond Hays (above Hensley), were later also to die from serpent bite. Photograph 1945 by J. C. Collins, identifications by Flora Bettis.

Esther Lee's home. At first some of the children stayed at times with Esther Lee and other times with her sister Rosa, switching back and forth from one house to the other. Winifred, Rosa's son, describes the situation: "So, that left all the kids in here. Just different ones, you know, raised them." Irene was going to stay at Esther Lee's until she could work something out to support the children, but before she was able to, she died of a heart attack following goiter surgery. Esther Lee and her husband, Luther, took legal custody of the children. At some point George did come for the children; but, when

given the choice to go with him, they decided to stay. Fortunately, George's first family (even Amanda) was always good to the second, including the second wife. Half-sisters and half-brothers became mother, uncles, and aunts; and cousins became brothers and sisters.

George also left Kentucky for Tennessee, primarily the Ooltewah and Birchwood area, staying with different people—his sister Rosa and, probably, relatives on Jane Brown's farm. When Irene died, he came to view the body, but after that he had virtually no contact with his second family,

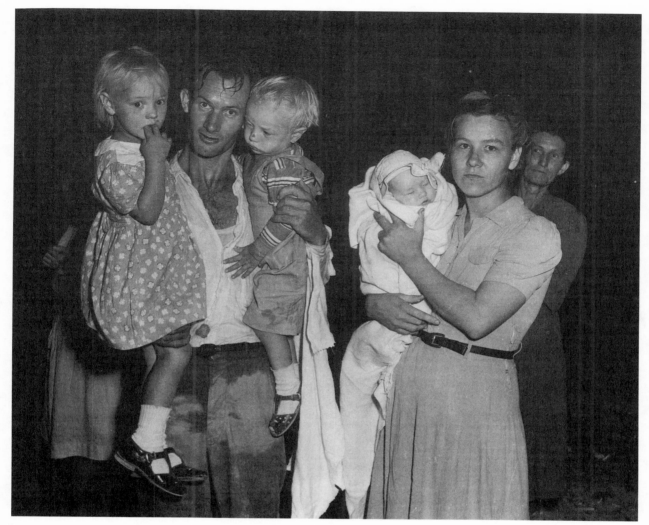

Tom Harden, pastor of the Dolley Pond Church, with his wife, Rosa, children, and mother (in the background). Photograph c. 1945 by J. C. Collins, identifications by Flora Bettis.

nor with his first one for that matter. He continued evangelizing.

Serpent handling in the Birchwood area during George's absence apparently had subsided. Perry Bettis said: "It continued maybe ten, twelve years, maybe fifteen year. Then old man Luther Morrow tried to carry it on by himself and it just kept a-gettin' worse and worse and worse on him, droppin' off here, drop off there, this 'n quit and that 'n quit;

and first thing you knowd there weren't nobody but that poor old fella and four or five left, you know. Some of them had died off and some of them had left and changed over to Jesus Name [baptizing in "the name of Jesus," rather than "the name of the Father, Son and Holy Spirit"], and that brung a split, division between the people." Religious attitudes toward following the signs also changed. Even the Grasshopper Church of God preached against

Some principal members of the Dolley Pond Church: George Hensley (left), Lewis Ford (in overalls), Jim Posey, Luther Morrow, Minnie Parker, "Boots" Parker (perhaps the B. A. Parker who died of serpent bite in 1946). Photograph 1945 by J. C. Collins, identifications by Flora Bettis.

Facing page: Minnie Parker's beautiful face framed with a rattlesnake. Photograph 1947 by J. C. Collins,

handling serpents and turned people out who believed in it. Perry Bettis told about Mark Braddam's being "run off" and going up to the window of the church, where he stuck his head in and proclaimed what may have been George Hensley's belief as well: "Every one of you is gonna go to hell if you fail to believe that this is right; I'm not telling you, you have to do it; but it is written and you got to believe it."

According to J. B. Collins, the dormant period began with Garland Defriese's having a bad experience in 1918 with a serpent bite and lasted until

1943 when Raymond Hays, an "ardent follower of Hensley," came into Grasshopper Valley and effected a revival (*Tennessee Snake Handlers* 2-3). Perry Bettis listed the sequence and people as follows:

Old man George had some trouble over here with his family, had some trouble, and it died down for a few years, you know, I wouldn't say how many years, fifteen or twenty year, and then old man George come back in and started preaching it again. Raymond Hays come from Kentucky; Brother Hutton was from Virginia, and they all come

Lewis Ford's funeral service: Preacher William Henry playing guitar (whose father, Walter, and uncle Hobart Wilson died the following year of serpent bite; Hobart was bitten at Walter's funeral). Photograph 1945 by J. C. Collins, identification by Flora Bettis.

down here and Brother Luther Morrow and Jim Posey and Mark Braddam and Walt Ford and Dora Young and all—they built a brush arbor up there at Dolly Pond and they started handlin' them there. My wife got bit there, and that's the first night I started goin' with her—she's snake bit—and I took her home, walked her home. We walked down the road and her arm all swelled up. It kept a-goin', and they built a church house there.

The congregation is reported as being founded, assisted by George Hensley, in June 1945 ("Demonstration of Faith" 1). They named themselves "The Dolley Pond Church of God with Signs Following." They remained nondenominational.

Raymond Hays, "Buck" as he was called, and George may have even come from Kentucky together. According to Collins it was Hays who led Tom Harden, later the pastor of the Dolley Pond church, into serpent handling, although Tom's father Enoch had been among the first to participate in serpent handling when it was originally introduced by Hensley (*Tennessee Snake Handlers* 5-6).

According to reports of wondrous acts performed by Buck Hays, it is no surprise that he was an ef-

Inez Riggs Hutcheson (center), George Hensley's third wife, after a religious service with Reece Ramsey (left front) and others. A copperhead drapes around Charley Fritts's neck. Photograph 1947 courtesy of Inez's son Bill Hutcheson.

fectual revivalist. Perry Bettis told of an amazing instance of handling fire:

I seen Buck Hays go up—they had a heater up there, and they fired it with (it was one of these old potbellied stoves, cast iron) and I seen him go up to that thing and it fired with coke—they didn't fire it with coal, they fired that thing with coke. And he walked up to that heater and he opened that door and it was sheer red; and the heater outside was red, blood red, man. And he just went around that thing and hugged that thing and just stuck his head in there and just held it no telling how long, a minute or two, and come out, boy—and pulled his sleeves up and showed everybody everything was alright, didn't even scorch his clothes, his hair or nothin'—come out of that heater, rejoiced around there. And my brother was sittin' back there, Paul, he's a-sittin' back there about half shot, and he said, "Why I can do that"—and then walked up there, grabbed the stove door open, rolled that sleeve up and stuck that arm in there and just as soon as he could get it in there and out, just "pop" (I mean he took it

out just like lightning), and the meat just fell off, boys, cooked it, I mean done too. I mean it put him in bad case—he didn't use it for a year.

There were many cases of "tests" by individuals' bringing in tormented snakes—"pour whiskey and black pepper in the boxes to get them to bite"—and especially large or vicious serpents to challenge the members. But it was not uncommon for scoffers to become believers. Sometimes the hecklers were rowdy young men out drinking. Minnie Parker Harden remembers the Ku Klux Klan's coming in the building one evening to control one such group. Julia Brumlow says the Klan took the young men outside, whipped them, took them back inside, and warned them not to disrupt the services.

Hensley was active at Dolley Pond, but characteristically his ministry in the valley was not restricted to that church or to any single place. His son Roscoe, who in 1944 was a pastor of a church not far from Grasshopper Valley, heard his father at a "cottage meeting" (a service at someone's home); it was one of the few sermons Roscoe was to hear him preach.

There were some hard feelings toward George when he came back to Tennessee, and there still are, as one would expect. For the most part, though, his domestic problems were seemingly dismissed by the community. But they are not dismissed by the family members, including Roscoe:

> We just all felt that he had erred. He abandoned the second family and was preaching during that time. You know how you'd feel towards a man who wouldn't support his family—if it is my dad. And he didn't support us, he didn't support his family. His income was very small. This type of ministry he was in was mostly of a summertime ministry. During the winter he didn't have a trade. He was a very poor provider, and abandoned two families. Why, you couldn't hardly approve of that type of lifestyle. They [the family] didn't feel too good about it, for sure.

Lloyd Stokes says about his grandfather George, "He was about as big a hypocrite that ever lived. The story he circulated in Ohio was that he gave up his first family only when the oldest son could take care of them—that was Franklin who was twelve years old at the time!" Actually Franklin was only nine at the time George left.

Nevertheless, George continued evangelizing. In September 1945 Lewis Ford, a member of the Dolley Pond church, was fatally bitten by a rattlesnake. The fatality, however, did not dampen the serpent-handling activities; perhaps it even increased them. Ford's funeral service included the taking up of serpents, as has become something of a tradition in funerals of sign followers. Serpents were placed in the casket during the service, but Minnie

Parker Harden, who was there, says they were not buried with the corpse.

Hensley's zeal was certainly not diminished by Ford's death. In fact, not long afterward, he and Tom Harden were arrested for disorderly conduct while handling serpents one Sunday afternoon in Chattanooga. They were conducting a faith-healing service in the front of the house of a member of the M. A. Tomlinson Church of God who had invited them to come preach. Hensley was reported at the time to be of Brightsville, Tennessee (Corliss, "2 'Faith-Healing' Ministers" 1). Both Hensley and Harden refused on principle to pay their fifty-dollar fines and were sent to the workhouse. According to one report, the case was appealed by friends who were concerned about George's physical condition (Collins, *Tennessee Snake Handlers* 23). The charges were dismissed.

George continued evangelizing. In 1946 he was preaching at Daisy, Tennessee, in a brush arbor, very likely the same one in which Ford was bitten. There he met Inez Riggs Hutcheson, a woman with ten children who had recently moved off the farm where she and her husband had lived before his death. As a result of George's preaching, Inez accepted both serpent handling as Bible teaching and George's proposal of marriage. She planned to assist him in his ministry, traveling with him and reading the Bible for him as he preached. They moved back to the farm in nearby Soddy with the four of her children who were still at home. Faith, George's oldest daughter by his second wife, was also to stay several weeks with him and this third wife until she returned home to the daughter of his first wife!

Inez's son Bill says his mother regretted the marriage almost from the start. He describes his

Building formerly of the Dolley Pond Church of God with Signs Following, presently of the Birchwood Church of God of Prophecy. Photograph 1989 by the author.

mother as a very religious person who thought that George was a godly man whom she could completely accept, both for what he said and what he appeared to be. In less than six months George and Inez were separated. According to Bill, George was not the kind of person Inez thought he was, not even the sort of man who should be preaching and handling serpents at all: "Not a mean man or anything like that, but a sort of a . . . weirdo."

George did not stop preaching, but apparently he was not at the Dolley Pond Church of God with Signs Following in August 1947 when Tom Harden and eleven others were arrested for violat-

ing the newly enacted Tennessee code against serpent handling. But two months after the Dolley Pond arrest and before the trial was held, George himself was arrested again in Chattanooga for handling serpents. The tent services he had been taking part in had been conducted for thirty days by the Undivided Church of God ("Man Bitten Here" 1). Several weeks later he was reported to be a defense witness for the Dolley Pond group and was photographed with Tom Harden and others at the trial ("Snake Handlers of Georgia, Kentucky" 1; Smartt 1). In December he was reported as the assistant pastor of the New South Chattanooga Church of

God ("Snake Cult Opens Church" 3). Sometime after this he is recounted as preaching in a tent meeting in East Chattanooga where serpents were handled and where he related a personal incident of being crushed in a Kentucky coal mine. He told how he had lain a year in bed paralyzed before being restored by prayer (Robertson 169-71).

Probably in 1951 in Chattanooga he met and later married Sally Moore Norman. She was nicknamed "Peg" because of a leg amputation from a childhood accident. It was the fourth marriage for both. She was in her sixties, he in his seventies. After George's death, she was to marry twice again.

From the time George returned to the Southern Appalachians he did not stop his evangelistic excursions. Apparently his lifestyle never changed. Irene had called him a "rolling stone," and George thought of himself as an Apostle Paul planting the seed, which the Apollos would water. Winifred, his grandson (and son-in-law by marriage), calls him a missionary: "I never did know of him staying at one church. He weren't no one-church stayer. You'd call him, I guess, a missionary; he went from places to places." His travels took him to Ohio, Indiana, Kentucky, Virginia, North Carolina, West Virginia, Georgia, and Florida; but during the last twenty-five years of his life Kentucky was his hub. Winifred says:

> Seemed like Kentucky was his main place. Then he'd spring out and leave, and then come down through Tennessee and wind up down in South Georgia; so he would spend a few months at each place and by the time he wound back up, you know, maybe he was back in Kentucky. When he came back, why, he'd just hug you and talk to you, and he was really good to us and he'd stay with us for a while, then leave and go somewhere. You

may not see him for a year. You didn't know. We lived up there off of Birchwood Road and he'd come, a-leading in one day—had him a goat. That's all he brunt in with him. He'd been gone for a long time. "Well, I'm gonna stay awhile with you'ns." "Well, you're welcome."

Winifred's wife, Helen (George's step-daughter by marriage to Sally), adds: "He traveled a whole lot. My mom went with him, and we weren't around them very much, except when they came back here. He just traveled everwhere, all through Georgia and Kentucky and Tennessee, preaching." His final move was to Albany, Georgia, with Sally, holding meetings there and in Florida.

George was not materialistic, or at least he did not have much invested in material things. Winifred relates:

> He'd come with a pair of pants and a long sleeve shirt and preach his message and that was it. He just weren't no real fancy goer and you never heard him talk about money. I mean if they made him up a little that was just, "Thank the Lord for that." He never did complain about money. I never knowed him owning a house, no car. He was just a loner I'd call him, traveled just here you know, and go up there in Kentucky and they a-having a revival, getting a meeting a-going so and so. "Well, I'll head down there," and he might get somebody to drive; and "Let's go visit them," and that would be a way for him to get there. Then when he'd go, he'd hunt somebody if he wanted to stay—nearly any church members, "Yeah, come on in—I mean you can live here with us" and he'd stay two or three weeks. When he was off and come back to Dolly Pond, my mom—I believe, I'm not for sure—my mom [Rosa] was the only one who would take him in. I don't know for sure, but he never did try none of the rest of them. I mean it was always come to our house. If he was

Site of George Hensley's last sermon and fatal serpent bite, 24 July 1955, in Calhoun County, Florida. Photograph courtesy of J. R. Hensley.

here, he'd never would go around none of the rest of 'em. And he'd wind up staying with us a few weeks, and then you may not see him no more for a few years.

After he moved to Georgia, the family did not see much of him, but it was in Florida near Altha that George Went Hensley was to end his ministry. There on 24 July 1955 in an abandoned blacksmith shop—the tin roof and board siding in need of repair, a board nailed across the top of a stake driven into the dirt floor as a pulpit—George was fatally bitten. His son says the snake was from a zoo. A local newspaper account of George's death was that he had been holding services for over three weeks without the use of serpents until the one that bit him was brought in ("Rattlesnake Bite Kills" 1).

Newspaper reporter Don Kimsey gives a first-hand account of that hot Sunday-afternoon service in the Florida panhandle twenty-five miles from the Georgia-Alabama line. Several dozen men, women, and children were present. Hensley was speaking in tongues, preaching, and calling out

"'Faith . . . faith . . . it can cure anything!'" A five-gallon lard can held a five-foot rattlesnake, which Hensley drew forth and wrapped around his neck and arms as he circled before the small assembly. After some ten minutes, just as Hensley was placing it back in the can, the large rattler sank its fangs deep into the preacher's right wrist. With his left hand he pulled the serpent loose and returned it to the can. In a few minutes Hensley became sick but refused medical aid. Kimsey says, "He fought off death for several hours, in great agony and constantly belching blood. . . . Just before he writhed, twisted and gasped his last breath, Hensley groaned to me: 'The snake would not have struck—if fear had not come over someone here.'" Some of those present said he had been bitten 446 times; another report said 401. The Calhoun County sheriff recorded the death as suicide. Three carloads of George's families drove all night from Tennessee to attend the funeral and then all night back to return for work. Grandson Lloyd Stokes said that a country band played at the funeral.

George had had close encounters with death

Family members of George Hensley who made the long drive to Florida for Hensley's funeral in July 1955. Photograph courtesy of La Creta Simmons.

by serpent bite before. Loyal remembers his father almost dying on several occasions and the deacons coming in and praying for him as he lay "rigid as a steel rod, vibrating with the death rattle in his throat." Jean remembers once in Ooltewah when she was about twelve years old that her father was serpent bit. He was delirious, calling out her name, and she was taken to him. "His head was black and as big as a foot basin." But those times he survived.

Most general reports about George himself are that he was a good, gentle, sincere man. According to his niece Grace Cook, he had a "nice personality, very humble." Pastor Henry Swiney from Sneedville, Tennessee, says: "There weren't too many handling them the first time he come through here. Everybody that knowed anything about him in this part of the country thought pretty well of him, spoke pretty well of him." Minnie Harden of Dolley Pond days recalls: "He was a quiet man." Harvey Grant, who used to preach with him in street services, states: "Oh, you couldn't help but love Uncle George. He was really honest. He was humble." Barbara Elkins, matriarch of the Church of the Lord Jesus, Jolo, West Virginia, who took her first serpent from his hands, recalls: "He was a good, sound believer; he was a good man." Perry Bettis, native of his homeground, believes: "Old man George, he was a fine old man now, he was a good old man; there ain't no question about it."

His grandson Winifred says, "He was always just a church-go-to-preach, go-home-with-some-body and stuff like that. I never did see nothing wrong out of him; he wouldn't even drink a Co'-Cola. I mean he was that strict. I don't think he'd even drink coffee. He was quiet. He'd sit down with a bunch of kids, you know, and maybe two or three get around and he'd rather play with the kids than associate with grown people." Winifred's wife adds: "Everywhere he went, children would come around him, you know—laugh and cut-up with 'em, sit down on the ground and just play with 'em." Winifred also recalls: "Yeah, he was a little, small guy. He'd just pile up in the grass and kids pile around him, even grown folks get out there. He was a lot of cut-up to him and happy all the time. There will never be another one like him, I don't believe."

George's daughter Jean also says he was a jolly person, always cutting up, and that he liked children—*he just didn't like supporting them.*" "He wouldn't hurt nobody, wouldn't cause nobody no trouble," says Winifred. "You never heard him argue; you never heard him say nothing about nobody. If he come and live with us for a few months you never heard a cross word out of him, and he was nice to everybody. He was just a happy guy. I guess it was the way he lived. To me, if you really wanted to be a Christian, he had the full works, you know—just by his actions and the way he'd go around and the way he treated people, 'cause nearly anybody would take him in, just tickled to death just to have him around. What few years we

remember him and know him, he was just, you know, a great guy to us." One time when Jean was about fifteen years old, she met her father on the street, and he didn't even know her, but still she acknowledges that George had a "charming personality—everybody loved that man."

Preaching, Hensley was anything but quiet; he displayed an altogether different personality. One newspaper reporter was obviously taken back: "Brother Hensley was waving his arms. He went up and down the aisles in an Indian dance with head bent low and knees moving high. The perspiration was pouring off his face" ("Pastor Here Whirls Snake" 12). Winifred was certainly impressed with his grandfather's preaching:

> But the only time he'd really do talking was when he got up to preach, and he would give you twenty-five or thirty minutes of I guess one of the best messages you could ask for in preaching. He was one of them kind of preachers that when he preached, he put everything that he had in it. I've seen him in them meetings preach and be wringing wet with sweat and just keep going. Well, he'd preach awhile—he had a funny doin'—he'd preach to 'em and then with his hand behind his ear: "Huh, can ye hear me?" Then he'd go back and he'd preach awhile again—he'd do the same thing. He'd run maybe half way: "Huh, did ya hear me?" He would get someone to read the verses from the Bible for him and he'd preach on them; he could just preach in it just anywheres he wanted to.

According to Winifred, George's preaching did not dwell on the handling of serpents: "You never did hear him really get on that one verse that they believed in. You know, I don't remember ever hearing him preach on it. But that was just something that was in the Bible that he believed in. He'd preach from just anywheres, just come out and you'd get him started and it just seemed like he could memorize it." Other members of his families, however, say he always preached on the handling of serpents. He certainly preached it at Dolley Pond, according to Minnie Parker Harden. Whichever opinion is accurate, most agree he was an effective preacher. Harvey Grant, for one, says: "He preached under the anointing. You could sit up there and listen at him two hours and it'd seem like he hadn't been preachin' no time." Winifred agrees: "He was a really good preacher to sit down and just listen at you know. And if they get happy, look out, 'cause they'd have snakes going everywheres and get a-hold of hot lamp globes. I mean, you know, it didn't blister them or nothing. They'd get them old torches and hold them up. He'd hold it right up in their face. And they'd be just as black as they could be when church was over, that old soot coming off that old kerosene."

It is interesting that, despite the pervasive influence Hensley had in the spread of serpent handling throughout the southern states, none of his children followed his example in taking up serpents, not even the son who became a minister. The irony does not escape the family: "They never did take up no snake-handling," says Winifred, "never would go to their church, never would go around together. As far as I know they never was none of the family or members took it up with him. I know my mother didn't, and, well, I know all the rest of 'em—none of 'em took it up."

When all is said and done, George Hensley may not have been significantly different—in his background, character, and preaching—from many rural evangelists of his time. What seems to be the most important difference is that he accepted less than most the moral responsibilities of family and chose instead to devote more of his life in going forth for half a century to preach and manifest a sensational belief. That belief brought Hensley a deluge of crowds, among whom were many who came to follow in his footsteps, preaching the signs. But the tide ebbed. His personal story is composed of antitheses, and the motivations of his actions are ultimately unclear. The subtle knot of the spiritual and physical in the life of George Hensley is Gordian. But, whatever else might be said about him and whatever personal demons he may have had, he persevered in his religious practice throughout a long life until he died a death that many serpent handlers would prefer.

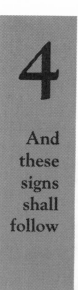

4

And
these
signs
shall
follow

Reports from the Battlefield

Weave a circle round him thrice,
And close your eyes with holy dread,
For he on honeydew hath fed,
And drunk the milk of Paradise.

—Coleridge, *"Kubla Khan"*

In 1923 a division within the Church of God formed two groups, one retaining the name "Church of God" and the other being called finally the "Church of God of Prophecy." In the eight years prior to this split, editorials and reports from the field, or "battlefield" as it is often referred to in the official church paper, show that serpent handling was being widely conducted by Church of God members. Serpent-handling believers—or "saints," as they often referred to themselves in biblical terminology—were never confined to the ranks of the Church of God, even though the general overseer of that organization was of the opinion that they were. Independents such as James Miller in Alabama took up serpents (Vance 36). George Hensley himself, a member of the Church of God for some ten years, handled serpents as an independent the greater part of his ministry.

Although serpent handling as a religious practice was not confined to churches formally associated with the Church of God, reports appearing in the church's paper, the *Evening Light and Church of God Evangel*, provide valuable insights into the early days of the practice. Reports came not only from the southern states of Tennessee, Kentucky, North Carolina, South Carolina, Georgia, Alabama, and Mississippi, but also from the mid- and southwestern states of Missouri, Illinois, Arkansas, and Texas. These accounts do not simply describe the activity of a small group of evangelists; rather, they

Service of the Pentecostal Church of God, Harlan County, Kentucky, in 1946. Russell Lee Collection, National Archives 245-MS-2621L, courtesy of Pat Arnow.

relate the experiences of numerous folks in tabernacles, brush arbors, homes, fields, and roads—descriptions of people being swept away by the demonstrations of the sign followers.

The names of more than fifty people are associated with the instances described in this period, and only a few are ever repeated. Even George Hensley's name appears only five times in conjunction with the mention of serpents, all within the space of approximately one year. Two of these are in con-

nection with the Cleveland revival in September 1914, and another is of a meeting the following month in Ooltewah held with M. S. Haynes in which two rattlesnakes were taken up. Almost a year later Pastor N. P. Mulkey refers to Hensley in an announcement: "We have closed the meeting out on the mountain. . . . God gave power to handle the rattlesnake. We are now holding a meeting in Soddy. . . . George Hensley, in charge." Then two months later, a report from nearby Dividing Ridge appears: "Brothers Hensley and Mulkey closed a meeting here the last of September. . . . After Sunday School was over the poison rattler was brought in." Over two years after this notice, William Headrick writes from the same area, Birchwood, but with no mention of serpents: "I thank God for ever sending Brother George Hensley to this place to preach holiness. He gave us the light on the Church of God."

The reports indicate that the serpents were generally brought in by outsiders. On some occasions this occurred as a means of ridicule: "They first brought us a little garter snake, but we would not fool with it." For the scorners, however, the worm would generally turn:

> people were convinced that we preached and practiced the truth. . . . later they brought in a Copper head, and the Lord gave power to handle it and the "garter snake crowd" stood back. . . . So last Sunday as some one was coming to the meeting they found a big rattle snake lying across the road and they brought it to the tent and God gave power to nearly every saint there to handle it.

A similar situation occurred in an adjoining state:

> On Wednesday night they brought us a little garter snake. We refused to have anything to do with it. The next night they brought us a rattle snake pilot. We refused to handle him because of the unsafety of the congregation, but we told the folks to wait until Sunday. . . . After the preaching we had prayer and the power fell. God gave power to handle the poison serpent. Praise the Lord! There were only four of us saints and all handled the serpent successfully.

There were other times in which the serpent was not immediately handled when brought in. In one case, "They brought the old rattle-snake in, but the devil howled so they put it out of the house

and said not to bother it. But God had all power and He gave me power to go down and take it out of the box before I left the yard." On one occasion the handling apparently was refused altogether: "It had been rumored that a snake was going to be brought there [Bunker Hill, Tenn.] for the saints to handle. Jesus said, (Matt. 12:39) 'An evil and adulterous generation seeketh after a sign; and no sign shall be given &c.'" At another time the serpent was retained for future use: "The snake was kept for a week and at intervals some of the brethren would go and take it out and handle it."

As would be expected, the number of those who handled the serpents varies according to the place, the circumstances, and the size of the group of believers, among other factors; but the handlers included all ages and both sexes. According to one account,

> She [Sister Mefford] went down in prayer and the power of the Lord fell on her and she picked the snake up in the name of the Lord and handled it in all shapes that she could think of and then started home with it in her hands. She put the serpent down three times and took it up again and during the time she was handling this poison venomous serpent she traveled three-quarters of a mile. Her mother was all the time watching for a chance to amputate the snake's head, and the fourth time she laid it down her mother struck it with an ax.

One participant is quoted as saying, "I am a boy of sixteen years and have had the Holy Ghost one week. . . . I have handled hot lamp chimneys under the mighty power of God and to-day while I was in the field, I was bitten by a serpent under the power and it did not hurt me. I can hardly tell where it bit me." Sometimes the number of handlers is only "several"; other times it is greater: "five

Mrs. Cecil Denkins putting aside guitar to handle a serpent at services of the Dolley Pond Church of God with Signs Following. Photograph 1947 by J. C. Collins, identification by Flora Bettis.

of his little band," "some ten or more," "about twenty-five," "about forty"—and in one naively open statement: "All the saints present handled it but three or four. My two babies, one eight years old handled it."

In most cases the handling of serpents is mentioned in conjunction with other signs, sometimes briefly: "The signs for true believers followed. Several hot lamp chimneys, fire and a large snake were handled successfully." Sometimes, with greater detail: "The Word was given out with love and power and it had its effect. The saints were greatly edified and God showed His mighty power of healing. We prayed for a baby with the small-pox and God immediately healed the child. The saints danced, talked in tongues, handled a hot lamp chimney and some live coals. Serpents were also handled

without injury." Other times, the description of the signs is given at great length:

We are praising God because He has linked together a little flock of believers according to Mark 16:17. . . .

In regard to taking up serpents. One night there was a big black diamond rattler, five feet long, brought in during the services and God gave us power to handle it. Praise His dear name. The Lord surely did bless during the time. It was really a foretaste of heaven. The saints remarked about the sweet spirit.

The next sign was laying hands on the sick. A sinner girl was pronounced by the doctor to have tuberculosis of the bone and said she would not walk for eighteen months or two years. The mother called us to pray for her girl and praise His name, what do you think happened? Just what

Cecil Denkins with serpent around his neck. Denkins was arrested for handling serpents at Dolley Pond soon after this photograph was taken in August 1947, then later with George Hensley and Reece Ramsey the following October in Chattanooga. Photograph by J. C. Collins, identification by Flora Bettis.

James 5:15 said would happen, 'And the prayer of faith shall save the sick. . . .'

Another sign was given unto the people just like what happened on the day of Pentecost Acts 2:3. 'And there appeared unto them cloven tongues like as of fire, and it sat upon each of them.' After meeting [sic] sinners came to us and said they saw a streak of fire start from L. G. Rouse's head on around mine and my husband's heads and back to Brother Rouse and as the fire reached each one the mighty sweet power of God quickened our mortal bodies and sinners were made to believe. Praise God.

Messages in tongues were given out and interpreted and many other signs were wrought and, praise the Lord, when the signs were seen to be following us, people began to believe. . . .

In the context of some of the more unusual reports of signs, the serpent handling seems rather ordinary:

A rattle snake was handled and also fire. The organ was played by the power of the Holy Ghost while our hands were held up in praises.

A lady about sixty-nine years old was instantly healed. She had not walked a step in eight years without crutches. A man was instantly healed of lung trouble and another healed of deafness and throat trouble, also many other healings.

Fire was seen by several more than once and one sister saw a crown of gold.

The signs were set forth primarily as "confirming" the word, the believers, the power of God, and the Church of God as well: "The signs are truly following the Church of God." Other expressions are

Mrs. Parker with a rattlesnake around her neck like a scarf. Maggie Parker was one of the twelve arrested at the church soon after this photograph was taken in 1947. Photograph by J. C. Collins, identification by Flora Bettis.

used to indicate different, though related, reasons for taking up the serpents. Obedience, for example, is implied: "A large rattler was taken up in accordance [*sic*] with the word." For some it is a test, apparently by Satan: "She won the victory out here by being tempted by a copperhead snake"; "We have been tried by two copperheads." In one instance it is specifically answering a challenge by Satan: "Nearly all the saints handled him [a rattlesnake]. He was then put away and Satan suggested that we were afraid to handle the copper head. The copper head snake was then set out and again we prayed and the Lord gave power to handle him." For others the emphasis on serpent handling is one of privilege and honor: "He has honored us by letting us take up live coals of fire and serpents"; "most of the saints enjoyed the privilege and blessing of

taking it [a copperhead] up in the name of Jesus." Another statement suggests that the experience confirmed God's honor, that He was true to what He said, "God wonderfully honored His Word."

For the most part the reports proclaim positive effects, both for the handler and his mission: "It was wonderful, and some were convinced"; "many were made to believe in the true God"; "people came humbling themselves crying to God." No doubt in many cases the serpent handling was the elixir that transmuted a meeting into a vital experience. In Jasper, Tennessee, "It seemed that nothing was being done until last night when some boys brought in two nice serpents"; in Bude, Mississippi, "Many people [who] witnessed the scene with great excitement and stony hearts were broken to pieces and many dry eyes overflowed with tears while God

Reece Ramsey, who died seven years after this photograph was taken from a serpent bite during a brush arbor meeting in Georgia. Photograph 1947 by J. C. Collins, identification by Flora Bettis.

was confirming His Word. People who were holiness fighters [*i.e.*, those opposing them] went [a]way from the meeting wanting the blessing."

The language referring to serpents in these reports is quite telling. Sometimes the words are appreciative: "a nice little copper head snake"; sometimes familiar: "old copperhead," "old ratler" [*sic*]; at other times the serpent is personified as "the big fellow" or "the old fellow." There is a certain lyric quality to be found in such expressions as "the old rattler sang in our hands and did not strike the first time"; sometimes a dramatic effect is achieved: "I set the box on the stand and was trying to get the lid off when the power struck brother Cagle and the lid flew off and out came the rattlesnake, singing and bitting [*sic*]." At times, the descriptions are metaphorical: "it was harmless as a bird"; some-

times innocently so: "I wish you could have seen Jessie fold those snakes in her arms and pet them as if they were kittens."

The serpents at times were less like kittens and more like cockatrices, yet the reports seem forthright about that, too. Some of the bites are described as having no visible consequences. Others are accepted as purposefully painful. But the emotional responses to the bites, however, are basically the same: "Glory to God." There are frequent statements such as "Some were bitten but it did not hurt them" and "The serpent bit one of the saints but the place did not even swell." When the wife of then-state overseer of Tennessee, George T. Brouayer, was bitten, the description is "as it was with Paul, she felt no harm." Two years later, when Brouayer was in Texas, he wrote: "The serpent's

The original caption for this photograph pejoratively states: "This coal camp offers none of the modern types of amusement and many of the people attend the services of this church more for the mass excitement and emotialism [sic] than because of belief in the tenets of this church." Russell Lee Collection, National Archives 245-MS-2635L, courtesy of Pat Arnow.

fang pierced the hand of one of our girls, and while some concluded she would suffer and die, the Lord beautifully healed." Occasionally the bites are graphically set forth:

> He [a rattlesnake] bit brother Cagle once and he gave him to me and he bit me four times and brought blood each time, and hung his two fangs in my arm so deep he could not get them out and hung there until brother Ed Cavitt pulled him loose. The blood ran down on my cuff but no harm was done. It did not make me a bit sick. I wiped my hand with my handkerchief and then wiped my face and mouth not realizing what I was doing and got poison in my mouth and swallowed

it. It sure tasted bad but I felt no hurt. My hand swelled just enough to let the people see that the poison was there. Glory to God, it gave me more faith.

In another incident a man was bitten three times and one of the rattlesnake's teeth was broken off in his arm. The bite made the man sick, and he vomited, but the swelling was accepted as having a purpose: "His hand just swelled enough that it [the tooth] could be discovered[.] I am greatly encouraged." One explanation offered for a serpent bite is surprisingly naive: "One night a copperhead snake was brought in and handled by about seven of the saints. It placed its fangs into the hand of one of the brethren just to show that he was fighting stock."

Serpent handlers received criticism early from those within and outside their fellowship. A warning comes by J. B. Ellis in the *Evangel* of 9 May 1914, only a few months after the first mention of the practice in the paper. Ellis does not disbelieve the miraculous nature of handling serpents and fire, but he firmly states: "'All do not work miracles.'" He says that there are limits to be observed by the saints and that only the mercy of God has "kept some of them out of the grave." He continues: "I have seen some with swollen limbs. Others have taken up a great number of snakes and been bitten over a hundred times by all sorts of serpents and felt no harm. These, no doubt, have the gift of miracles, and could as easily command the lame to walk, the blind to see, and the deaf to hear if they would only use their gifts to profit withal." The implication of the latter part of this statement is that the gift is misappropriated. In the final statement of his article is another implied criticism. Some of the saints who handle serpents were not apparently demonstrating Christian love: "Let us get the gifts and use them as God directs and be sure we are in the more excellent way; for if we had all gift[s] and not charity we would amount to nothing."

The criticism that the power of God was being misappropriated is addressed again in an article five years later in May 1919 by M. S. Lemons, who warns the handler: "I tell you God will let them take your life unless He associates His power with you to prevent the harm." Lemons goes on to negate the argument that some were using the power to handle serpents that should be used for "heal-

ing the sick and raising the dead." He explains that it is God's power, not man's; thus it is God who determines its use:

> There seems to be a mistaken idea in the mind of some people in that they think God leases His power out to some folks and they use it for illegal purposes. . . . It is God that takes the hand of His little ones and wraps them in His own hand of power that can handle the poisonous reptile or that takes up the living coals of fire. It is not in man to do that. . . . No living man can get God to go into a shoddy business like that. . . . Some would accuse God of making a mistake (?) His signs do not follow unbelievers. No man can corral the power of God and use it for an illicit purpose.

Lemons also addresses another accusation, that the power is from the Devil and not from God: "It is very easy to conclude that they desire to leave the insinuation that we have the devil in the lead, and are coworkers with the same. We will let the Lord be judge. 'The fire shall try every man's work of what sort it is.'"

The first reference to serpent handling in the *Evangel* seems to be on 24 January 1914, apparently by the editor and General Overseer A. J. Tomlinson. It is included in a list of marvelous demonstrations of God's power being manifested by the Church of God. Tomlinson continued over the years to comment on serpent handling in the *Evangel*, sometimes devoting lengthy articles to the subject. The first long description, appearing on 19 September 1914, gives a second-hand report of the Cleveland meeting conducted during the previous month by George Hensley. The article, "Sensational Demonstrations," is headed with "Signs following believers, and miracles done in the name of Jesus are Scriptural and should be encouraged as a means of preaching the Gospel. Rom. 15:18, 19." Tomlinson recounts that some instruction about serpent handling was given during the meeting and that George Hensley had prophesied "that some body was going to bring them a snake to take up." On Friday night a rattlesnake pilot was brought in, but "None of the saints had made any plans or said what they would do about the matter and even went to the meeting with little or no expectation of such a thing." The serpent was handled, and some were bitten—but with no harm. Then on Sunday night, according to the report, the sensation being so great and the outsiders wanting to test the matter further, a copperhead was brought in—with the same result. On the following Thursday a poisonous adder and a rattler were brought in, "but as soon as they were touched by those under the power they wilted and never offered to bite any one."

Tomlinson says he was told that the effect of the serpent handling at the meeting was commendable and that many became believers. He adds, however, a qualification: "Can't tell what the final outcome will be, but believe it will result in much good for His glory and the salvation of souls, as all that has been done so far as I know was on Scriptural lines." In closing he warns: "Beware of presumption. Never try to handle a serpent yourself. Be sure it is the power of God that impels you and not a mere impulse of your own. Take it because the power makes you do it and no other way, then there is no danger." He tells his readers that it is a time when one may expect many miracles, but he obviously had some reservations: "It is also a time for Satan to be on the scene and try to press people into extremes and presumptious [*sic*] undertakings, which, if done, will bring reproach on the worthy cause we love so well."

The month following this article, Tomlinson

went to a meeting in Ooltewah—conducted by George Hensley, Amanda Hensley, M. S. Haynes, and others—where serpents were handled. His comments are entirely complimentary except for those regarding the press: "We found the attendance large, and the best of attention and order. In spite of the ridiculous falsehoods published through local papers, people are seeing the truth. Praise God." The next month, as part of his report on the General Assembly of the Church of God, he exuberantly proclaims without qualification: "Our people are taking up serpents and literally handling fire with no harm, besides speaking in tongues, casting out devils, healing the sick and raising those to life who are apparent-[ly] dead." Serpent handling heads the list of those "greater things" to which he says "We have come." Previously to the assembly itself he had said: "Wild poison serpents have been taken up and handled and fondled over almost like babies with no harm to the saints" (*Book of Minutes* 166; cf. 183, 268).

On 21 November he writes that serpent handling—a practice that would have been considered fanatical a few years earlier—has become not simply one of the signs *following* believers but one that was *expected* to follow believers. At the beginning of 1915, he writes: "The past year has been one of progress which has led us into many miraculous things. Quite a number have been able under the power of God to take up serpents and thus demonstrate the power of God to a gainsaying world." Again, at the beginning of 1916: "God is honoring His Church by giving the members power to take up serpents." During August of this same year he eloquently responds to a critical attack from outside the church: "Wild rattlers are subdued and tamed in a moment of time and fondled over like harmless babies. . . . No, we do not contradict His statement. No, we do not disobey Him, and reject His counsel and statement by refusing to do just what he says believers will do. He says plainly that belivers [*sic*] 'shall take up serpents.'"

Tomlinson continues his reply the following week. In that article he gives his perspective on most of the key matters relating to the practice: the numbers of persons involved, the duration of time in which the activity has prevailed, the absence of reported deaths, the instances of bites and effects on those bitten, the ostensible divine purpose in the bites, the overall effect on evangelism, the relevancy to salvation, and the parallel with biblical times:

> We do not pretend to say that none have died that were bitten, but not one instance has come to our hearing of any one of our people dying as a result of snake-bite. I suppose hundreds have taken up serpents according to Mark 16-18 in the last two or three years, and only a very few have been bitten, and still fewer that have been poisoned enough to swell. Some, like Paul, have shook them loose and felt no harm. Others have swelled severely and caused much pain, but almost as soon as unbelievers were convinced that the reptiles were really poison, God healed up the wounds. I wish to say right here that the taking up of serpents has been a great factor in stopping the mouths of gainsayers, and convincing unbelievers of the power of God. We do not claim this as a matter of salvation, but it is one of the signs that is being displayed to the glory of God among our people. . . . I leave it with any honest thinker to say if it does not read like Bible times. One verse is sufficient: "God also bearing them witness, both with signs and wonders, and with divers miracles, and gifts of the Holy Ghost, according to his own will." Heb. 2:4.

Tomlinson was not alone in his position regarding serpent handling. He was receiving significant reinforcement from his brethren. He writes in October 1916, "Calls are coming almost constantly for preachers. They say, Send us a preacher that the signs are following his ministry. They never saw any one take up serpents or handle fire."

The accusations and name-calling were increasing as well. Toward the end of the year Tomlinson states, "We are jeered at now for handling fire, and taking up serpents. They call us 'fire eaters' and 'snake charmers,' but such work is done with the deepest reverence and faithfulness." After this comment he gives a philosophical rationale not made elsewhere, the basis of which is love, and he expresses it lyrically:

> A love for God's Word suddenly seizes the inspired pilgrim. They know it is true and it shall not be put to shame. Then a sudden love for the serpent or the fire envelopes and possesses the performer and this conquers the reptile and quenches the violence of the fire. Deep love supplies the soothing oil, and thus the Scriptures are proven true in the face of doubters and scoffers. . . . There is a power stronger than logic. There is a power stronger than argument. You might try to reason with the serpent, and produce your argument till you are gray, and every time you put your hand down to take him up he will bite you. . . . But take one of God's little ones that belongs to the Church of of [*sic*] God (for these are all the people I know of that do such things) and let him get enrapt with the mighty power of love, and the serpent will yield to him and seem to be happy in his hands. (16 Dec.:1)

Tomlinson does not say much in the *Evangel* the following year about the practice, but in

November 1917 he said to the thirteenth annual assembly of the Church of God:

> It has been reported that a few of our ministers have become enthused, and probably a little over zealous, and on the spur of the moment declared that unless a person could take up a serpent or handle fire he did not even have salvation. Such wild assertions as these should be avoided. The Church of God stands uncompromisingly for the signs and miracles, and upholds the taking up of serpents and handling fire under the proper conditions, but does not stand for making such experiences a test of salvation. (*Book of Minutes* 268)

Tomlinson devotes a lengthy editorial to the subject in June 1918 entitled "Signs Following Believers." For the most part this a reply to an article in another religious periodical. In his defense of the practice he cites additional scriptural evidence and repeats that Jesus said that these signs would follow believers, adding:

> Besides this Mark says that "They went forth, and preached everywhere, the Lord working with them, and confirming the word with signs following." (Mark 16:20.) . . . And to help Mark about the matter the writer of Hebrews shows that the signs followed, because he says, . . . "God, also bearing them witness, both with signs and wonders, and with divers miracles, and gifts of the Holy Ghost, according to his own will." (Heb. 2:3,4.) . . . Paul encourages and endorses the signs following believers when he says, "I have therefore whereof I may glory through Jesus Christ . . . to make the Gentiles obedient, by word and deed, through mighty signs and wonders, by the power of the Spirit of God. . . . " (Rom. 15:17-19.)

Two years afterward, in April 1920, he writes an editorial in which his position is clear from the title: "The Signs That Follow: Why Object to God's Word When It Is So Plain?" Among other points, he addresses the proposed spuriousness of the key text in the sixteenth chapter of Mark: "No, sir! those verses are there, and all the higher (?) criticism and lower criticism too that have been running rampant during the last century, have never been able to force Bible houses to stop printing them." He goes on to repeat the argument of the consistency of Mark 16:17-18 with other scriptures from both the Old and the New Testament, concluding: "Remember these signs are to continue until the return of our Lord. Do not weaken because they are spoken against."

Even after 1923, when the split occurred in the Church of God and A. J. Tomlinson was no longer associated with the *Evangel*, articles appear in support of the signs as mentioned in Mark 16:17-18. S. J. Heath on 28 July 1928 strongly confirms his belief in the teaching of this scripture: "I believe as much in this teaching as I do repentance. I believe it is the will of our Lord that we live so close to Him that He can bring His Word to pass through the very church He has purchased with His blood." He denies that it is a test of salvation and affirms that one would have to be filled with the Holy Ghost. On the other hand, he condemns the actions of those who "have gone into rank fanaticism, and false teaching, bringing reproach on the Church, and disgust to intelligent people over the handling of serpents." He refers to the biblical incident of Paul on the island of Melita as an example of the proper circumstances in which the signs are to follow believers. Then he concludes: "If it becomes necessary to have serpents handled to convince an unbeliever, He [God] can furnish the serpent and the man" (3).

On 3 October 1931, B. L. Hicks responds similarly in an article, "And They Shall Take Up Serpents." First he says that the serpents mentioned in the verse are to be interpreted literally. Furthermore, he supports the unquestionable benefits of the practice: "serpents have been handled by believers in these last days, under the power of the Spirit and this has been a convincing sign to unbelievers and has been to profit withal." He also recognizes and condemns what he sees as attendant fanaticism: "It is also a fact that some have made serpent handling a hobby, gone into fanaticism and brought reproach on the precious gospel of Christ." He states that it is no more incumbent to take up every serpent that one sees than to lay hands on and heal every sick person. He concludes with a warning: "Be very careful and prayerful with our life which is not ours but God's" (1).

In more recent commentaries in the *Evangel*, the emphasis changes even more. The focus has come to be on the condemnation of fanaticism associated with the signs and on the provisional nature of Mark 16. On 5 December 1949, R. W. Harris writes: "You ask, 'Don't you believe in snake-handling?' Yes, I believe God has promised divine protection from swelling, death, harm, and injury in the handling of serpents, provided God causes and brings about the experience to one of His followers for God's own purpose and glory; but I do not believe in the modern system and method of practice" (9). George B. Horton in a June 1989 article devoted to the signs asserts that the entire passage in Mark 16 is conditional, that it "is a promise of protection rather than a command to perform" (Cross 20). He unreservedly adds: "Though done with ut-

most sincerity, snake handling is the divisive product of error in understanding the Holy Scriptures." Proof positive of Horton's case is apparently intended by the reference to the life of George Hensley. Horton makes such statements relative to Hensley as: "Unlike the more than 200 previous snakebites, however, this one would be a final 'act of faith,'" "The father of the serpent handlers . . . was bitten by serpents many times, thus revealing the times that the 'faith' he spoke of failed him," "The final failure occurred . . . in 1955," and "No amount of faith was to mute the agonizing power of its venom this time" (19-21). The irony, the impugning of motives, the absence of empathy implicit in these statements are in marked contrast to the earlier articles in the *Evangel* and even Horton's own final reference to Hensley. He quotes the old soldier's dying words: "I know I'm going. It is God's will." In seventy-five years of the *Evangel*, Hensley goes from saint to sinner.

The *Evangel*'s reports from the field could serve as a textbook on serpent handling. The rationale for the practice is there, along with the justification of the practitioners, the scriptural support, the initial leaders, the multiple rationalizations for mishaps, the practice's explosive beginning and infectious spread, the resistance from within and without, and the initial cautious acceptance followed in turn by welcome and—ultimately—rejection. These foot soldiers in the trenches of the battlefield reveal their exhilaration with the excitement and joy of the phenomenon they are experiencing. What is at times pathetic, outrageous, and naive in their actions and statements is transmuted by the power of their religious zeal.

5

And these signs shall follow

Serpent Handlers in Tennessee Courts

When sign-following serpent handlers first went forth, they were met with both exaltation and ridicule. Then, as ministering servants of God, they met the angel of death. They found that even believers sometimes die from poisonous serpents, as did Jim Reece in Alabama before 1920 (Vance 55) and Alfred Weaver in Florida in 1936. Among the sign followers little disruption was caused by this discovery. Each serpent handler had an explanation for what happens when a death occurs: all is within Divine Providence. But, outside the fold, others were outraged: "We don't like this sort of thing, and we'd like to stop it. . . . some of the citizens up here are going to try to get a law." And get laws they did.

Legislation

In Tennessee, legislation was passed against serpent handling in February 1947. The bill was probably engendered by events taking place in the previous eighteen months, including five deaths in East Tennessee and one in Southwest Virginia. The first death was that of Lewis F. Ford in September 1945. Ford, a member of the Dolley Pond Church of God with Signs Following, was a man in his early thirties employed as a truck driver in a munitions plant near Chattanooga. His serpent-handling beliefs became known to his fellow workers and, consequently, to a Chattanooga newspaper, which ran a photo story about him through the Associated Press (Collins, *Tennessee Snake Handlers* 17). Ford—attending a brush arbor meeting in Daisy, Tennessee, near the Dolly Pond area—was fatally bitten by a serpent. The report of his death was carried in the Chattanooga papers, and some twenty-five hundred attended his funeral at Dolley Pond (Pennington, "Ford, Rattler's Victim" 1).

In Wise County, Virginia, Anna Kirk died on the same day as Ford, after being bitten at a serpent-handling service ("Tennessee Preacher, Virginia Woman Die" 25). Soon afterward, George Hensley and Tom Harden also came to public notice by being arrested in Chattanooga and charged with disorderly conduct for handling serpents. In July the following year at a meeting in a home in Daisy only a few miles from where Ford died, Clint Jackson died from a rattlesnake bite. Ironically, Jackson, who had been injured at a plant in Chattanooga and released for medical treatment, had gone to the meeting for divine healing (Collins, *Tennessee Snake Handlers* 23). The next month at a church outside the limits of Cleveland an eighteen-year-old convert, Harry Skelton, died from a rattlesnake bite ("Snake Bite Is Fatal" 9). Five days later, Walter Henry died from handling apparently the very same serpent at the same site (Travis 9). Two days later at the funeral services, Henry's brother-in-law Hobart Wilson died from the bite of a serpent, reportedly brought in by Tom Harden ("3rd Snake Cultist Dies" 15). Before the close of the next state legislature, the bill that prohibited serpent handling was introduced simultaneously in both houses and passed. The code reads:

> 39-2208. *Handling snakes so as to endanger life—Penalty.*—It shall be unlawful for any person, or persons, to display, exhibit, handle or use any poisonous or dangerous snake or reptile in such a manner as to endanger the life or health of any person.
>
> Any person violating the provisions of this section shall be guilty of a misdemeanor and punished by a fine of not less than fifty dollars ($50.00) nor more than one hundred and fifty dollars ($150), or by confinement in jail not exceeding six (6) months, or by both such fine and imprisonment, in the discretion of the court.

In spite of the legislation, serpent-handling services continued at Dolley Pond. Consequently, some five months later, in August 1947, Hamilton County officers arrested Tom Harden and eleven other members, five of whom were women, for handling serpents during a Saturday evening service. Three who had been permitted to take their children home that evening turned themselves in the following day (Collins, *Tennessee Snake Handlers* 32). Ten of the members, including Tom Harden, were convicted of violating the Tennessee State Code against serpent handling. The decision was appealed to the Tennessee State Supreme Court in December 1948, whereupon the decision of the Hamilton Criminal court was affirmed.

Other than *Harden*, no decision of legal action in Tennessee involving serpent handling was appealed to a superior court until 1973. In September of that year Pastor Liston Pack and Assistant Pastor Alfred Ball of the Holiness Church of God in Jesus Name at Carson Springs, Tennessee, were ordered by the Cocke County Circuit Court not to handle poisonous serpents. The initial petition filed on 14 April against them followed incidents at their church services during the preceding week in which two men died from drinking strychnine and another was bitten by a poisonous snake. The two who died were the pastor's brother, Buford Pack, and former pastor Jimmy Williams. The petitions against Pastors Pack and Ball were made not on the basis of the Tennessee statutory code (criminal law) but on common law (civil law). The

*George Hensley
preaching outside the
Hamilton County Court
House, where fellow
serpent handlers were
prosecuted and finally
convicted. Photograph
1947 by J. C. Collins.*

original petition was to prohibit the handling of serpents or the taking of poisons and, upon failure to do so, to padlock the church as a public nuisance. Two weeks after this petition was filed—following the special homecoming services of the Carson Springs church, where followers were still drinking poison and handling serpents, and where at least one more person had been bitten—the district attorney for Cocke County filed a second petition charging that the county "was in imminent danger and likely to 'become the snake handling capitol of the world'" (S v. P, 527 S.W. 2d 104). Pack and Ball were held in contempt, fined, and sentenced: Pack $150 and thirty days confinement

and Ball $100 and twenty days. The sentences were suspended until the defendants handled serpents again in Cocke County. In August the two men were jailed in default of payment of the fines. The following month the final decree of the trial judge was issued enjoining them perpetually from handling serpents in Cocke County. Pack and Ball spent four days in jail before the fines were paid, and the decision of whether they would serve their jail sentences was deferred until appeals were concluded. The state filed first to the Court of Appeals; next, to the State Supreme Court; then the defendants appealed to the United States Supreme Court, which denied certiorari; i.e., the court did

Some principal members of the Dolley Pond Church, left to right: Reece Ramsey; Maggie Parker; Tom Harden's sister Ida; Harden's mother, Allie; and Mrs. Joe Ramsey. Photograph 1947 by J. C. Collins, identifications by Flora Bettis.

not deem it compelling to call up the records from the lower courts and pass judgment on their decisions.

The major arguments in the legal opinions set down by these courts may be presented as follows:

1. The First Amendment to the Constitution guarantees religious freedom: "Congress shall make no law respecting an establishment of religion or prohibiting the free exercise thereof." Government, state or federal, may not regulate the unconditional, absolute right of religious belief.

2. Religious conduct is encompassed within the shelter of the First Amendment since religious belief is an empty right unless physical expression of that belief is permitted.

3. Religious conduct, unlike belief, is not unconditionally guaranteed; it may be prohibited under certain conditions in the interests of society.

4. Restriction on religious activity must withstand constitutional scrutiny: "the State's interest must be compelling, it must be substantial, and the danger must be clear and present and so grave as to endanger paramount public interest before the State can interfere" (S v. P, 527 S.W. 2d 101.)

5. The state has a compelling interest in protecting human life and "in having a strong, healthy, robust, taxpaying citizenry" (S v. P, 527 S.W. 2d 102). The state, therefore, is obliged to prohibit actions that endanger the life, safety, and health of its citizens—and this obligation extends even to the "right to protect a person from himself and to demand that he protect his own life" (S v. P, 527 S.W. 2d 113).

6. The state's right to "having a viable citizenry" and to protecting individuals against themselves is not unconditional; "the State's interest in the 'viability of its citizens'" is not necessarily sufficient "as a logic leading to unlimited paternalism" (S v. P, C of A 18). The state's right must be evaluated in respect to the individual's: "No general answer can be given to the question of the State's constitutional power to protect the individual from himself. Rather, the State's interest must be weighed against the individual interest in concrete circumstances in which the factors affecting the balance can be identified and evaluated" (S v. P, C of A 17).

7. The methods selected to restrict a religious activity may not be more than are necessary, and "in reconciling governmental interests with religious liberty every possible leeway must be given to the claims of religious faith" (S v P, C of A 13-14). "The scales are always weighed in favor of free exercise of religion" (S v. P, 527 S.W. 2d 101).

Legal procedures being taken in 1947 against members of the Dolley Pond Church after seven men and five women were arrested for violating the recently passed state code prohibiting handling of serpents. Photograph by J. C. Collins.

The Court of Appeals, from their perspective on these tenets, found the injunction against Pack and Ball "unconstitutionally broad" (21) and modified it to prohibit them from handling serpents "'in such manner as will endanger the life or health of persons who do not consent to exposure to such danger'" (21). The Tennessee State Supreme Court overruled that opinion: "we hold that those who publicly handle snakes in the presence of other persons and those who are present aiding and abetting are guilty of creating and maintaining a public nuisance" (113).

Simply put, the State Supreme Court said that Pack and Ball were free to hold their religious be-

lief in serpent handling but that their practice of it was a public nuisance. Further, the prohibition of this religious activity, they said, was not unconstitutional; it conflicted with the compelling interest of the state to ensure the life and health of Pack and Ball as well as those who were present when they handled poisonous snakes:

Under this record, showing as it does, the handling of snakes in a crowded church sanctuary, with virtually no safeguards, with children roaming about unattended, with the handlers so enraptured and entranced that they are in a virtual state of hysteria and acting under the compulsion of "anointment", we would be derelict in our duty

*Judge George Shepherd of Cocke County, Tennessee.
In 1973 Judge Shepherd tried and convicted Pastor
Liston Pack and Deacon Alfred Ball for handling
serpents. Photograph 1983 courtesy of George
Shepherd.*

if we did not hold that respondents and their con-
federates have combined and conspired to commit
a public nuisance and plan to continue to do so.
The human misery and loss of life at their "Homecoming" of April 7, l970 is proof positive. (113)

The State Supreme Court addressed the original
petition (not just the trial court injunction) against
Pack and Ball and prohibited not only handling poisonous snakes but also "consuming strychnine or any
other poisonous substances, within the confines of
the State of Tennessee" (114).

The Court of Appeals, on the other hand, had
addressed principally the final injunction issued by
the trial court, which prohibited Pack and Ball only
from handling poisonous serpents in any church
service in Cocke County. In their modification of
that injunction, they noted—among other things—
that "the right of the State to protect the snake
handlers from themselves—is not involved in a
public nuisance action" (17) and, furthermore, that
"as the societal effect of one's conduct diminishes,
so does the legitimacy of the State's interest in it"
(18). Their reasoning from these concepts, among
others, was "Where a 'preferred freedom' is at stake
and the State can demonstrate no greater interest
than the most generalized concern for robust citizens, it has failed to produce a compelling reason
for the restriction on them. . . . we are unable to
see how the State's generalized interest in a healthy
citizenry can outweigh the right of persons engaged
in the earnest exercise of their religion from con-
trolling their own bodies, even if at some danger
to themselves, under circumstances where those
not sharing their beliefs are fully protected" (19-20).
The Court of Appeals did not affirm, however, that
individuals other than the serpent handlers had
been fully protected. In fact they ordered that Pack
and Ball were responsible for proving to the trial
court "that non-consenting adults and minors will
not be endangered" (21).

The modification set forth by the Court of Appeals was deemed improper by the State Supreme
Court because, in the words of the opinion written by Justice Henry, there is "no reason to restrict
the injunction to the terms of the statute, nor is
there any occasion for applying a 'consenting adult'
criterion." Although the Court of Appeals did not
base its judgment on the Tennessee statute, it did

use the language of the statute as well as to concur with its conditions (i.e., the restriction upon the manner in which others, rather than the handler, are endangered).

The objection by the Tennessee Supreme Court to permitting consenting adults to handle serpents was that "this practice is too fraught with danger to permit its pursuit in the frenzied atmosphere of an emotional church service, regardless of age or consent" (114). The implication of this statement is that the Supreme Court may have allowed consenting adults to handle serpents if the atmosphere of the church services had been different from the court's perception of it as gained from the court's own record and research (113). Moreover, the State Supreme Court's perception seems completely different from that of the Court of Appeals: "The proof in this case demonstrates that some care is taken to avoid injury to nonparticipants. There is no indication that an on-looker has ever been bitten. We find that the only danger to nonparticipants is the possibility that a snake might be dropped and escape into the congregation. We cannot know how likely such an accident may be, but the eventuality cannot be ignored" (9).

Justice Henry says there is "no reason" and "no occasion" to restrict the injunction as suggested by the Court of Appeals—that is, there is no reason merely to ensure that no one other than the serpent-handling adults is endangered rather than stop the practice altogether. It is curious that he makes this statement, particularly without addressing the limitation imposed on the state in a religious activity to select only those methods that are *necessary* to avoid an injury to the public.

In comparison with these two opinions of the higher courts on *Pack*, the opinion by the Tennes-

see Supreme Court on *Harden* twenty-seven years earlier is uncomplicated. In that opinion, as set forth by Justice Tomlinson, the defendants from the Dolley Pond church were guilty as charged unless (1) the statute does not apply to church services or (2) the statute violates the religious freedom of the ten defendants.

The first proposition is summarily answered and seems definitive: the language of the statute does not indicate the exclusion of anyone, and the legislature is concerned with protecting people at all times and places.

The second proposition is also answered with some dispatch. The argument runs along this line:

> (1.) Religious belief is guaranteed absolutely, but religious conduct can be prohibited constitutionally upon certain principles. One principle is that of protecting society from grave and immediate danger.
> (2.) The practice is inherently dangerous to the participants, and the handlers' precautions to avoid danger to others were inadequate.
> (3.) The prohibition of the defendants' serpent handling, therefore, is constitutional.

This argument, which at first seems conclusive, is limited from the point of view of contemporary constitutional analysis. As categorically stated by the Court of Appeals: "While it is possible that the result reached in *Harden* might be reached by the U.S. Supreme Court today, it is altogether self-evident that under modern constitutional theory that legal conclusion could not be justified using the analytic methods employed by the *Harden* Court" (16). In the context of constitutional interpretation during 1948 the only necessary criterion was to show a rational relationship between the restrictions placed on religious conduct and the state's interest in those restrictions. Presently, it is not adequate to demonstrate that simple relationship: "such constraints are now subject to strict scrutiny of the nature of the governmental concern at stake, the relationship of the legislation to it, and the availability of other means to achieve the end sought that will less drastically invade the liberty" (16).

Tennessee was not the first state to make serpent handling a criminal offense. Kentucky passed a law in 1940 and, in the decade following, five other states were to have similar statutes: Georgia (1941), Virginia and Tennessee (1947), North Carolina (1949), and Alabama (1950). The laws were similar yet diverse. The majority placed emphasis on the manner in which a serpent was handled rather than on the act itself—so as not to endanger the life of (seemingly) *another* person (Georgia, Virginia, Tennessee, Alabama). In the Tennessee code, according to the 1948 State Supreme Court opinion, "any person" included the snake handler; the 1975 opinion says "any *other* person" (112). North Carolina's statute focused on the act and made "intentional exposure" to venomous reptiles and "inducement to such exposure" illegal; even preaching the signs would be illegal. Georgia's code made it not only illegal but a felony to encourage someone else to handle a poisonous serpent in a manner dangerous to the other person. A minister of the gospel or anyone else in accordance with his or her own belief at a religious ceremony was not exempted. Kentucky's law was the only one directed specifically at religious services, and it did not designate the poisonous nature of the animal: "Any person who . . . uses any kind of reptile in connection with any religious service or gathering. . . ."

Punishments for violation were also varied; four of these statutes punished the offense as misdemeanors with fines ranging from fifty to five hundred dollars, and two of these with the possibility of imprisonment of up to six months (Tennessee, North Carolina). Alabama along with Georgia made violation a felony with jail sentences from one to twenty years. The most stringent punishment was Georgia's in the event that the violation effected the death of another person, in which case the law stated: "the prisoner shall be sentenced to death, unless the jury trying the case should recommend mercy" (No. 387). Georgia and Alabama have since repealed their laws. Virginia and Tennessee have diminished the punishment. The Tennessee code as repealed and reinstated reads basically the same and authorizes as punishment an imprisonment of "not greater than thirty (30) days or a fine not exceeding fifty dollars ($50) or both unless otherwise provided by statute" (39-17-101; 40-35-111).

States did not require statutes against serpent handling, however, to make convictions against it. The legal action against Pack and Ball, which was based on common law rather than criminal law, is a case in point. A suit tried in Virginia also prior to the passing of a code is one against a minister, Harvey O. Kirk. He was convicted of involuntary manslaughter of his wife Anna, "whose death was caused by the bite of a snake alleged to have been held by Kirk during a church ceremony" (Kirk v. Commonwealth 410). The State Supreme Court of Appeals reversed the decision and granted a new trial on the claim that the jury was not provided with proper instructions. Because of its reversal the court did not deem it necessary to pursue certain claims of the defense. One of the claims was that some members of the jury were prejudiced against

Kirk because of his religious beliefs. Any prejudging would have ensued no doubt on the man's wife being mentally ill and miscarrying a six-month pregnancy as a result of the serpent bites (411). The Reverend Kirk "pleaded guilty to manslaughter and accepted a sentence of three months in jail" (Kane, "Snake Handlers of Southern Appalachia" 74).

Appeals resulting from the state laws were executed, as in *Harden*, primarily on the principle of constitutionality. In the Kentucky Court of Appeals, Justice Tilford in the opinion for *Lawson* deals with the dichotomy of belief versus action and the limitation on religious freedom in deference to public safety. He also discusses in considerable detail the motivation of the framers of the United States Constitution in guaranteeing religious freedom: "As Colonists, with the exception of those who resided in Maryland, Rhode Island, and Pennsylvania, they had been subjected to punishment for nonconformance with the established religions. . . . Almost every deviation from the established practice or faith constituted a crime. . . . From these abuses they sought relief, not the right, under the guise of religious freedom, to jeopardize the safety, health, or welfare of their fellowman" (974-75).

Rather than give a lengthy exposition, Chief Justice Stacy of the Supreme Court of North Carolina in his opinion on *Massey* states succinctly: "as a matter of law the case comes to a very simple question: Which is superior, the public safety or the defendants' religious practice? The authorities are at one in holding that the safety of the public comes first" (180). Similarly, the Court of Appeals of Alabama denied Luther (Loyd) Hill's "main contention . . . that the statute penalizing the practice of snake handling is unconstitutional" (883).

Fundamentally, the argument in these appeals first establishes a simple, reasonable relationship between the restriction of the right to religious freedom and the state's interest. On that basis it declares the restriction constitutional. As the Tennessee State Court of Appeals commented in regard to *Harden*, the United States Supreme Court might arrive at the same conclusion, but this argument is contemporarily insufficient in determining the constitutionality of restriction on religious actions. Now the principal questions are: (1) What is the subtle balance between the state's right to maintain a robust society and the individual's right to practice religious beliefs even at personal danger? (2) Does the legislation maintain that balance? and (3) What is the best method to achieve that balance?

Arrest and Prosecution

Besides the question of legality there is the matter of arrest and prosecution. Ten years after the Tennessee Supreme Court decision on *Pack*, Charles Prince was bitten by a rattlesnake during a religious service in Greeneville, Tennessee, and subsequently died. The response of the officers of the court to this event gives some insight into the attitude of legal authorities in Tennessee toward serpent handling. Gale Collier was sheriff of Greene County in 1985 when the incident occurred. He describes the involvement of his department:

> On Monday morning, the nineteenth of August, we received a call that a man was sick up in the Limestone area of Greene County; and one of my sergeants went up to a home up there, Carl Reed's home, up on what we call the Bowmantown Road, and he went to this house and he found this man

Charles Prince hooked with a cane by one of the arresting Haywood County officers in 1985 for violating the North Carolina state code against handling serpents. Photograph by Mike DuBose.

there that had already died. He got to talking to some people that were there, and they said he had been bit by a snake. . . . By result of talking to those people that were there at the home at the time, we found out that he had had a service down here at one of those churches, Apostolic Church down here on the old Knoxville Highway, just out of the city limits of Greeneville here. So, from the results of that, we began to investigate as to what took place.

The ensuing autopsy revealed rattlesnake bites on the left hand, hemorrhage below the skin, hemorrhage of the stomach, hemorrhage of small and large bowel, kidney shock, and aspiration of the contents of stomach hemorrhage possibly during the throes of death. The imminent cause of death reported was "Rattlesnake venom reaction and/or strychnine ingestion." No legal actions were filed. Sheriff Collier explains:

The way I read the code on this particular law, it was a little bit vague as to what they could do and what they couldn't do. I felt like, in my own opinion after I read that, that that was his freedom to worship anyway that he seed fit to; and the people that were down there—I felt like if they thought their life was in danger, they wouldn't have went in that church. And if I understood the law right, you had to feel like this snake was endangering peoples's lives to have it out. So, it's possible he could have been in violation of the law. But the law, to me, was vague on the thing; and we've talked with the Attorney General about it and we just decided that maybe we didn't have to do nothing, to let it go as it was.

At the time, Berkeley Bell was the attorney general with jurisdiction over Greene County. He openly discusses some of the difficulties with the code, in particular one of the matters delineated by the Tennessee Supreme Court opinion:

If you take what Justice Henry said in that opinion, then I can perceive a situation where a person could handle the snakes in, say, behind glass, a glass partition in which there was no danger to anyone else and them not being in violation of the law. But I would like to put a caveat on that, in that that's not what this statute says. A literal interpretation of this statute is that it applies to *any* person; that's what it says, "any person." If it's interpreted literally, then it could very well apply to the person who's actually handling the snakes.

District Attorney Bell also remarks on the problem of prosecution:

You know, we sit around here and we talk about a lot of things that we know go on, as a matter of general knowledge, if it's been in the paper or whatnot, but when it comes time to bring the matter into court, you really have to have proof. And that's the rub, so to speak. That's where the real rub is—you've got to have it. It's very difficult to get.

The matter of evidence may well be the reason the petition against Pack and Ball was made on a public nuisance charge rather than on a violation of the state statute.

Besides the problems with the meaning of the statute itself and with obtaining relevant proof of endangerment that would hold in court, there are other matters to consider. Arresting people who are religiously adamant in their actions in order to protect them against themselves is impractical in many local situations and seems ultimately futile. Charles Prince is a case in point. Two weeks before he was bitten and died in Greeneville, Charles was holding a Sunday afternoon meeting in Canton, North Carolina, outside the building that served as his home and place of business; he was, ironically, a successful distributor of worms used as bait. He had already been raided and had serpents confiscated during a meeting the month before. He knew that the sheriff was going to be present and that he might be arrested, although he did not seek arrest. He even called on me as a university professor to document the service in the mistaken hope that it would then be considered an educational event, thus justifying the legality of his use of serpents.

The sheriff, Jack Arrington, was indeed there and made it clear that the law prohibited handling of serpents even in a religious service and that anyone doing so would be arrested. Bales of hay had been placed around to provide a barrier between the onlookers and the participants, who were for the most part under a funeral tent that had been pitched for shelter. Prince's father from Georgia; Allen Williams from Newport, Tennessee; Marvin Gregg from Morristown, Tennessee; Jimmy Morrow from Del Rio, Tennessee, and other preachers and associates greeted each other with embraces. But there was no sign of the familiar serpent boxes. Very soon after the service began, a table drawer within the tent was opened and Charles came out of the tent with an armload of large serpents. Deputy sheriffs began closing in around him while Charles tried to evade them. Sheriff Arrington walked straight up and grabbed one of the serpents, which immediately bit him: "I thought I'd get a closer hold up to its head where I could control his motion, and I reached to get him closer to his neck, and the snake went to the right and come back and bit me on my left hand. I finally got him down and stepped on his head and got a deputy to come stand on his head there. Then I went on to the hospital and was treated at the hospital and stayed in the hospital maybe fourteen or fifteen days."

Charles and Allen Williams were arrested on warrants for violation (during the previous service on 7 July) of North Carolina statute 14-418 prohibiting "handling of reptiles or suggesting or inducing others to handle." Charles, in addition, was charged with the obstruction of an officer discharging his duty. Allen, the son of Jimmy Williams—who died from drinking strychnine at the Carson Springs service—was bitten a week after the arrest in Canton and just a week before attending the service in Greeneville when Charles died.

Serpent handlers who are genuinely committed to their beliefs do not discontinue their practice because they are put in jail or threatened with jail. They identify with the apostles in their persecutions as the result of following the teachings of Christ, and they often quote Peter: "We ought to obey God rather than men" (Acts 5:29). Strong believers in the signs are willing even to die rather than not follow what they believe the Bible and the Holy Ghost direct them to do. On one occasion Perry Bettis of Birchwood, Tennessee, had run from officers of the law rather than be caught, but later he unequivocally said: "I'll never run again, not from no man; I'll take my stand ag'in' the devil and I'll stand there. If I'm handlin' snakes and the law wants to take me in, that's just fine; I won't quit because the law come. I promised the Lord that I'd die before I'd run again—I would."

Pastor Marvin "Bud" Gregg for many years had no conflict with legal authorities over serpent handling at the House of Prayer in Jesus Name in Morristown, Tennessee. But conflict began after the death of Jimmy Ray Williams, Jr., from a serpent bite in July 1991 during a church service. There was no question, however, of his ceasing to follow the signs due to legal restrictions.

If we take out the serpent handling, then according to God, the Bible says if we take one word out of the prophecy, then our name shall be taken out of the Lamb's Book of Life. If I quit taking up serpents because of the law telling me to quit, then I believe that my part will be taken out on earth, that my part will be taken out of Heaven. I don't see no way in the near future, as my mind and my heart and my soul stands today, I don't see no way in the near future that I would quit, under any circumstances, working the signs of the Gospel.

Henry Swiney, pastor of the Holiness Tabernacle at Sneedville, Tennessee—a block from the courthouse—has handled serpents for some fifty years, thirty-five years right in Sneedville and before that on Newman's Ridge. He has never had any personal confrontation with the legal authorities about his religious practices.

Even though law enforcement does not seem to affect the practice of the committed serpent handler, it does sometimes smother the religious fire of those less zealous. At Newport there were those who became caught up in the enthusiasm of handling serpents before hundreds of people and the national media, but who quit under threat of being jailed after the legal actions against Pack and Ball. Arrests at Carson Springs did not stop serpent handling there, but as Alfred Ball says: "The trouble with the authorities had some ill effect; and on the other hand, it had some good effect. I think that that moved out some people who were only doing that—I mean, there's no point in denying there were people who did not live close to God as they should that were takin' up serpents. Some of those people got hurt, but when all the trouble with the authorities came up and some of those people began to realize, 'Hey, I could go to jail,' they backed up. They got out."

Whereas some serpent handlers think that legal authorities should not interfere with the services in any way, others recognize that there should be some limitations. Even Liston Pack, who contested governmental restrictions, says:

I can see the reason the law should have a law concernin' the church because here you got those people liable to give one to a minor or a mental [mentally incompetent person]. I agree with the law one hundred per cent due to that fact, because the law is good if a man uses it lawfully, and the Bible states that. You take just an ordinary person, don't know anything about the anointing of God, started—but say for instance, at Sand Hill, I can't really recall the man's name, but anyway, he crippled a boy for life because the boy was on the outside, and he was a non-Christian, but he just walked to the front of the church because his daddy was a minister, and this man laid this rattlesnake around his neck, and he bit him in the right hand, and he was crippled all until he died. So, you really need a law concerning that kind of aspect. Whether it's me or anybody else, operating a church in that order, should be closed down or stopped or put in jail.

Liston Pack tells another anecdote that is somewhat a parable of the responses that serpent handlers make to the prohibition of their practice. The story is of a certain two men who were tried and sentenced to jail:

They had a chain gang, a road gang. So, the third or fourth day, Judge Shepherd called them back before him and asked, "Will you not do it no more? If you'll give me your word that you'll not do it no more, I'll turn you loose." And so one of them did give his word that he would not do it no more; however, he's never did it no more. [The other man] . . . he wouldn't give his word so they put him back on the road. And it started dying out then.

The two men were from a church where Liston first saw serpents taken up, but which no longer practices the belief. Liston, who himself was put in jail for his belief, still handles serpents.

One wonders why society has taken such strong legal actions against serpent handlers. There has been no similar reaction to many other members of society who routinely endanger their lives—race car drivers, daredevils, and various athletes, to name a only few. Does our society have some deep-seated psychological response to rituals involving serpents? Is our rational world threatened? Richard Davis, a professor of philosophy, suggests: "We have responded with laws that may seem a bit irrational compared to the threat they pose. But we have done so out of our concern that the world view we hold as Protestants, Catholics and Jews, and as Americans in common will not be threatened by the extraordinary, the miraculous, the unscientific." Does the opposition to serpent handlers proceed from a concern for the welfare of the state or from a challenge to a faith paled by comparison? These are difficult questions.

Other profound philosophical and legal issues are involved as well. Society must promote individual values, but society itself cannot exist without certain restrictions. Every individual is important to the body politic, and what is harmful to the individual is harmful to the whole body. But how far can the state exert its paternalism in preserving the welfare of the whole? The preservation of life by the state is of great value, but certainly the quality of life often transcends the quantity of life. People have always been willing to die for certain values regarding the quality of life.

And there are practical questions involved in the legal restrictions placed on serpent handlers. Since these laws are enacted primarily to prevent harm, and not to punish a malicious act, do they effectively deter or merely punish? Or do they instead stimulate those activities by publicizing them and creating martyrs?

In general, are statutes against serpent handling good laws? Will such laws stand up in the light of contemporary constitutional scrutiny? Will more or perhaps all of them eventually be removed from the books? Will other measures such as better formal education resolve any legal expediency?

Whatever the answers are to these questions, the situation in Tennessee and some of its sister states remains a classical conflict between church and state. Sophocles heard it long ago on the Aegean, over four hundred years before Christ, and dramatized it in *Antigone*. The central figure in his tragedy, a young girl attempting to follow her perception of the will of the gods, wishes to give her brother a proper burial. The king warns Antigone that, in burying her brother, a traitor, she breaks the law created to preserve the state. Antigone responds that she is answering a higher law and is willing to be put to death rather than disobey it. Hers is a holy crime.

6

And these signs shall follow

Portraits

I am often asked "what a serpent handler is really like." The implication of such a request is that there is some prototypical specimen, whereas in reality the variety of individuals is wide. No one person, not even several, would give a complete perspective on the whole. One might choose an old-time preacher like Henry Swiney, Perry Bettis, or Harvey Grant. Or perhaps a serpent-handling family, like Dewey Chafin's, himself the most internationally publicized serpent handler; his mother Barbara Elkins, the matriarch of his congregation; his stepfather Bob Elkins, pastor and mine superintendent; his sister, Columbia, who died at twenty-two from a serpent bite; and his niece, Columbia's daughter, the strikingly unusual organist Lydia. Or one of the other leaders—past or present—from various states, like Carl Porter in Georgia, Arnold Saylor in Indiana, Bruce Helton in Kentucky, or Austin Long in Virginia. Or any number of others: a successful businessman, a tradesman, a laborer, a farmer, an elderly grandmother, a young convert, a quiet unassuming follower, or a charismatic evangelist. Any one of the choices would be good; all of them would be better, but of course impractical.

Faced with these choices, I have settled on the following portraits. Their purpose is not so much to give biographical data as to provide a sense of these personalities, a feeling for these lives. I feel that the individuals chosen here—Liston Pack, Charles Prince, and Anna Prince—do provide a significant, if not totally representative, perspective on the whole range of serpent handlers.

Liston Pack:
Out of the World's Black Belly

by Fred Brown

There is about Liston Pack a certain uneasiness, a restlessness that feels like a wolf's breath on the back of the neck. In his presence there is a solid feeling of the known and yet a sense that the unknown is awaiting its turn to emerge, that something might tear loose at any minute. In geologic terms he would be labeled dichromatic, for there are many sides and many colors to this man of God, a Holiness preacher unlike any other among the Holy Ghost people.

Here is a man who knows of what he preaches, and what he is about. Spawned and reared in some of the worst conditions imaginable, Liston Pack has visited the depths of depravity numerous times.

For the young Liston Pack and his eleven siblings, there were not many opportunities to succeed in the ordered, regulated society where protective law prevailed. Instead, his world was outside the laws of humanity or religion, a world where the One-Eyed Jack thrives. He survived in that world for twenty-seven years before discovering he had a conscience and that there was an easier, gentler flow to life than the one upon which he had been riding.

Liston Pack understands sin because at one time in his life, sin was the very core of his soul. "Before I was a man of God, I was a man of the devil. And the devil is strong. Understand, I was possessed. I had strong demons."

Indeed. There were strong demons inside a very strong man, a man who encountered not only the fist, but also the gun and the knife. Liston Pack has been shot and has shot in return. He has been slashed and has slashed back. He has been pummeled, and he has counterpunched with power.

He was born in Cocke County in East Tennessee in 1940. Although the rest of the nation was emerging from the Great Depression and heading toward World War II, Cocke County, rural and agrarian, was still staggering from poverty, mainly because of its isolation. The county, set in the adagio of mountains that make up the Blue Ridge, is at once lovely and uncompromising.

About the only thing that would make here were apples, corn, and moonshine. By the mid-1940s, the county had earned rightly the reputation of being the moonshine capital of the nation. Liston Pack's father, Albert, was one of its best producers of illegal whisky. And it was at his father's knee that Liston and his brothers learned the trade of turning fermented corn spiraled through copper tubing into a cash crop.

It was against this backdrop of lawlessness out of survival that Liston Pack matured, quickly and as hard as the land. He missed out on the innocence of childhood. Because of his father's reputation and abilities, the family had to move often, hop-scotching across the county, landing in first one area and then another. Born in a place known locally as Bat Harbor, Liston had moved a half-dozen times before finally settling in Del Rio, a community as tough as the sound of its name.

Before his eighth birthday, Liston knew the moonshine trade. By the time he was twelve, he had already been arrested for making and selling white liquor. Most of Liston's education came to him not in a schoolhouse but in the Pack house-

Pastor Liston Pack preaching on the "signs" at Carson Springs, Tennessee. On the pulpit are jars of strychnine, torches for handling fire, and prayer cloths anointed with oil for sick members unable to attend services. Photograph 1984 by Mike DuBose, Knoxville News-Sentinel.

hold, where the lesson was often minute-to-minute survival. But there are a few treasured schoolboy memories:

> I remember my first school bus. It was a 1930 Roadster. Kids sat in the back, all stacked on top of each other. We had to walk three miles to where we caught the bus. Most of the time, it would break down and not get to the bus stop. If it did, it broke down on the way to school. Sometimes, I rode with the teacher.

School for Liston was but a mirage. Education seemed to be for someone else. "I figure that out of the seven years I went to school, I didn't go 100 days in all." Moonshining in the backwoods with

his father Albert was far more constant than his sporadic attendance to classes. He, consequently, understood the intricacies of making illegal liquor far better than what seemed to him the spaghetti-like confusion of reading, writing, and arithmetic.

Spit out of the educational system and onto the hard streets around Newport and Bridgeport in Cocke County, he found life was marginal and as mean as a cur dog. He learned quickly the world of the quick and the dead, finally emerging as a leader and thriving on crime and violence.

From his early teens Liston Pack was not someone an adversary could take lightly. He was quick to anger, faster to fight, and ready to kill if neces-

Liston Pack, pastor of the Carson Springs Holiness Church of God in Jesus Name; his second wife, Mary Kate; and her son Jimmy Ray Williams, Jr., 1983. (Mary Kate's first husband in 1973 and Jimmy Ray, Jr., in 1991 died in "following the signs.") Photograph by the author.

sary. "I knew the mob" is how he describes his former life. He will not go into any of the details or confirm whether he was associated with the Mafia; but some weeks, he made as much as eighteen thousand dollars operating in the black belly of the underworld.

Let's just say what I was doing was illegal without saying what business I was in. I can tell you, getting saved cost me a lot of money. But, I wasted a lot of money, too.

I had no fear. Nothing. I didn't fear God, even. I had violent thoughts toward God. I know now it wasn't right, but I didn't then.

I was the baddest person to come out of Del Rio. If I told you to squat and you didn't, I'd squat you.

It is a matter of public record that he spent time in a federal facility on an attempted-murder charge. In fact his becoming saved more than likely saved the lives of at least two people—his and another man he does not want to name.

There was a man who had done me bodily harm.

Physical harm. If I hadn't gotten saved, he would be planted by now or at the bottom of a lake in a barrel full of cement. And, I don't think I would have made it to my 30th birthday.

At the age of twenty-seven, a battered and bruised Liston Pack confronted one of the many changes in his life. During a Wednesday night prayer evening, he walked into the Lincoln Avenue Church of God in Newport. That August night in 1967 altered him forever.

He became a man of God, almost overnight—well, almost. "It took three nights. I returned to church Saturday and Sunday. By Sunday I was saved," he says.

If it was hard for his friends and enemies to believe that Liston Pack had indeed changed colors, it seemed folly for the county's law enforcement personnel. To them, Liston Pack being overcome by religion was a bad joke.

"I knew I was different, but no one else believed it. You will find people today even who still

Holiness Church of God in Jesus Name at Carson Springs in a hollow outside of Newport, Tennessee. Photograph 1984 by Mike DuBose, Knoxville News-Sentinel.

think I am a dangerous man. But, I'm not," he says, his eyes crinkling into a smile that resonates across a face that seems to have been reconstructed of putty.

> The police didn't believe it. No one did. One day about two or three months after I was saved, the police chief saw me on the street. He told me to get into the car, that I was going to jail. I got into the car without saying anything. They knew right there that something was different. Had that happened a few days before, there would have been not one or even two men who could have put me in jail. After a couple of hours in jail, the chief said he was letting me out. I asked him what I had been arrested for, and he said nothing. They just had to see if I had been saved. I was.

Liston Pack knew he was a different man because he had discovered that he had a conscience after all:

> I was just sick about some of the things I had done, about some of the violence. I wasn't afraid of no human being, but I was afraid the Lord was going to get tired of what I was doing. I told everyone at the house that I was going to go to church that night, and you could hear them screaming for about two miles.
>
> When I was baptized, there were people who drove for hundreds of miles to see me baptized. It was unbelievable. There were people from different organizations and people I knew. It was unbelievable.
>
> They couldn't believe the way I wanted to be

Worship at Carson Springs, including visiting serpent handlers: member Andrew Click (drumming); Charles Prince, of Canton, North Carolina (dancing); pastor's daughter Elizabeth Ann Pack (playing guitar); Pastor Pack (speaking in tongues); and serpent handler Jimmy Morrow, of Del Rio, Tennessee. Photograph 1984 by Mike DuBose, Knoxville News-Sentinel.

baptized. Normally, they baptize in the name of the Father, Son and Holy Ghost. I wanted someone to baptize me in the name of Jesus Christ. I couldn't find nobody to do that. It was sort of scarce in that part of the country.

It was my conviction. To be baptized any other way would not have helped me at all. In the name of Jesus Christ is the name of the family of God in heaven and planet Earth and everywhere else. See, father is not a name. Son is not a name. Holy Ghost is not a name. Jesus Christ is a name of the family of God.

The church he was attending at the time disagreed with the way he was baptized. They asked him to leave. So he began going from church to church, keeping the manner in which he was baptized to himself. "Some of the churches I went to were Holiness and some were a homemade mess."

During that period, he went to Baptist and Methodist as well as Holiness churches: "My mother was a Methodist and my father was a liquor maker, so that is a bad mix and a bad strain. Daddy didn't attend church." Then he became a preacher: "I ran a check on my family tree, and I'm the only minister in our family for 500 years back."

Liston Pack is not a big man, though he is powerful. His shoulders are thick, and his arms have the appearance of strength. His right arm was almost severed in a battle against a man with a knife. He is lucky to have the arm today and thought, when he was being sewn together in a hospital emergency room, that he was going to lose the limb.

His face is ruddy and handsome, sculpted in places by several violent insults. A shotgun blast in the face was only one of these rude intrusions to his outward appearance. He was also shot once in the neck by someone armed with a pistol.

Then in 1978, while cutting timber with a chainsaw, he was involved in an accident that easily would have destroyed a lesser man. As his saw whined through an overhead limb, he incautiously allowed the blade to kick back. The double-sided saw slammed into the right side of his face and cut a swath three inches deep from the top of his forehead, through his right eye, down to the corner of his mouth. "It eliminated my right sinus," he says of the terrible ordeal. Although stunned by the event, Liston Pack managed to pick himself up and signal a friend to transport him to a Newport hospital. Because of the severity of the wound, he was sent by ambulance to a Knoxville hospital where he remained for four hours, stretched out on a table, awaiting attention. Doctors had to put ten inches of nylon mesh inside his head to prevent his jaw from sagging onto his neck since muscles and tendons had been damaged by the power saw. For eight days he wavered between life and death in the hospital. Eventually he healed.

The kind of vitality and intensity with which he approaches life is similar to the driving storm he brings to the pulpit. Pack did not begin as a preacher, but he says God called him. "I didn't want to become a preacher at first. I just wanted to be like anybody else, go to church and Sunday school and go home. . . . But," he says almost apologetically, "I have a gift." That is true.

Liston Pack can arouse a congregation. His preaching is a memorable event; the delivery is at once common and uncommon. There is an allegro-like symmetry to his sermons. They come hard and fast like the sermons of many of his colleagues, but there are few who have the sharp edge like Liston Pack. When he becomes anointed, it is a physical thing. He turns beet red, beginning at his hairline. Like a faucet letting loose fresh blood, the anointing cascades down his face, flushing it rouge and then eddying into his arms in ribbons. His sermons, punctuated by pacing and finger pointing, can last for three hours or more with Bible verses streaming one after the other. But he is always cautious to warn his congregation that to pick up a serpent is a dangerous thing. Liston Pack is as forceful for the Christian religion as he once was for the religion of violence. He has never been one to do things halfway. Says one friend, "I'd believe Liston Pack sooner than I would Billy Graham!"

He became an associate pastor of the Holiness Church of God in Jesus Name in 1969 under the Reverend Jimmy Williams. His brother, Buford Pack, was also a member. The church, established by Liston Pack, Williams, and Alfred Ball about eighteen months after Liston was baptized, is in the coil of Cocke County in Carson Springs outside of Newport. The little white clapboard building, formerly a hunting camp, sits quietly in a pretty wooded glen beside a noisy spring.

Williams was the church's first pastor. He did not always agree with Liston Pack, and Liston did not always agree with Williams. But Liston says that Williams was a very good preacher and he was glad for him to do the preaching, at least for a while. "I just wasn't ready, and I really didn't want to be a minister," Liston Pack says of that time.

Liston Pack had other demons to overcome, mainly reading and writing. He struggled with words. They turned to iron in his mouth. A minister needs to be able to communicate. "Jimmy Williams was way ahead of me," he recalls. "I just couldn't hold a crowd." But in 1971 Liston Pack took over the tiny flock at Carson Springs and has been its pastor since, except for one period of several years.

In 1973 an event took place that forced another change on Liston Pack. His brother and Williams died after drinking strychnine during the same service at the little church. A few days later, a temporary injunction was issued against the church from handling deadly snakes and from drinking poison. That order eventually made its way to the State Court of Appeals and the State Supreme Court, but Liston Pack and another minister had to serve time in the Cocke County jail for refusing to pay their fines. Liston Pack was and still is willing to undergo any hardship to uphold his belief in the Bible.

There is little to dispute that the Bible is his cornerstone of knowledge, for the Bible is the book that not only taught him how to read, but also how to write. "I have a gift," he says, "I know the Bible. I have read it maybe 100 times, and have studied it with people more than 25 times. There is a difference in reading the Bible and studying it. It may take you a year to read it through, but years to study it."

He continued to pastor Carson Springs Church after the deaths of Williams and his brother, but another event took control of his life that set about more change. "I backslid. I fell from grace in late 1976. I didn't stay backslid all the way up to 1983, but I had already resigned."

Part of the reason for his backsliding was that he had gotten a divorce. His wife left with his two children to start a new life in Florida. For thirteen years he had no contact with his wife or his children. By coincidence, his daughter called him on his fiftieth birthday; she had just discovered that her stepfather was not her biological father.

During the seven years he was away from the church, Liston returned to drinking and some of his previous rowdy ways. In the meantime, the church had elected John Wayne Brown as its minister. Later came two more preachers before Liston returned to the church—this time with even more fervor.

Because of his intensity in the pulpit Liston Pack has always found a following, not only in his church in Carson Springs, where he has been solidly ensconced, but also across the country. Particularly after the bout in the Appeals Court and Supreme Court, he was courted by Holiness congregations and had speaking engagements from California to Michigan.

His beliefs regarding religious conduct are as varied as the man. For example, on women in the church:

> The woman is the helpmate, but the same spirit of God that is in a man is in a woman. They are the weaker vessel, but they got a right to do a lot of things in the church and I don't think they should be put down. Without a woman there never would have been a man. Women can do many things in the church. They can prophesy and do basically everything a pastor can do.
>
> A church should be run by a governmental body. The members should have just as much to do with the church as anybody else. If a woman

Buford Pack and Jimmy Ray Williams (wearing the inscribed drape) during a 1969 service in Chester, South Carolina, four years before their deaths at Carson Springs by strychnine poisoning. Photographer unidentified.

can prophesy and she can speak in tongues and handle serpents, then I think a woman can do any of the work of any of the offices of the church, except being ordained. But she could share the message. There is no scripture in the Bible that says you can ordain a woman. The Apostle Paul never did ordain a woman. Apostle Peter or Christ never did ordain a woman. I know many different women who say they are ordained and that they are pastors, but there is a little bit of a disagreement with me because I do not think they can be ordained, but I'm not saying their liberty is taken

from them to obey God. They are ministers and helpmates in the church and a helpmate is a help to the pastor or the trustees or whoever it might be in the church government.

A lot of people stand against me on this. I think a woman can preach as good as a man, but I think she should have a man over the business and the government of her services to make the decisions because a woman is the weaker vessel. But if a woman can't do anything, then a man can't either; and we might as well fold it up.

About divorce—his second came in 1992—he has these thoughts:

> It is how it is approached. If the husband and wife are mistreating one another, if they come to where they can't agree or get along, and they commit adultery and be unfaithful, then God is not pleased with it.
>
> In some churches divorce would get your head cut off. If a minister is going with two different women, then he would have to be put out. He would have to be loose from one before he could marry the other. And he could only marry in the Lord.
>
> I don't believe God would put two sinners together [i.e., join them together in marriage]. Some churches state that the first person you have sex with is your wife. I would not think that. There is no scripture to back that up.
>
> Some people think that when you go buy a set of licenses at the courthouse, that is your wife. I don't think that either, because God never built a courthouse or bought a set of car tags.
>
> If you are married, you have got to keep yourself unspotted; and the one wife is all God intended for you to have.

On how women should dress:

> A woman looks her best in a dress; but on the other hand, there is no scripture in the New Testament that says a woman cannot wear pants.
>
> As far as makeup, it would be entirely up to them, but I think they would look better if they would leave it off their face. They are just covering up something. There is scripture that says a woman is not to wear makeup. There is scripture that says for her not to cut her hair. They shouldn't wear makeup or cut their hair. That's what the Bible says.

As for taking up serpents or drinking deadly poison, Liston says it is certainly not a test of his faith but a celebration of it. "You don't put the Lord to a test in the five signs. You don't put God to a test. God does not tempt a man. The only way you tempt God is by being disobedient to Him and not doing what He asks you to do."

On sin, Pack has this to say:

> If you see it is going to cause a fall from grace, you should not do it.
>
> The worse sin you can commit is homosexuality. That is misusing their bodies one to the other. That won't work in a church or nowhere else. That is very unclean.
>
> You can't please people to start. Mankind has got to make a stand and stand for God. If anything is a sin, it is a sin; but what I say is a sin might not be a sin. But if the Bible says it is a sin, then it is a sin.

Charles Prince: God's Hero

by Fred Brown

Charles Herman Prince believed that taking up serpents in praise of the name of the Lord was a pronouncement of victory over evil. For most of his forty-seven years, he structured his life based on those beliefs, which were impressed on him in childhood by his father, Ulysses Gordon Prince. In the end, those same beliefs accounted for his death in Greeneville, Tennessee, in August 1985. For Charles Prince, there was no other road, no remorse and no sorrow over it. He died in everlasting faith that good would overcome evil, that the Word would prevail. It was God's way.

Prince's story is not easily told, for here was a complicated man. Just when you feel you have him

Charles Prince "taking up serpents" and quenching through faith "the violence of fire"
(Heb. 11:34). Photograph 1984 by Mike DuBose, Knoxville News-Sentinel.

in focus, you have to look again. Who was he, and how did he come to be highly respected and sought after throughout the South to preach at Holiness churches?

Prince was born into a large family. There were two sisters and five brothers, some born before the beginning of the Great Depression and others into the teeth of that raw economic disaster that hit hard the South and men like Prince's father, who walked five miles to work in a sawmill for one dollar a day in wages.

His father became an itinerant Baptist preacher, traveling the back roads, hitting the small crosshair towns in Tennessee, Georgia, and North Carolina. From an early age, Charles and his brothers and sisters grew up listening to their father and attending worship services in home prayer meetings and on the streets near Gastonia, North Carolina. Ulysses Prince began with a Sears and Roebuck guitar and a Bible. Anna, Charles's older sister, remembers that "God was the number-one conversation in our family. As children we just played and prayed. It was a way of life."

They grew up watching their father and mother dancing in the fire, ignited by the word, handling dangerous reptiles, and reaching into wood-burning stoves and shoveling out handfuls of red-hot coals. And more. Ulysses Prince was rock hard in his beliefs. He would go off into the woods and fast and pray for days. The father made certain his children were washed in the Blood of the Lamb and immersed in the Word. At night when his children were growing up around Copperhill and Turtletown in Tennessee and Lowell, North Carolina, he placed boxes of rattlesnakes underneath Anna's and Charles's beds. Each night Anna and Charles fell asleep listening to the buzz and hiss of large snakes.

When Charles was six and Anna was nine, they attended their first snake-handling service with their father. Anna recalls the story: "Here was my daddy in the back. He had never seen it before. He went leaping up through there, jumped over this white picket fence in front of the platform, reached down, pulled up a copperhead, and held it up. Charles did the very same way the first time he was in a snake-handling church as an adult."

Ulysses began to preach full time, without pay. The family had to depend upon the good hearts of their mountain neighbors to provide them with what food they got to eat. "They wouldn't pass the plate in their church," says Anna; "my father thought you weren't supposed to ask for money. As a result we got poorer and poorer. I went from the time I was nine until I was 15 without a store-bought dress."

Ulysses told the mountain people at one of his services that he wanted someone to bring him a rattlesnake. They did, and at that night's service Charles watched as his father took up the serpent while Anna and her mother were in a back room praying.

Their evangelist father, Anna remembers, did not intend to stay in any one area long. On an average they moved every six months to a new place with new people and new needs for their father. "We just had to tag along and survive the best way we could."

There were times when their father would fast for as long as twenty-one days on nothing but water, and there were the marathon prayers after a long day of street preaching in Georgia or Tennessee. "We would wake up in the morning and the cornbread would be frozen on the top of the cook stove," remembers Anna, but "the first thing we did was hit the floor and pray. At the breakfast table we had prayer. If we had any lunch, which usually we didn't, there was prayer. At supper there was prayer, and before we went to bed there was a long prayer. If anyone was sick, everything stopped and we prayed. We didn't go to the doctor. There wasn't an aspirin in the house. We had Rosebud Salve, a jar of Vaseline and some Blair hand lotion. There was no medicine in the house."

Following his father's example, Charles Prince for ten years, from 1975 until his death, was a minister for the Holiness Church, crisscrossing the South's rutted back roads. In 1975, married for the second time to a fourteen-year-old, Charles Prince experienced a conversion.

Charles was owner of a bait shop in Canton, North Carolina. He was living the good life and clearly enjoying himself, his beer, and his cigarettes. Anna and their brother Harley had been meeting regularly at prayer sessions and had decided to talk to Charles. But, shortly before his sister and brother came to see him, Prince had begun to search for new meaning in his life. He looked back at the days when he was a child, going to church with his father, venturing into the mountains to fast for consecutive days with only water to drink.

"I questioned him on the Bible and was shocked at how little he knew. He could barely remember any verses," Anna recalls. The trio began meeting in the basement of the bait shop with others. It was during one of these sessions that Charles Prince stepped over the religious line and set off on a course that first changed his life and then took it over completely. "Charles said one evening that he had invited over a man who had lost his arm in a suicide attempt. The man wanted us to pray his arm back on for him. I told Charles that I didn't think we were up to that just yet," Anna said. "I told him we needed to start with something like trying to lift a coffee cup; and if our faith was strong enough to do that, then we might be able to pray that fellow's arm back on for him. I told Harley that we had to make sure we let Charles down easy on this one."

Charles—a short, stocky man with jet black hair—dropped to the floor as if he had been stunned and began praying, praying for the cup to levitate. The coffee cup did not budge. "He said it must have [moved] and that we blinked and didn't see it. He said he knew it lifted because he had asked God to move it." Anna managed to convince her brother that, if they were to pray for the man's arm and fail, it might do him more harm than good. Charles listened to his sister and decided not to attempt reattaching the arm through prayer, but from that point on he was never quite the same again.

He sold his bait shop for fifty thousand dollars. He gave his second wife, Linda Gail, half of the money and the rest to the poor. "He just gave away $25,000," Anna said. "He'd see someone walking along the street and give them $100 bills."

It was then he decided he would become a Holiness preacher. At first he thought he would go to Jerusalem, but he wound up in Haiti, attempting to establish a mission. "I never did know why he tried something like that," Anna relates. "But, he only stayed a week before he came home. He said it was a good thing that he had a bodyguard with him because people tried to rob him."

Charles Prince drinking the "deadly thing" while Pastor's son Robert Lee Pack (who does not follow the signs) plays guitar with visitor Marvin Hill on banjo. Photograph 1983 by the author.

In church one day, Prince decided he had to test his beliefs. Rather than conduct that test in front of the congregation, he went home to his bedroom. He jumped inside the closet and closed the door, where he prayed for hours. And then he downed a bottle of lye. It set him on fire.

> From my lips to the bottom of my stomach I was burning. I heard voices. They were telling me that it would do no good to go to bed, I was going to die. The voice told me it would do no good to go to church, I was going to die. I knew it was the devil talking to me. I laid down on the bed and my Bible opened to Mark 16, the 16th verse. It just opened like that. When I read that word shall the fire went out. I knew then I wasn't going to die. I returned to the service and shouted.

He never stopped shouting for the Lord, not as long as he lived.

Whenever Charles took command of a Holi-ness service, it became both an uncharted religious odyssey and an old-fashioned foot-stomping event. Prince would breathe fire from kerosene torches made from rags stuffed into soft-drink bottles. He would drink poison from fruit jars and walk on snakes with his bare feet. In his bare hands he would hold poisonous scorpions, their tails arched ominously. He would smile at them as they crawled about his puffy palms and fat fingers.

Prince's faith was strong. He believed as Paul wrote: "The last enemy that shall be defeated is death." He was simply a man born into the old-time religion mold. When he paced behind the pulpit, people in the congregation would stand, hands raised over their heads, waving and wavering and tapping into the spirit and his energy. The constant hum of rapture would swell and recede, punctuated by an occasional "Glory to God" shooting up to jar the thick drone. When Prince was really on, the floors would vibrate and bounce and the atmosphere would be charged with electric expectancy. Prince delivered sermons with zest and some showmanship. He was like other Sunday saviors, sweating hard, preaching hard, charging back and forth before the flock, causing the pine boards beneath his feet to squeak and to groan.

This man rose to such a feverish pitch in his zeal to spread the Word that his deeply religious family became concerned about their son and brother. You never knew what to expect from Prince, although it was always exciting.

Then, at the apex of his ministry in the churches of the hollows, where rattlesnakes and strychnine and the scriptures mingle in a deadly serious game of faith on Saturday nights and all day Sundays, he died. His death came as a shock and a surprise to the Holiness world. He had been preaching to saints and sinners alike on that sweltering night in the Apostolic Church of God in Greeneville, Tennessee. Prince had just pulled a very large yellow rattlesnake from a box when the rattler sank two fangs into the muscular section between the thumb and forefinger of his left hand. Two smaller wounds were underneath the thumb where the animal had slammed in two stubby, sawed-off teeth to assure that its victim would not free itself soon.

Prince rarely ever acknowledged when he had been bitten, and similarly on this night, he disregarded the bites and laid the snake on the pulpit. Despite the effects of venom, he continued his sermon, pausing from time to time to drink strychnine from a clear mason jar.

After concluding his sermon, he began to dance, whirling and hopping, perspiring heavily, as was usual. He waved a kerosene torch back and forth underneath his chin. Several times he stopped to sit on a pew; after a few moments' rest, he would rise and take another drink from the jar. As time elapsed, he became less and less active until he became limp. Several parishioners carried Prince from the church. They drove him to Carl Reed's house in Limestone, Tennessee.

Even his wife was convinced of his invincibility. When he was bitten, there was concern; but it was more of how long it would take for him to recover, not that he might not recover. "I think she was the only one who was shocked when Charles died," said Anna. "He had convinced her that if he went to the hospital he would die. As long as he stayed out of the hospital, he would be keeping the faith and the Lord wouldn't let him die. This was his way of thinking. He had made her promise that she would never call an ambulance for him, no matter how unconscious he got."

In the end Prince was a man of the Word, and he died by his interpretation of the Word as church members from Tennessee, North Carolina, Georgia, West Virginia, Kentucky, Florida, and Ohio gathered to pray at his side and tenderly but intently stroke his head and body with their hands. They used prayer to battle death, which was the way Prince wanted it. His only medicine—the only medicine Prince said he ever needed—was large doses of faith.

He followed the church's beliefs to a degree that commanded the awe of others of his faith. In times when he perceived that God's law collided with man's law, Prince never faltered, and those who knew him said he had a highly charged love for his religion. Prince liked to say, "God said it. I believe it. That settles it."

This, however, was not Prince's first embrace with death. Seven times before the fatal bite, he

Pallbearers taking the body of Charles Prince across the road to be buried at a site that was once a brush arbor where his father preached. Gene Sherbert leads the group. Photograph 1985 by Mike DuBose.

Charles Prince drinking strychnine at Carson Springs in 1984. Photograph by the author.

had been bitten preaching in Jesus' name. There were days when he was bedridden from those bites, and very few ever knew that at one time he was quite afraid of cottonmouth moccasins. "There are some snakes that you can handle and others that you are instinctively afraid of. I was afraid of moccasins," he said a few weeks before his death. But in the years of handling the reptiles and other crawling things, he had found peace with himself and with his faith. At the end, there was absolutely no fear in him. "It doesn't matter now," he said not long before he was fatally bitten. "I will take up any serpent."

He was so devout that he traveled hundreds of miles throughout East Tennessee, North Carolina, Georgia, Kentucky, and West Virginia to attend Friday- and Saturday-night services and Holiness homecomings on Sundays. He was becoming the Billy Graham of the Holiness preachers.

There was one quality about Prince that set him slightly apart from most others of the persuasion. He seldom waited for the anointing before reaching into the long and wide, primitively decorated wooden serpent boxes.

Prince usually was the first to the box and the first to take up a snake, any snake, and the first in line to drink strychnine. Once he began, there was no stopping or turning back, not until the service had run its course. "If it is not deadly, then I don't want to drink it," he once said. His black hair would jitter on his head as he bounced in his seat or skipped on one foot across the room. His eyes would look toward heaven, and there was a rapture about him. He smiled and at times would hold one finger up. Some nights he would sing and make a joyful noise unto the Lord.

At one of his last services, Prince brought in a quart jar of strychnine, saying: "It's still got the feathers in it." The feathers, he explained, are the undiluted crystals of strychnine floating in the deadly, colorless liquid. Streaks swirled in it like heat rising off of hot pavement. "He's a good God!" he shouted that night. "He don't put out the flames. He just takes away the pain." Prince believed that.

One night at a church service in Carson Springs, Tennessee, Prince bounded on one foot across the church floor, the first finger on his raised right hand pointed upward signifying the number one—the one God. Then he reached into a box and grabbed a canebrake rattler. The snake weaved before him. He took the snake by its tail and smiled and waved the rattler in one hand as he danced with it. After a few moments he swung it like a short piece of stubby skip rope. The snake moved against the force of gravity like a thick pendulum, its body worming upward as if to climb on the air, its tongue licking quickly. Next, Prince scooped up a half-dozen snakes from several boxes

Charles Prince, holding serpent, and Liston Pack "tread" on serpents. Photograph 1984 by Mike DuBose, Knoxville News-Sentinel.

and clutched them to his chest. This was his signature, an armful of snakes. They squirmed and writhed in his arms. He looked like a Medusa. His attention suddenly became focused on a beautifully decorated black snake box containing a huge Eastern diamondback rattler. The words of Mark 16 were etched across the box's lid. Before reaching for it, Prince began to shout, "He's a good God!" Pulling what seemed to be an endless rattlesnake from the box, he lifted the diamondback and held it high. The big snake waved back and forth in his hands, rattling a brittle warning. Prince hoisted it; and even with the snake held at the length of his arm, which was stretched up straight above his head, Prince had to lean at an angle to keep the snake's tail from dragging the floor. Its head was the size of a man's fist. The snake had appeared at only one other service, and no one had dared to handle it. "It comes out of the box biting at the wind," said the pastor of the church, Liston Pack. "It's a big 'un, and it's mean," he said. Prince strode before the pulpit while the rattler stiffened like coiled cable as if to strike him below his elbow. Shifting the weight of the diamondback onto his shoulders to free one hand, Prince retrieved a canebrake rattler from another handler and set it on the floor. Shoes off, he stepped on the mid-section of the snake with his right foot. With his free left foot, he roughly raked the writhing ends of the snake. He unwound the diamondback from around his arm and began again to dance on one foot, holding the snake high. "Praise the Lord and Glory to God!" he shouted. He swung the arm-thick diamondback as he had the other snake, then held it high, and looked it in the face and smiled. "He's a good God!" Prince shouted again

as he uncoiled the diamondback from his neck and laid it on a church bench directly in front of the pulpit. The snake filled the bench, spilling over the side of the worn arm rest.

Then the snakes were returned to their boxes. Prince stepped behind the pulpit and took a gulp from one of the jars he had laced with a half teaspoon of strychnine. He picked up a soft-drink bottle filled with kerosene. Someone lit the wick and Prince held its orange and blue flame in place underneath his chin and paraded back and forth. The flame spread as though from a yellow paintbrush up both sides of his chubby face. Soot coated his lips from the smoke; his shirt collar was singed from the heat.

"The serpent does not have the keys to heaven or hell. We are not looking to die. We are looking for eternal life," he said on that night.

His greatest encounter came a few weeks before his death. He was convinced that his religion and his people were being persecuted. "When God's laws conflict with man's law, then I'll have to follow God's law," he said.

Sheriff Jack Arrington, of Haywood County, North Carolina, had confiscated four boxes of snakes just before services began in an open-air tent behind Prince's bait shop. A cottonmouth moccasin was shot six times during the service by a deputy, and the sheriff warned the worshippers not to bring their snakes again. No one was arrested that day, though Prince and others were told that it was a misdemeanor in North Carolina to handle snakes in a public place.

"We will hold our services the first Sunday of every month," Prince said in response to the

Charles Prince "taking up" serpents at Carson Springs.
Photograph 1984 by Mike DuBose, Knoxville News-Sentinel.

sheriff's order. He also asked that his snakes be returned. The snake boxes, but not the snakes, were brought back.

A month later in Canton, Prince hauled out an armload of reptiles from a table drawer during a worship service. The sheriff and his men again appeared and moved in. The sheriff was bitten by a yellow timber rattler and had to be hospitalized for weeks from the bite. After the incident, he retired from law enforcement. Prince and Allen Williams of Newport were arrested that day and charged with handling deadly snakes. Prince was also charged with obstructing a law enforcement officer.

Prince was pleased with the outcome, saying he was willing to go to jail. He began preparing for his court appearance and even looked forward to challenging the law that denied him his religious freedom. Before the court date, however, he was dead.

Anna recalled a time three years prior to the fatal bite in Greeneville when her brother was struck by another rattler. Then, he had been taken to the home of John Brown, another snake-handling preacher. "The Rev. John Brown and all the people in his home were just as warm and concerned as they could be. They gave us a pallet on the floor and we stayed with Charles."

But things were quite different in Greeneville. "This time," Anna says, "they didn't offer me a pillow, they didn't ask me if I'd like to sit down. All they did was read me my cigarette rights when I came in that front door: 'We don't allow no smoking in here.' That was our welcome at the front door. They didn't even introduce themselves. This was altogether different from the time when Charles was at the John Brown home. It was as different as night and day. In fact I think it was night,

darkness versus light. At John Brown's home, they had cried and prayed through the night. Something went wrong here. If God had been in total control here, my brother wouldn't have died. I feel like these people had the wrong spirits, not all of them, but some of them."

Charles Prince died early Monday morning after suffering nearly thirty-six hours. Charles's father preached the funeral in Turtletown, Tennessee, a land of stenciled dreams and signs proclaiming "Jesus Saves," "Prepare to meet thy Maker," and "Get right with God." The old minister, crying at times, pleaded with Holiness hard-liners to let his son rest in the bosom of their faith. Some in the congregation had wanted to initiate a prayer vigil in which they would attempt to pray Charles Prince back to life. In the end, Prince's father held firm and the emotional funeral was held without incident.

A kind of quiet settled for a while over the faith. One of its strongest soldiers had been removed from the field. He died never really achieving what he had set out to do: to have a profound effect on the world for Christ. Charles Herman Prince was just beginning to be heard when he died the only way he could have, preaching and confirming the Word as he knew and understood it.

A Snake-Handler's Daughter: An Autobiographical Sketch

by Anna Prince

I paced the floor of my home in Canton, North Carolina, late Saturday night in August 1985. My brother, Charles Prince, had gone to a big snake-

Thirty-five-year-old Ulysses Prince street preaching with loudspeakers mounted on his van. (His daughter Anna generally helped draw a crowd by singing). Photograph 1946 courtesy of Anna Prince.

handling meeting in Tennessee. Over the previous few months, Charles had become a celebrated leader of religious snake handlers in the southeast.

He had nearly daily national media coverage as the press followed him to his meetings and even to his home. Radio stations from other states called his home to say, "Mr. Prince, you're on the air!"

I had hoped that none of my five brothers would follow in our father's footsteps. Our Dad, Ulysses G. Prince, was a fearless snake handler during our childhood. I have suffered much over snake handling.

Charles had been the quiet one, reserved, operating his wholesale fish-bait company where he was known as the "worm king." But something "clicked" in him! He began visiting snake-handling churches, becoming bold and daring, risking his life three or more times a week by drinking strychnine mixed with water, handling snakes and fire, often at the same time! As he became more daring, I became terrified he might go too far. I spent many sleepless nights fearing for his life.

The shrill ring of my phone sent a chill through me! The worst had happened! Charles had been bitten by a rattlesnake and was spitting up blood! Having witnessed eight snake bites, I had never seen anyone spit up blood. Had he drunk poison as well? I nervously dialed my parents in Georgia. They had to be told: "Daddy," I said gently, "A rattlesnake bit Charles! It's bad. I'm going to him. I'll call you from Greeneville, Tennessee. Stay home and take care of Mama! Pray, Daddy."

Fearing he might die before I could reach him, I prayed out loud as I drove the mountain curves. But my prayers were interrupted by self-pity and anger. How dare he do this to me! Hadn't I suffered enough from snake handling? I had begged him not to do it anymore. In a desperate effort to erase my painful memories and find my own identity, I had become an overachiever, running a small construction company, becoming a successful songwriter and performer, teaching a night class for songwriters at a local college, and being a candidate for County Commissioner. When I was nominated for Distinguished Woman of North Carolina to the Governor's Office, I felt I had finally succeeded in burying my past as the daughter of a snake handler and poison drinker. Now Charles had brought snake handling back into my life and might be dying from it himself. My other four brothers and younger sister were successful business people, most in other states, having nothing to do with snake handling. And like me they never mentioned it to anyone.

Directions given to me over the phone took me to a rural area near Greeneville, Tennessee, and to a new, two-story brick house with a groomed yard and swimming pool. The door was opened by Carl Reed, pastor of the church where Charles had been bitten—a handsome man in his late thirties. I felt grateful that he was caring for my brother and followed him through to the large master bedroom with a spacious adjoining bath. A king-sized waterbed centered the beautiful room, which was off-white, trimmed in navy. Charles lay on the plush white carpet beside the bed on a blanket, because the waterbed made him nauseous.

He was wearing a white T-shirt and covered from the waist down with a handmade quilt. His eyes met mine and he offered a weak smile, but I could see that he wished I had not come. He didn't want me to see him down and helpless. Holding his composure as long as he could, he began swinging his bent and covered knees left and right in a steady motion, murmuring: "Mercy, Lord, have mercy, Lord," in constant chant, "Mercy, Lord, mercy, Lord." His left arm, stretched straight out from his shoulder, was turning a grayish blue, swollen to over twice its size.

I knelt on the floor between his waist and his outstretched arm, closely looking him over and touched his hand, ever so gently. He winced in pain! There were three, possibly four, sets of fang marks, where the snake had taken his left thumb base into its mouth, biting repeatedly. His hand and arm looked like a grotesque balloon! Noticing

the dried blood in the corners of his mouth and the red splattered spots on his shirt, I asked: "Charles, did you drink any poison?" He nodded. I said, "You drank poison after you were bitten?" He nodded yes. I groaned and moved to the foot of the bed, out of his sight, buried my face into the thick carpet, and joined him in chanting, "Mercy, Lord, have mercy, Lord."

Three young men who attended him were seated on the edge of the bed. They were praying softly and bending over occasionally to squeeze a few drops of ice water on his aching hand and arm. As soon as they were gone, I moved quickly to my former place beside him and noticed his arm was becoming a strange gray color with pockets of poison turning his skin vivid scarlet, purple, and yellow in places. His swollen face quivered as if he had wiggle worms under his skin.

Fully aware that Charles like other snake handlers refused medical treatment, I cautiously asked, "Charles, can I call an ambulance? Can I get you a doctor? Please!" He mustered a firm "No!" turning his face as far away from me as he could.

I called Dad collect from the kitchen wall phone. I told him I had arrived and would keep him posted and returned to my brother's side. I thought about calling an ambulance and forcing Charles to go, but I knew he would likely deliberately roll off the stretcher in an effort to resist. Droves of people filed by, stopping to speak to him or pray. These people were "believers" from many different states. They were here to pay homage to one of their own. I draped my body over his arm for fear someone might step on it.

A big woman about sixty in a pink-flowered, shoe-length dress with a bouncy ruffle at the tail tapped my shoulder, motioning me to follow her into the adjoining bathroom. She proudly handed me photographs of snake-bite victims, arms and hands bloated by venom! She seemed as proud as if they were pictures of her grandchildren! I noticed there were no pictures of her and wondered if she just enjoyed the misery of others. Laughing and chattering she said, "We sat up all night with one man, thinking he was asleep. The next morning he was dead! Imagine sittin' all night with a dead man and we didn't even know it!" She laughed out loud! Sickened, I returned to my brother's side. A camera flash drew my attention to the right as the woman added Charles and me to her photograph collection.

Thirty-two hours had passed and he had not slept. The pain was intense. His breath came short and raspy, but I still hoped and prayed for a miracle. I had tended eight snake-bite victims and all had survived. But they had not drunk a pint of strychnine!

I wanted to gather him up in my arms and run with him, back to our childhood to wade streams, giggling, back to long summer evenings playing hide-and-seek, catching fireflies, sharing our secrets. Instead, I wept beside him, admiring his strength to live or die for what he believed to be true. I chanted for him, the words he could hardly say anymore, "Mercy, Lord, have mercy, Lord."

Lying face down on the carpet, I searched for a reason for the madness, the pain—an answer to why we were lying there on the floor of strangers, in a different state, begging God for mercy. Memories of scenes and faces from a different time and place came vividly to my brain. I thought back to when I was two years, nine months old. Someone took Harley, my brother, two years older than I, and me to a friend's house to spend the day. When I was brought back home, Mama, a short, dark-haired pretty woman, was lying on the bed in the living room, covered up. There were women moving around, and Mama called me and smiled as she uncovered a little baby beside her on the bed. The date was February 26, 1938, and would be remembered as Charles's birthday.

When Charles was able to sit up and I had passed my third birthday, I got the whooping cough real bad. Harley and Charles got it too, but they said I had it the worst. I puked a lot and thought I was going to smother to death. They said I coughed till I burst a blood vessel in my eye. I remember hearing the grown-ups say the neighbors were threatening to have Daddy sent to jail for not taking me to a doctor. But Mama just wrote to Granny (Daddy's mother in Tennessee) to pray for me.

Daddy prayed every morning in the toilet behind the house. He was trying to get something from Jesus. He and Mama liked Jesus a lot. I was afraid of Jesus. One morning, about daylight, Daddy got what he was praying for and came running from the toilet, around and around the house. He was real happy and jumped and laughed and talked strange. We couldn't understand him. The milkman arrived with the morning milk, and he couldn't understand him either. Hours later Daddy started talking regular again and said he had been speaking in tongues, that he had got the Holy Ghost, and that Jesus had called him to preach the gospel.

Now that Daddy was called to preach, he ordered a Bible and guitar from Sears. I was five years old the day they arrived. Daddy was sitting in the door of one of Mr. Lowery's rental houses (we would eventually live in all four) in Gaston County, North Carolina.

Baptism in Georgia by Ulysses Prince. Photograph 1947 courtesy of Anna Prince.

Daddy, a tall, dark-haired, handsome man of thirty, tunes up his new guitar and begins to sing, "What would you give in exchange for your soul." He sang loudly, "What would you give"—I walked up to his knee and sang, 'In exchange. . . .'"

Amazed and pleased, he realized for the first time that I could sing. He saw promise for his ministry: he had a Bible, a guitar, and a new tenor singer. He didn't have to go it alone. Now he needed somewhere to preach.

The following Saturday, Daddy and I made our debut on the sidewalk of Gastonia where preachers without churches often lined up "to preach the word." We sang our only song, and Daddy preached his first public service.

Our street preaching and singing became a way of life until I was seventeen! Daddy and I would be on some street corner most every Saturday except in the dead of winter, and sometimes we preached

and sang in blowing snow! We reached thousands throughout the Southeast on radio broadcasts, street corners, in tents, brush arbors, at home prayer meetings and a few churches that would let us in.

My restless father changed houses a lot. Even if the houses were identical and side-by-side, we'd move to the next one and then to the next. We lived in a tent three times before I turned sixteen and moved twenty-four times. Daddy always moved and Mama always had babies. They were almost always boys, five boys—the youngest was born in a tent. My only sister was born when I was fourteen.

We had no radio or television or even electricity. Our light was a kerosene lamp, and our heat was a coal heater in the living room. The Harrises, another couple about thirty years old, the same age as my parents, came to our house two or three evenings a week to pray. The four grownups, who had all come from Baptist backgrounds, along

The Prince children, who lived in a tent while their father, Ulysses, was building a block church in Turtletown, Tennessee. (Anna, eleven, holds five-month-old brother). Photograph 1946 courtesy of Anna Prince.

gan dancing in the flames and pieces of glass. He ran his hands through the flames as he got in the middle of the hottest part. He was not catching on fire and he was happy. He was having a good time. Mama joined Les in the flames and ran her fingers all through the fire. She played in the fire, and it did not even catch her dress tail on fire. Daddy and Pauline watched in amazement as their mates handled fire for the first time. The flames died out as soon as the kerosene was burned up, but the wood floor never burned. There were no blisters on Les and Mama's hands, nor were Les's knees cut where he had danced on the broken glass. Mama and Les had discovered they had the gift of miracles to handle fire and not be burned, if the spirit anointing was present.

From then on if a heater was present and in use during prayer meetings, it was common for my mother to open the door of the heater and shovel up the hot coals and hold them until they became cool, gray cinders, and Les Harris to press his face against the red-hot stove pipe.

My parents were like many other southern traditional Baptists in dire need after the Depression who exercised the one element they knew would work, their faith in Jesus. Their prayer vigils and meetings, their speaking in tongues brought the exciting belief that Jesus was visiting His people and giving them the gift of miracles as He had the disciples.

When I was seven, we moved to East Tennessee, near Copperhill, where our English Prince ancestors had settled in 1840. My paternal grandfather had been a medical doctor and judge there. I was born on Prince Mountain, the very same land where my grandfather had been born and which he was later to own. We had moved back home.

with their children got on their knees and prayed for hours for God to show them miracles and signs that He was hearing their prayers.

One night Les Harris began to dance and shout in the spirit. Daddy was speaking in tongues and Mama and Pauline Harris were clapping their hands and praising God. Someone accidentally knocked the kerosene lamp off the fire board! The lamp globe shattered, and the kerosene ignited on the wood floor. Les got down on his knees and be-

One day while eating dinner, Charles, four years old, reached up on the table and got a pod of Daddy's red hot pepper, perhaps by accident, because it looked so pretty. He stuck the small pod in his mouth and began to chew! I screamed at him, "Spit it out Tachi! It'll burn you!" (Tachi started as the baby name I called him because I couldn't say Charles.) But Charles didn't spit it out; he just kept chewing and big tears started rolling down his face. He wouldn't spit it out. He'd got the attention of everyone and he was not about to lose it. My brother Harley teased him, "You don't want any more, do you?" Charles just reached his little fat hand out, got him another red pod, put it in his mouth, and started to chew. We began to realize how determined little Tachi was and that he had an unusual personality.

When I was eight, we moved back to Gaston County, North Carolina. Mama worked night shift in a cotton mill and was sleeping days, so we had a lot of freedom to prowl. One day Charles, five, and my brother Don, three, went down the road; and before we noticed they were gone, I looked down the road and here came Charles dragging a big, dead black snake, and little Don tagging along behind it. They had bashed its head and brought it home.

Daddy handled his first snake when I was nine years old. We were living at the place of the chinaberry tree, three miles from where Charles was born, near Charlotte. (The chinaberry tree was a great climbing tree that grew in the yard.) Daddy heard that snake handlers, the Haley brothers, were practicing their faith in the area; so Daddy drives to their small church. We went inside and sat in the audience. Both Haley brothers had their arm in a sling from a snake bite. Still, after preaching, they handled two copperheads. Suddenly, Daddy jumped up from the back bench where we were sitting, jumped over the little white picket fence around the church podium and grabbed a copperhead out of the snake box. He looked happy and excited as he held it in the air. We all watched in astonishment as Daddy handled his first snake the very first time he had ever seen it done. Daddy had a strange gleam in his eyes as he drove us home. It worried me.

A few weeks later, Daddy quit his good job as supervisor at the cotton mill and made Mama quit hers. He sold all our furniture down to the spoons and forks. Mama cried over the loss of her Singer sewing machine. She wept, "Ulys, how am I going to make clothes for these kids?" and he answered, "The Lord will provide, Sister Prince."

He bought an old bread-delivery van; loaded clothes and kids, Bible and guitar; and moved us two hundred miles west. The last fourteen miles were on a bumpy dirt road as we worked our way into the southern edge of the Great Smoky Mountains to Aquone, North Carolina, overlooking Nantahala Lake.

We moved into an empty four-room house with no furniture. We laid our clothes on the empty floor. We had no dishes or pots, just one old frying pan. Mama made a campfire out back while we skinnied up an apple tree for some apples. We found an old wooden bench and some can lids; so we knelt before the bench and ate fried apples from can lids with our fingers. We had no spoons or forks. Daddy had sold them all. Since we had no beds, that night we piled corn shucks in the back room corners. We lived this way for several weeks.

Daddy worked long enough as a part-time carpenter to buy a public address system: two huge loudspeakers, which he mounted on a strong plank across the van top over the front doors, and a turntable and boom microphone anchored between the front seats. As his assistant in training for four years, since I was five years old, I was appointed to be his sound engineer and to play Gospel records.

One afternoon, a few days later, Dad and I rode up and down the mountain road, speakers booming, announcing an upcoming meeting. I played the Gospel music softly as he announced loudly, "We're having a meeting over at the Hicks house on Saturday night. Come on out! If anyone finds a big rattlesnake, bring it and we'll handle it in Jesus' name. Somebody bring me a big one!"

The next day, the mailman stopped by and told us that they'd found a rattlesnake and were bringing it out on Saturday night. Daddy headed up the mountain and started fasting. He fasted and prayed for three days and nights. We were still living in the house where we were sleeping on the shucks, and he gathered us kids around and said, "Children, if the Lord don't move, I may not make it; but I want you to take care of your mother." Mama was crying, "Ulys, do you have to do this? Ulys, do you have to handle this snake? What if it bites you and kills you? What are me and these kids going to do? They're all just little. I'm up here and I can't drive, ain't got no way to get nowhere. We've got no way to get something to eat. Ulys, do you have to do this?" He said, "Sister Prince, I've got to do it." So we were quiet that day because we were thinking, "What will we do if Daddy dies?"

So we went out to Edgar Hicks's house for Daddy's first serpent-handling meeting. It was just a little wood house up on the mountainside. The people came from far and near because Daddy had advertised another day or two on his loudspeakers.

We arrived and squeezed into the tiny living room. It was very crowded. The people were standing on the back porch, front porch, and at the windows. Outside in the yard, I saw two men kneeling over a twelve-by-eighteen-foot wooden dynamite box with a screen wire across the top. They had brought the rattlesnake. The men were blowing smoke in on the snake and poking it with sticks. "Let's make it mean," they said; "watch it strike this stick." Mama looked at me, and we headed into a little back storage room to pray, hard!

All while Daddy's preaching, we're out there just a-prayin' up a storm. We don't want to see him handle no snake. Then we heard the dipper fall off the shelf and the water bucket go bang, bang, rolling down the hill. We came out of this little room, and people were just falling over backwards, tumbling over each other, getting out of there. And we knew that Daddy was handling the snake. Men and women were climbing out of the windows, pushing through the doors, anyway they could, to get out of that house. They had seen all they wanted to see and were trying to give the preacher and his rattlesnake some room. A woman named Mag Wilson told me that when he pulled the snake out that it was just as calm as it could be. He held the gentle serpent up in the name of Jesus.

Mama and I went behind the house around the back after the men had their snake back. They were poking the snake again, and Mama and I heard the young man say to the mailman, "Let's make it mad again and take it back in there, and make it bite him and kill him." That made my

Mama real angry, and she turned around to them and said, "You saw him risk his life in the name of Jesus. You evil unbelievers! You wouldn't believe it if he raised your grandmother out of the grave." They got real quiet and just picked up the box and walked out into the dark. The young man who wanted to see the snake kill Dad was a healthy-looking young man, but he took a fast-eating cancer and in six months he was dead. We always wondered if maybe that's why he died.

Daddy built near our house a little place for open-air services with sawmill slab benches. He used his loudspeaker and advertised for people to come out. They came, some to join us, some to heckle us. Several young women and girls screamed and called us "holy rollers" and "snake handlers" and yelled, "You wouldn't know the Bible if you saw it." They yelled until it was almost impossible to preach, but he had the loudspeaker so he could talk loudest. They didn't bother Daddy that much, but they bothered me an awful lot.

Soon I had to go to school with those girls. I was nine years old; and when I began the new school, the kids would torment me relentlessly. My brothers didn't seem to pay much attention to the persecution, but I would try to defend the Bible and tell them it says in Mark 16, "they shall take up serpents. And if they drink any deadly thing, it shall not hurt them."

The children would then come with notes from their parents and argue, "My mother told me to read this to ya." At lunch time they'd gather around me and read the notes: "Well, how do you explain this scripture, such and such?" A certain crowd of girls would start the arguments at lunch, but the boys would lie in wait for me behind doors and under steps, jump out, hit me hard and run. I

had to go to school fighting. I fought all day and left fighting.

When neighbors realized we had no furniture, they told us about an abandoned house that was fully furnished up in the cove nearby. A Mr. Yonce had unexpectedly died about ten years previous, and his grieving widow had refused to reenter the house. The house had been vacant since.

We gladly moved into the rent-free house. We actually had almost nothing to move, just packed up our clothes and went. It was an eerie feeling as we entered the old house for the first time. The Yonces had been eating dinner when he died, so dried food was still on the plates and bowls. We took the plates to the nearby creek, scraped and washed them. Now we all had a plate apiece and lots of spoons and forks.

The house was big and rambling with plenty of soft feather beds and fluffy pillows. A huge bookcase was filled with books like *Tarzan of the Apes* and Zane Grey westerns. I was ecstatically happy because I loved to read! I've read at least thirty-five books a year since that time.

Mama was very pleased with the fully furnished kitchen. She had everything she needed to make us a home. I prayed that Daddy would not move us away from this big delicious house, the best we'd ever had. We settled into a good and easy life, catching lightning bugs, playing hide-and-seek, and laughing a lot. My brothers never tired of my nighttime songs about little children lost or dying and the ghost and panther tales.

On one occasion when several of us kids were picking blackberries up on the mountain for Mama to can, Charles got sick and Mama thought maybe he had eaten a poisonous spider while eating unwashed berries. Charles got worse and lapsed into a coma with a high fever. Days and nights passed, but Charles did not wake up. Mom and Dad just walked around, in a daze, praying as they went. But they didn't take him to the doctor. Even though Daddy's father had been a medical doctor, Daddy's new faith demanded of him that he not take medicine; and he demanded it of his wife and children. We needed a miracle, fast. Daddy loaded us and started going from prayer place to prayer place, having people to pray for Charles. Charles told me later that he had awakened while the people were standing around him, laying hands on him and praying.

Even after Charles regained consciousness, he was still having diarrhea; and Mama kept asking Daddy, "Let's buy him some Pepto Bismol." Daddy said, "No, Sister Prince, we're not using any medicine; we don't use medicine." But Mama begged, "Please, Ulys, it won't hurt him; it's made out of herbs. Just give him one teaspoon full. He's just wasting away; we've got to do something so he'll keep some food on his stomach." So Daddy finally turned his head and let Mama give Charles a dose. Charles always said that the Pepto Bismol did him no good, that it was the prayer. He defended that all his life.

Soon after my tenth birthday Daddy announced we were moving. He had borrowed five hundred dollars from Granny and bought six acres of land, four miles away, where he planned eventually to build a house. In the meantime, we moved into the eighteen-by-twenty-four-foot gospel tent. We'd spent a few weeks in the tent three years earlier—between houses—with our furniture set on a dirt floor. But this time we would face a bitter winter with twelve-inch snowstorms and winds gusting over fifty miles an hour at three-thousand-feet elevation on the edge of the Smoky Mountains.

We built a wood slab floor and frame, then roughly partitioned off three rooms. I worked alongside Daddy and the boys. I was always treated the same as the boys and never cut any slack because of being a girl. With three old beds, a wood heater, a wood cook stove, and a homemade table and benches, we moved into the tent.

As soon as we got settled in, Daddy went into the mountains and caught two large rattlesnakes and placed them in a dynamite box with a hinged, screened lid. Without explanation he slid the snakes under my bed. I dared not ask him to remove them, even though he knew I was terrified. The boys paid them little attention. I had horrifying nightmares and would for years dream of being surrounded by snakes and running all night through endless snakes, unable to escape. The next morning Daddy checked his snakes and one was missing. We'd slept in a room with a loose rattler. Each night I feared it might be under the covers and bite me or my brothers while we slept. Daddy made the box more secure. The other snake spent the long winter under my bed, rattling me to sleep.

Daddy's greatest desire was to find God's perfect will for him. The Bible was Daddy's whole life, and he expected his family to have the same goals as himself. He prayed and fasted often, once even forty days. He got so thin he had to tie his pants up with strings to keep them from falling off. He read the Bible and prayed hours each day. We would be awakened sometimes at two A.M. by his groaning prayers. There he'd be, wrapped in a quilt, seeking God in the dead of the cold night. He was driven to take the word of God to the

Anna Prince (on the left) with her mother, Della; father, Ulysses; and brothers (three-year-old Charles is squeezed between father and older brother). Photograph 1942 courtesy of Anna Prince.

poor, and to risk his life to prove with miracles, signs, and wonders that Jesus was real and alive.

Early on Daddy refused offerings of money; but as he realized, we would suffer greatly without it, and he accepted the meager amounts. He never, however, took up an offering, even though he often spent his last dollar for car gas and headed out with us to places unknown. Somehow we got back home, eventually.

Daddy heard of people in West Virginia who were drinking poison, following St. Mark 16: "If they drink any deadly thing it shall not hurt them." So he went to the store to buy some poison, and the only kind they had was Red Devil Lye that was used for unclogging drainpipes. He took it home to test it.

He mixed one teaspoon to a pint of water, shook it, and took a sip. He jumped and spat as it ate a hole in the tip of his tongue. Then he climbed the mountain with a blanket and fasted for a week. On his return he once again tasted the deadly mixture, and it was as sweet as sugar to him. He had Mama and my brother Harley try it to make sure it had not lost its power!

They danced around the floor and spat the fiery liquid out. Daddy knew he had the victory from God to drink lye. From then on he added lye drinking to his preaching and carried a pint of it in a canning jar along with his snake box. Occasionally an unbeliever dared him to let them sip his potion. They usually ran yelling and spitting to their car and never returned. The lye even ate the paint off the table where it set. He mixed it so strong, he often had to stand on his Bible, literally, for the poison to go down his throat. He was never harmed.

Daddy tried to handle stinging scorpions only once. He had read in the Bible: "I give you power to tread on serpents and scorpions . . . and nothing shall by any means hurt you." One night he brought in a big jar of about ten scorpions. While preaching in the pulpit with the people watching, he opened the jar. The scorpions scurried up his arm and down his shirt collar and into his clothes. He began dancing around and ran from the church, unfastening his shirt as he went. He never attempted scorpions again. We all laughed for weeks over that—all except Daddy.

During life in the tent, Daddy began to peak in religious fervor. He wanted to preach the gospel to every creature. Most every Saturday he and I traveled to neighboring towns and preached on the streets. At night we returned home to get Mama and the boys to attend a scheduled home prayer meeting or a revival. At times we had a radio broadcast. From April through September we were in full-time ministry.

Snakes, lye drinking, and fire handling were only a small portion of our religion, which few members practiced at all. Ninety-eight percent of our faith was table blessings, hour-long prayers at bedtime and for the sick, as well as living a clean life. We didn't smoke, drink, even drink coffee, wear jewelry, or go to movies. Anything Daddy even imagined might be a sin, we stopped doing immediately. We had clean language without even slang words like heck or darn. The women wore long dresses with sleeves, no makeup, and long hair. We strove to be clean, truthful, honest, and sincere.

At age nine, I began having playhouse prayer meetings with little girls in our prayer group. We'd sing, testify and shout a little. One day during a great meeting in progress in the woods behind our home, Charles, now seven, approached carrying a white, lidded bucket, followed by our brothers Don, five, and Daniel, three. Charles asked that they be allowed to join our meeting. I said okay. We continued laying on hands and quoting Bible verses. Suddenly Charles yells, "Thank you Jesus!" as he opens his bucket and lets out a squirming big brown toad frog! He waves the frog in Jesus' name and passes it to Don, who in trying to keep the frog from getting away squeezed it a bit too hard. A stream of liquid wets the back of Don's left hand! "He's got warts for sure!" Charles excitedly announces, "Gather 'round, Saints; let's pray hard. The frog has peed on Brother Don!"

Daddy and I continued as a team with new songs, new sermons in lots of towns and states. I helped him pray for the sick and stood beside him at funerals. I watched him try "Elijah's God" on a totally blind woman. She was reading her Bible in forty minutes. I watched him pull a complete stranger from her wheelchair and demand her to "walk in Jesus' name." She walked. I've hung onto my car seat as he spun in the road to chase down another preacher in order to have a heated Bible discussion beside the road.

Daddy and I would go street preaching most every Saturday to many small towns in the tri-state area of North Carolina, Tennessee, and Georgia. We continued to use loudspeakers, although they were against the law in some places, and to preach in up to five towns a day and some days be in three states. Mom and the other children only went to night services usually because of its being too much traveling for them.

One Saturday we stopped to preach in Bryson City, North Carolina, a small riverside mountain town. I played the guitar and sang two songs, and Dad began to preach over the loudspeakers. A small crowd gathered on the sidewalk to listen.

Two big policemen walked up the street toward us and asked Daddy to turn off his loudspeakers, that it was against the law. Daddy replied, "Brothers, you're in the quietest world you'll ever be in. I obey the laws of God. God tells me to preach the Gospel to every creature." The officers grabbed Daddy by the belt and shoulder and quickly walked him down the street toward the courthouse. A crowd of witnesses followed, yelling for the policemen to let him go. I was left alone standing on the street, crying my heart out. Daddy was gone. I was ten years old and didn't know how to get home to Mama. I didn't even know where we were. I ran down the street following the crowd who were following Daddy. We went into the courthouse basement to see the mayor. The people yelled, "You let that preacher go or we'll throw you into the river!" The mayor told Daddy never to use his speakers again and turned him loose. We went

home, but Daddy and I would return again and again and use the speakers, but he was never arrested there again.

As soon as it was warm enough, Daddy gave a revival near Turtletown, seventy miles away. Since there was no church, we built a brush arbor by cutting the tops out of four corner trees in a wooded area, then cutting down all the trees inside the square. Poles were nailed across the top and brush tossed on top for a temporary shelter. Benches were sawmill slabs, and the floor was covered with wood shavings and sawdust. The loudspeakers were operated from the car battery because we had no electricity. Lanterns and torches were our only light.

Daddy brought in his snake box and set it under a front bench. He was keeping two or three rattlesnakes or copperheads himself, and often a new snake would be presented to him to handle while he was preaching. Cars parked a mile in two directions on the remote mountain road to hear him preach, see him handle snakes, and occasionally drink lye.

Many nights throughout the years after a meeting we headed for a nearby river for a midnight baptizing of new converts, even during icy winters. Most summers we had a radio broadcast; and as his fame increased, he baptized hundreds. Many, however, still condemned and criticized his actions.

Life constantly changed for us with new places and faces. During revivals we spent over one hundred nights a year in the homes of strangers; and since there were so many of us, our family would be spread out with different folks. I usually went home with a girl my age. It was scary, being driven in the night to unknown places with strangers I'd just met. I usually didn't even know where the rest of my family was and often cried myself to sleep.

Many nights the serpents were not handled, nor lye or fire brought out, but we were avid seekers of the Spiritual anointing that was present sometimes, making miracles possible. When it was not present, the people tried to "pray it down." When it came, anyone could see the results. Old timers began patting their feet. Women began trotting their babies on their laps. Young people would begin to laugh and cry at the same time and praise God. Even small children would suddenly stand up and say how much they loved Jesus!

When the anointing came, the music got faster and the songs had more meaning. Everyone seemed to be able to sing in tune and look at each other and smile and hug! Daddy would begin to preach. The people cheered him on, and the words flowed from him like a river making profound sense. When the anointing was present, the people became electrified and anything could happen.

One night while the spirit was moving, Daddy was handling a long yellow rattler when a twelve-year-old boy came running from the back of the brush arbor, took the snake from him, and danced with it. A teenage girl, who was singing, took it from the boy; then her girlfriend took it from her and wrapped it around her waist like a belt. They had never handled a snake before and likely would never handle another, but the anointing was there and they knew they were safe from harm. Then the fire handlers took out their torches and danced as the flames lapped under their arms. Their clothes would not even burn. Then Daddy opened his jar of lye and drank a few swallows in Jesus'

name. Dad did everything in Jesus' name! He always said, "The power is in the name of Jesus, not in me."

On a night like that one, visiting Baptists and Methodists sometimes became snake and fire handlers. Curious visitors often became participants in miracles—when the anointing was present. The crowds came early and stayed late! Sometimes the services lasted till sunup, while converts prayed at the altar for salvation or for miracles from God.

During the Turtletown brush-arbor revival, a farmer brought a box containing a three-foot yellow rattler that had tried to bite his dog. The service lacked religious fervor, although the slab benches and every available log and stump were loaded with people waiting impatiently for Daddy to handle the new snake. After preaching an anointed message, he released the snake from a small barrel and lifted it up. The snake coiled to the right and struck the top of his left hand at the base of his middle finger. The blood ran off his hand as he put the snake back into the barrel. Farmers in overalls took out their pocket watches and began to count minutes until he died. He continued the service with all eyes upon him. Two hours passed, and his hand did not swell at all. The following night the crowd doubled since word spread that the snake handler had been bitten. Dad presented his bitten hand to anyone who wanted to inspect it. The fang marks showed clearly. Some said it was a miracle; some said it was a trick; but many became believers.

Daddy began to be daring and bold. He put snakes in his white shirt that stuck their heads out while he preached, and he wrapped serpents around his neck and head as he danced and yelled, "Bring me a lion and I'll ride it!"

The Madisonville Sheriff's Department sent Daddy a message that snake handling would not be tolerated in the county. They assured him they would be watching. Sure enough, when we went and the service began, three deputies arrived to catch Daddy handling snakes. Daddy preached and as usual handled the serpents fully in the sight of everyone. As soon as the snakes were re-boxed, the deputies informed Daddy that when the service was finished they would confiscate the snakes and arrest him. Meanwhile, they instructed him to lock the snake box in the trunk of his car, parked beside the makeshift podium, so that they could watch until the service was finished. One of the deputies propped his foot on the bumper of our car to guard the snakes while the service continued.

I realized Dad was in trouble and needed help. He was going to be arrested and the snakes were the proof of his crime. I found Harley and we quickly devised a plan to steal the snakes even though our car was right beside the podium in an area with a string of electric lights. Harley and I watched for a chance to duck in front of the car and scoot under it. We waited for a distraction, then Harley gently opened the passenger-side front door and slid into the back floorboard. He began removing the rear car seat to get at the snake box. I lay on my back on the ground just inches away from the deputy's grounded foot and wondered what the penalty was for stealing court evidence. One deputy walked around the car and shone his light and we froze. After many breathless minutes, he moved on. Then I felt the car door begin to open, and I moved under the door, hands up to the crack of the door hoping Harley had succeeded. It always frightened me to carry the snake box, but I carefully took the box Harley slid down

to me. I scooted my feet along the ground and then ran into the dark woods in back, covered the box with leaves, and returned to Harley. We smiled to each other and waited. When the meeting was dismissed, the two deputies placed Daddy under arrest and had him open his car trunk. Daddy was as surprised as anyone to find the trunk empty! Daddy was taken to jail and spent three days, but when the hearing came up, the judge asked for evidence. The deputies reluctantly explained that the snakes actually disappeared while they were being guarded. The charges were dismissed.

When I was eleven years old and we were having one of our biggest brush-arbor revivals on a back road near Atlanta, a strange man rolled a wooden barrel across the sawdust floor to Daddy's feet while he was preaching. Knowing it held a new snake of some kind, Daddy ripped open the nailed-down top. The biggest black diamond rattler any of us had ever seen leaped several feet into the air. With both hands Daddy wrapped his fingers around the snake's baseball-sized middle as it whipped its body back and forth. I watched frozen with awe as man and serpent battled. Daddy wrestled the huge, lunging snake as women grabbed their babies and stunned onlookers fell backward over slab benches to give the pair more space. The snake finally calmed down, and Daddy returned its heavy body to the barrel.

A few nights after that incident, the anointing was not going well. I prayed he would not handle any serpents. Things didn't feel right. A group of strange men were mocking and heckling from the back of the arbor. It was hard to sing or preach. A visiting Tennessee handler had brought in a three-foot black diamond that had already bit-

Anna Prince, daughter of Ulysses Prince and sister of Charles Prince. Photograph 1982 courtesy of Anna Prince.

ten a woman a few days earlier. The visitor removed the big snake from the box, but the angry reptile struck at him, and he dropped it to the ground. The snake crawled toward the spectators. Daddy had no choice but to try to put it back in the box. The snake suddenly struck the pulse of Daddy's left wrist, sinking its fangs so deeply that it had to wiggle its head to get them out.

Stunned, he placed the snake back into the box, locked it, and walked a few steps and fell to the sawdust. Within minutes, his face was swollen almost beyond recognition. Weeping believers meekly suggested medical treatment, but he firmly shook his head, "No!" My seven-months-pregnant mother ran hysterically outside and dropped to the rough ground. She rolled back and forth and would not let me comfort her. I pressed next to her and rolled with her.

The third day after hovering between life and death, Daddy revived and asked to be driven to the meeting at the arbor. His arm was still so swollen it would not fit into a shirt sleeve. With his good hand, he handled the snake that bit and almost killed him.

With one arm he drove us back to the mountains and our home. The snake box went back under my bed where it remained all winter. Mama soon gave birth in the tent to her fifth son, eleven pounds, four ounces, with no medication and only a midwife to assist her. It was as common to hear the snakes rattle as to hear my new baby brother cry.

Numerous adventures happened during the next few revivals. Brother Luther Williams was bitten by a copperhead, but with prayer survived; one brother, who often put his face in the snake box to show he had no fear, was severely bitten and maimed; Aunt Donnie's arm swelled real big from the fangs of a black diamond rattler; a nine-year-old girl died of carbon monoxide poisoning and we prayed her back to life; a devil-possessed man ran through the brush-arbor on hands and knees screaming about Jesus (he finally died in an insane asylum); and Charles bit a lizard's head off just to prove he could do it.

My searching mind focused briefly on these and other childhood scenes, looking for the answers I sought for Charles and me. I found many. I raised my face from the carpet and back to the re-

ality that my brother might be dying. Two men lifted Charles to a half-sitting position as I, thinking Charles had to vomit, grabbed a nearby bucket to hold under his chin. Blood gushed out like an open water valve. He was hemorrhaging to death.

I ran to the kitchen wall phone, stretched the cord out the door to the porch, and quickly dialed my father in Georgia. Carl Reed was beside me in a flash. He leaned heavily against the porch banister, murmuring repeatedly, "I thought he'd be alright! I thought the Lord would heal Brother Charles."

"Daddy," I screamed, "Charles is dying! We're losing him." He replied, "I know, Sister, I know. I've been praying all night. The Lord just showed me a vision that Charles was dying! Your mother and me are getting ready to come up and bury our son."

When I returned to Charles's side he was alert, but fading. "Charles," I pled once again, "can I get you some medical help? Can I get you a doctor? Please, Charles." He shook his head a firm "No" and turned away. Realizing that I might be the last blood relative to see him alive, I felt I had to make peace with him for the whole family and help him find God's hand to guide him through the valley of death. "Is there anything you want me to tell anyone?" "Pray, tell them to pray," he replied. We prayed together: "The Lord is my shepherd, I shall not want. . . ." A tranquillity settled over his face as he whispered, "I think I can rest now." I wept for the life that was slipping away and for myself. We were both victims of snake handling and poison drinking! I wept also for the other victims I would have to call with the news of his death.

We took Charles's body for the funeral and burial to the Turtletown Church we had built on the grounds where Daddy had handled snakes in the brush arbor when we were children. The media found us but watched solemnly from a distance as Daddy preached Charles's funeral and I sang his favorite song, "I Was Born to Love the Lord." Charles's seven children, ages seven to twenty-four, sat wide-eyed on the front row. I prayed none of them would follow in their father's footsteps to handle serpents.

Mom and Dad still grieve for their son. Dad, over eighty years old, pastors the Turtletown Church. He stopped handling snakes when Charles began and tried hard to dissuade his son. But the seed had been planted too deep.

My faith in God and the Bible are strong. I know miracles do happen. I have witnessed many dozens. But the greatest miracle of all to me is the miracle of hearing the voice of God, the audible and clear communication of God. Deeply puzzled about Charles's death, I asked God, "Lord, why did my brother die? What really happened between Charles and you?" So God gave me a dream-type vision, an allegory:

> Once a homeowner needed a ten-foot-high brick wall built, promptly; so he hired a bricklayer. The workman worked hard and his work was smooth and accurate! The owner complimented the workmanship! Bystanders began to tell the worker what a fine wall it was. But the wall was only three feet high! The workman, liking the praise, stopped working and began to admire his own work. He replaced his work clothes with a Rhinestone Cowboy suit and strutted and pranced in front of the wall as admirers gathered, praised, and watched. The homeowner, needing his house completed quickly, had to let the workman go; but he explained, "Just because I let him go doesn't necessarily mean he won't be paid for the good work he's already done."

And these signs shall follow

Conclusion

One common conclusion regarding these people and the practice of serpent handling is that the people and the ritual itself are simply bizarre and irrational; snake handlers are crazy. This opinion is generally held by those with only a hearsay knowledge of the practice, and it is the image sometimes expressed or implied in the media. Serpent handlers are often confronted with this view and are repulsed by it. Jimmy Williams's son Allen, whose father died from drinking strychnine during a religious service, is a case in point:

> Me and my brother and the pastor of this church here where I attend was in the Bible shop, and this man just come in and was givin' my daddy and another man that drunk the poison, just talkin' about 'em like they was dogs.

The same is true for Allen's sister Joyce:

> I was in Revco down here, and it's a pretty big store and a lot of people; and there was this man I know. I recognized him as soon as I seen him, over in the other aisle; but he didn't see me or he wouldn't know who I was anyway. He said, "Do you remember that crazy Jimmy Williams that drunk that strychnine and died? You remember him, don't you?" He said, "They was over there workin' on his house the other day, paintin' it"; and when he said it, he was talkin' so loud that he could be heard, Lord knows how far. I just walked up there and I said, "That's my daddy you're callin' crazy!"

Serpent handlers are quick to say, as does Lydia Elkins Hollins (whose mother died from a serpent bite): "We're not crazy like we're taken for." Newspapers, magazines, and television programs, however, sometimes promulgate this view in order to exploit the inherently sensational aspects of the practice. One article, for example, prints, "THE

GOSPEL OF DEATH," followed by "A BIZARRE religious sect praises the Lord by handling poisonous snakes, putting fire on their bodies and drinking deadly poison"; another article, "Praise the Lord—and pass the snakes," uses as its lead: "West Virginia believers play with killer rattlers to win God's love." One columnist explains, "To most religious people, the idea of handling a poisonous snake as a demonstration of faith is near inconceivable if not downright revolting"; another writes, "The skeptical and sometimes disgusted world calls them 'Holy Rollers' in public and various unprintable things in private."

Some reported statements, particularly earlier ones, are unreservedly direct: "We don't like this sort of thing, and we'd like to stop it. . . . some of the citizens up here are going to try to get a law just like the one in Kentucky." One report says that a police captain was under orders of the governor "to crush out the 'dangerous' toying with reptiles." Some of this journalism is almost humorous, but not to the serpent handler, especially such terms as "leader of the Holy Roller band," "Snake Cultist," and "'Snake' Preacher," or descriptions like: "their eyes alight with religious frenzy, 500 followers . . . staged a near riot on the highway"; "Rattlers . . . are being passed about in meeting [sic] with as much sangfroid as Mrs. Asterbilt-Jones-Smith exhibits in serving tea to her guests"; "snakes at the meetings have created quite an excitement among certain classes"; "SNAKE CHURCH . . . An Appalachian sect praises the Lord and passes the copperheads"; and "'Holy Rollers'. . . are still playing with snakes and allowing the snakes to bite them in their public meetings." Some of the accounts sound like bad novels: "music of the git-fiddle thrummed through the hot

Georgia night, setting nerves to throbbing. . . . He plunged his hands into the box and brought out two giant rattlers. . . . Women moaned and reeled. In the hot night, the guitars thrummed on."

Carolyn Porter, wife of a serpent handler, expresses her reaction to this kind of report: "We've had a lot of bad publicity from people that don't understand and are only out to put you down, make you look like a fool. Most people think we're uneducated, ignorant, unlearned and ain't got good sense to start with. We have had people come in and write stuff, ask you something; and then when they print it, you don't even recognize you said it."

This deprecation of serpent handlers is not restricted to certain reporters and unsophisticated respondents. In one personality study, for example, a group of clinicians was given diagnostic profiles to categorize and sort according to those they thought belonged to snake handlers and those to conventional church members. They assigned most of the profiles they judged abnormal to serpent handlers when in fact a larger percentage of abnormal profiles belonged to the conventional group (Tellegen 227-29). Researcher Virginia Hine says of another study: "The obvious bias revealed here is not uncommon. Informal interviews with four psycho-therapists about our Pentecostal data revealed a remarkable readiness to assume pathology" (217). The same bias is manifested in the following statement from a clinical report in a reputable medical journal: "Poisonous snakebites are an occupational hazard among professional and amateur herpetologists . . . and *religious faddists* who use poisonous snakes as part of their *ceremonial regalia*" (Parrish and Pollard 277; emphasis added).

Richard Davis, a professor of religion and philosophy, comments perceptively: "We do not, however, in the mainstream of America, think of spiritual growth and development as our primary concern. We are not expecting miraculous powers to appear which defy our normal view of the world. When those powers appear to us, they threaten the civic religion, they threaten the values that the society holds in common."

The Freudian perspective, as expressed by Weston La Barre, is that the serpent handler manifests a religious psychopathic behavior. The serpent represents the "projected, hysterically unacknowledged, and unadmissible desires" (*They Shall Take Up Serpents* 170), i.e., a projection of the id. To the "cultist," the serpent is the Devil, evil incarnate and death-dealing. Evil and good seem to be outside the person, though really both are within; "The evil, phallic part of oneself is projected as the separate and discrete serpent" (170). The practice of serpent handling, however, is not seen by La Barre as psychologically therapeutic; he states that the practice "expresses an *un*-mastery of sexuality on the phallic level" (169). In these terms, serpent handling is an overt expression attempting to reconcile deep personal feelings that are repressed by outside forces; but as a result of the nature of the outside forces (the view of God and the diversionary rather than overt manner of reconciling the feelings within), the expression is psychologically harmful.

This view of serpent handling may be derived from a symbolic reductionist theory of religion developed by Freud in which "the real meaning of religion is to be found in the Oedipus complex which it symbolically expresses. The Biblical God stands for the primordial father toward whom the sons feel both rebellious and guilty. Christ sums up

a whole set of conflicting oedipal wishes. . . . [T]he psychologically courageous man will discard the religious symbols which cloak his neurosis and face his inner problems directly" (Bellah 90-91). In many ways the Freudian psychoanalytical approach is exclusive rather than inclusive. As Robert Bellah suggests, it excludes, for example, religious belief "in the ordinary sense of the word" because it believes itself to possess "a truth superior to that of religion" (91). As other critics point out, there are limitations in La Barre's evaluations other than oversimplification and exclusiveness. His conclusions are of a highly inferential nature and are based on a single complex theoretical perspective; the data he selects for description and his direction of analysis are subject to his psychoanalytical orientation, and his substantiation does not include a wide scope of observations (Tellegen 222).

Even if it were accepted that deep-seated sexual impulses and associations may be manifested in serpent handling, those impulses would not necessarily be present in every serpent handler; nor would they explain the total meaning or significance of the activity. If, for example, baseball were seen in general to have deep-seated Freudian implications, that insight would not necessarily explain why the game is vital to a particular player's life or why it has become the national sport of the United States, although the psychological associations would certainly suggest the complex nature of the game.

In contrast to La Barre's negative conclusions, it is informative to note the psychological evaluation by Nathan and Louise Gerrard of a group of serpent handlers in West Virginia. The Gerrards administered the Minnesota Multiphasic Person-

John Brown, minister from Newport, handling serpents in Baxter. Photograph 1983 by Mike DuBose.

ality Inventory Test to members of a serpent-handling church and to a conventional-denomination church twenty miles away. One difference observed in the two groups was the way the older members of both churches responded to illness and old age. In the conventional church the older members "seemed to dwell morbidly on their physical disabilities" whereas "the aged serpent-handlers seemed able to cheerfully ignore their ailments" ("Serpent-Handling Religions," *Trans-Action* 24). Although both groups relied on their faith for consolation, the older serpent handlers were apparently more successful and were "not frightened by the prospect of death" (24). Although the young people of both groups also tested as "remarkably well adjusted" (24), the young serpent handlers appeared to have less psychological incompatibility with the older members of their church than the young people of the conventional church did with their elders. Regarding particular traits that might predispose an individual to serpent handling, rather than pointing to deep-seated Freudian conflicts, the psychometric data from the MMPI test suggested traits "more closely related to impulsivity and emotional expressivity," that is, traits related to "'extraversion' rather than to 'neuroticism'" (Tellegen 241).

A personality analysis by Susan Gilmore addresses the psychological health of Pentecostals in general. The Pentecostals she studied who held beliefs openly and non-dogmatically (when they were compared to college students and other groups) appeared "as well-adjusted and interpersonally skillful as do people in general" (164). Similarly, Troy Abel's findings in his study of Holiness Pentecostals in an Appalachian community "do not support a psychological deprivation hypothesis, with its assumption that Holiness-Pentecostals, glossolalists, or those who act out [*i.e.*, during the service run in the aisles, dance, pass out, scream, shout, give long testimonies] are psychologically unsound" (190). In conjunction with these analyses, anthropologist Steven Kane's conclusion regarding the psychological health of Pentecostal Holiness serpent handlers is particularly apt: "We are dealing here not with the privately constructed, idiosyncratic fantasy and action systems of neurotics and self-insulated psychotics, but on the contrary with a vigorous and perduring institutionalized system of ritual and belief whose symbols are public, socially shared and sanctioned (at least within the practicing group), and transmitted across generational lines. . . . In sum, to interpret dissociative behavior among serpent handlers as a symptom of psychological abnormality would be gross error" ("Ritual Possession" 302).

Serpent handling is also commonly set forth as a particular response to one's environment, a form of socioeconomic determinism in which religious experiences and practices are responses of individuals to social needs. From this point of view, serpent handlers—who are seen to come from repressed economic areas—live hard, often dangerous, demanding existences with little to give them hope, recognition, power, or self-esteem. The practice of serpent handling gives them a sense of community with both the old and the young, with males and females. It provides them with a means of coping with the realities of the present; it demonstrates at least to them that they are important, that they have power over obstacles, that they are supported by temporal as well as eternal forces, and that they have a better life coming. In the words of Nathan Gerrard, "Religious serpent-handling . . . is a safety valve for many of the frustrations of life in present-day Appalachia. For the old, the serpent-handling religion helps soften the inevitability of poor health, illness, and death. For the young, with their poor educations and poor hopes of finding sound jobs, its promise of holiness is one of the few meaningful goals in a future dominated by the apparent inevitability of lifelong poverty and idleness" ("Serpent-Handling Religions," *Trans-Action* 28).

J. Kenneth Moore summarizes this position: "Sociological research suggests that the Snake Handlers are sending a defiant socio-economic message in their sermons, testimonials, and songs. This message, clothed in double entendre, states that though the Snake Handlers may not be economically powerful, they are spiritually powerful. This power, derived from God and proven through acts of faith, elevates them, they believe, to a position superior to those who have not found the true way to salvation (society)." Further, Moore contends that the congregational singing of serpent handlers not only makes a statement through "implied socio-economic double entendre" ("Ethnic Hymnody" 36) but also reinforces their elevated psychological state.

There is something to be said for this socioeconomic point of view, but a number of relative factors should also be considered. For one, serpent handlers represent a relatively small percentage of the people in the area from which they come, and if the environment is a determining factor in their

Gracie McCallister from the Church of the Lord Jesus, Jolo, participating in the services at the Church of Jesus Christ, Baxter. Photograph 1985 by Mike DuBose.

practice, only a small number are responding to the environment in that particular way. In addition, even if the deprivation theory has validity, its application has limitations. Serpent handling originated in rural areas of the South among people with little education who shared a low socioeconomic status; it is questionable therefore whether there was any pervasive awareness of social repression among these people at this time. Also, serpent handling can be found among relatively prosperous, even wealthy, individuals and in thriving rural communities and other areas, such as middle-class industrial centers, where the stereotypical deprived socioeconomic mold does not fit.

The deprivation concept certainly has its limits as far as serpent handlers themselves are concerned. They resent being viewed as backward, repressed, deprived people. One group said that, after serpent handler Charles Prince had died in their home, they "had become so distressed at what they were reading in newspapers and hearing on radio and seeing on television that they decided it was time to talk." And they did, to the local newspaper:

> We just want the world to know that Brother Charles didn't die in a one-room shack or that he was being cared for by a bunch of unlearned, backwoodsy, bare-footed people who don't belong in the 20th century. As you can see, we have electricity. We are college educated. Most of us here have been in the coal-mining business. We think we're doing all right. The banks do too. (Hurley, "A Snake Handler's Death" 11)

Regarding both the socioeconomic and the Freudian views, it should be stated that the valid-

ity of a spiritual experience—as either a supernatural or a powerful psychic phenomenon—is not negated by its fulfilling other psychological needs. To show that serpent handling satisfies a number of individual as well as social needs does not repudiate in any way its manifestation of a divine or psychic event. In other words, the spiritual reality of serpent handling and its efficacy are two different considerations.

It may be noted, however, that psychological needs intensified by various states of deprivation, such as poverty, isolation, and insecurity, may effect powerful spiritual experiences. Richard Davis addresses this point:

> As time develops, we have people who feel themselves cut off, who have nowhere to turn for a genuine sense of community, turning within themselves as individuals; and spontaneously they begin to discover real powers of the inner spirit. And the manifestation of these inner spiritual powers starts to appear—the ability to go into trances, and while in a tranced state to handle a serpent with perfect safety, the ability to go into a trance and to hold one's hand to a hot coal without any detriment to the skin, the ability to drink poison without a response, physiologically, to that. These were genuine powers. They are comparable to the powers developed in Indian religion by the Hindu yogis. One can't be in the presence of that without sensing that something here is real and vital.

It may also be that the numerous adverse experiences common to many serpent handlers have worked as a cohesive as well as a productive force. In fact, as one may infer from a statement by theologian Anton Boisen, deprived conditions may well explain the origination of serpent handling in the South—but in quite a different manner from that expressed in the standard socioeconomic deterministic view:

> It follows that one result of the economic strain is to lessen the sense of isolation and to increase the sense of social solidarity and thus to induce a state of mind favorable to religious experience rather than to mental disorder. The fact that people suffer together through no particular fault of their own leads them, at least in many cases, to seek for some common solution, some common hope, and to find this in religious faith. (192)

It would seem that some Pentecostal Holiness serpent handlers, as a result of being cut off from mainstream society, have tapped other waters that have welled up into spiritual strength.

From a theological point of view, serpent handlers may be labeled *fundamentalists*; that is, they believe that the Bible is the inspired word of God and is to be interpreted literally. The Bible is the principal means of God's speaking to His people, and believers are responsible for doing whatever He says to do. If they follow His commands, they will receive God's blessings, God's anointing Spirit, God's miraculous power. If God says to sacrifice your son Isaac, you do it trusting God with the results; if He says to walk into a fiery furnace without fear, you do it. These people read among other scriptures in their Bible that Jesus said to his disciples that they "shall take up" and "tread on serpents"—and they do not have any other choice than to believe and act upon what Jesus said. Theological historian Richard Humphrey states the case pointedly, "The word *faith*, as they understand it, incorporates belief and practice. You can't separate them or you're a hypocrite. . . . They don't

do it [handle serpents] to prove their faith, they don't do it to demonstrate their faith, they do it out of obedience to what they think God has called them to do. . . . It is a part of their faith, an expression of it. . . . I think that someone who doesn't take the Bible as their faith or as their rule of faith and practice would have a hard time understanding that."

This literal position of serpent handlers, however, poses a dilemma even for other fundamentalists. There are those who believe in the possibility of God's power to protect the saints from physical harm, to heal them, to stave off death, but who look primarily for this power to be manifested indirectly. These more liberal fundamentalists, consequently, are skeptical when a group, particularly when they are perceived as less enlightened than themselves, profess to experience the power of God directly. Even though mainstream fundamentalists believe in miracles, many say that serpent handlers misinterpret the scriptures and that the apparently miraculous experiences have naturalistic explanations.

The view of some contemporary fundamentalist religious leaders on serpent handling may be illustrated by the Reverend Jerry Falwell, head of the late Moral Majority, who said in an interview with Fred Brown that he pities those who feel they have to take up serpents as a profession of their faith and he admonishes them to return to mainstream Christianity. "Personally," Falwell says, "I feel that the wording of the last verse of the Gospel of Mark spoke of miraculous happenings that would occur in the Apostolic era. . . . I think these snake handlers are very sincere people, but I think they are sincerely wrong. . . . I think the snake-handling and poison-drinking churches are about as dangerous to the boys and girls who are watching adults' examples as prime-time television is. They are both dangerous to the health of America's young people."

Going beyond a limited description of religious fundamentalism, theologian Mary Lee Daugherty suggests that the ritual holds for the participants the significance of a sacrament, a physical manifestation of a spiritual reality. The ritual, she says, "is at the center of their Christian faith"; it is "their way of celebrating life, death, and resurrection. Time and again they prove to themselves that Jesus has the power to deliver them from death here and now." One clue of this sacramental nature or symbol of victory over death, she says, is to be observed in their funerals, where serpents may be handled much "as a Catholic priest may lift up the host at a mass for the dead, indicating belief that in the life and death of Jesus there is victory over death" ("Serpent-Handling as Sacrament" 234).

Daugherty goes on to say that a principal feature of the Appalachian serpent handlers is their intense desire for holiness. She suggests that their greatest message, however, is not relative to their faith in serpent handling, even viewed as a sacrament. She says that it involves something else: "they have faith, hope, and love, but the greatest message they have given to me is their love" (238).

From a somewhat different point of view, serpent handlers may be said to be achieving an epiphany, that is, an intuitive grasp of reality, a perception of the essential nature or the meaning of themselves, religion, and God. They go to the serpent box for truth; and they believe that, not to be harmed, they have to be filled with the power of God, inspired, fully anointed with divinity. Filled with this power, they approach the box fearlessly. They willingly accept whatever they find, not just to witness the physical power of God but also to experience an epiphany—completely denying self to gain direct apprehension of ultimate truth.

Since this kind of insight transcends physical phenomena, its validity cannot be verified or rejected by a person who has not shared the experience. It is fruitless, therefore, to contest the epiphany of serpent handlers or to suggest to them optional explanations for their experiences. There is generally no adequate response to those whose perceptions are based on any altered state of mind when they say, "Thou canst not speak of that thou dost not feel."

Serpent handlers are members of a traditional community. In appearance, life-style, and values, they share a heritage with those with whom they grew up. They are not significantly different from other folks around them. Their religious beliefs, based on the same King James translation read by the majority of American Protestants, are essentially the same as those of others in their communities; the exception is not their *belief* in a particular scripture but their *interpretation* of it. They believe that God expects them to persevere regardless of the opposition of Satan in any form, that they must follow the example of Jesus' disciples and be willing to be persecuted, even die for their Lord, and that they will be rewarded in heaven for their fidelity.

Their religious meetings are not essentially different from many others in nearby areas, particularly Pentecostal churches. On occasion they worship at the services of other churches that do not hold to their interpretation of key scriptures; conversely, other church members who do not accept their interpretation attend their meetings, not simply as spectators but as worshipers. Even preachers who do not believe in handling serpents sometimes preach for them. They may extend fellowship to others less on the basis of Mark 16 than on how they are baptized, whether in the name of "Jesus," "Lord Jesus," or "the Father, the Son, and the Holy Ghost." They seemingly have no more or less manifestation of human limitations than other folks. Their preachers are no more or less susceptible than others to ego, publicity, showmanship, hypocrisy, or carnality.

The traditional beliefs of serpent handlers, fused with their religious ones, are also basically the same as those of their neighbors. They believe in the presence of the supernatural—spirits, ghosts, demons—not only stemming from their belief in Scripture, but also from what is passed down in oral tradition. They believe in codes of heroic behavior, proving oneself, accepting challenges, demonstrating courage, being fearless, and disdaining death. They believe in and identify with heroes of song, story, legend, history, war, movies, television, and the Bible; one hears repeatedly in their sermons references to being like Daniel in the lion's den. From this point of view, serpent handling is one particular manifestation of traditional religious beliefs and values of personal conduct.

In the end, none of these varying approaches to explaining serpent handling is fully satisfactory. It is an irrational practice engaged in by religious fanatics. It is an expression of psychological needs for religion and ritual or, to expand on that view, an archetypal experience common to humanity and expressed in correlative rituals throughout the world. It is a response to socioeconomic forces within a particular subculture. It is an act of religious fundamentalism reinforced by the evidence of divine power in modern times or of extraordinary natural phenomena effected by a belief in divine power. It is a zealous quest for spiritual perception and realization. It is an expression of traditional attitudes, values, and practices.

A better perspective would be to say that serpent handling, both collectively and individually (regardless of any divine nature which would be outside empirical assessment), is the eclectic result in varying degrees of a number of religious, socioeconomic, psychological, and traditional factors in American culture.

It is inherently difficult for an outsider to experience this unusual religious and cultural expression without dehumanizing the participants; serpent handlers as such are not freaks, they are not crazy, they are rational human beings. Especially in the handling of poisonous snakes, drinking of deadly substances, and divine healing, but in other aspects of their lives as well, serpent-handling believers evoke a "power" that works for them. There is limited controlled data on the effects of that power; consequently, in many cases (primarily because of the nonclinical circumstances in which it is manifested) the observer does not know whether the effects are supranatural or only remarkable. And, of course, it is not within the realm of science to determine whether the power comes directly from God or indirectly from a divine source through naturalistic causes or completely from natural causes. Presumably, one could determine clinically whether solely naturalistic causes produce similar effects. The information necessary to arrive at a substantive conclusion of the matter is not, however, available due to a number of reasons. There are understandable limits to experimentation with human subjects, and there are insufficient data relative to such factors as the potential extent of neurological control of physiological functions.

Regardless, then, of which conclusions one comes to, the initial attitude one takes is critical. Rather than approach serpent handlers with the aim of impugning their power or rationalizing their activities, one should seek first whatever truths they have to reveal, to learn about the changes they effect physiologically, psychologically, spiritually, and socially. One should try to comprehend dispassionately, without any theoretical preconceptions, the power of their ultimate commitment.

As with all complex human beings, there is much to be learned from serpent handlers, people like Liston Pack for example. As a small boy Liston was awakened one night by the sound of a high-powered rifle and by the body of a man, whom his father had just killed, falling across the bed where he and his brothers were sleeping. A few years after that, still a young boy, he was arrested the first time for helping his father run moonshine. Later he was involved in almost every illegal activity one could imagine; he came close to dying from knife wounds on several occasions and once from being shot in the head with a riot gun.

Then Liston was redeemed—if not eternally, then certainly to society—and subsequently he became a hardworking, loving husband and father, a minister devoting much of his time and money to his calling. Although his life remains rocky, he is a man who believes in miracles from personal experience, and as a result of his experience he has strong religious convictions. For these convictions he has gone willingly to jail like Thoreau in an act of civil disobedience, and if he were as literate as Thoreau, he might well quote Hamlet to those who seek simple explanations for his complex life: "how unworthy a thing you make of me! You would play upon me, you would . . . pluck out the heart of my mystery, you would sound me from my lowest note to the top of my compass. . . . do you think I am easier to be play'd on than a pipe?"

There is much light associated with serpent handlers: conviction, courage, affirmation, purpose, forthrightness, regeneration, humility, generosity, hope, joy, inner peace, love—"truth," as Faulkner says, "all things which touch the heart." They believe, and that belief is a powerful force, both to them and to those who witness it. There is also darkness: extremism, naïveté, illiberality, simplism, and foolhardiness.

The same ambivalence surrounds the practice. By biblical scholars it is almost universally repudiated. It endangers people, the mature as well as the impressionable. And even though it does not pose a "grave and imminent danger" to society, it does produce widows, orphans, and grieving relatives. For some individuals, however, taking up serpents provides meaning and insight into reality. It is an ultimate commitment that reinforces belief and shapes lives in a way that many other religious expressions do not. To serpent-handling believers, the ritual is an act of obedience to that which gives quality to living, and it is worth dying for. To the analyst, serpent handling provides insights into the efficacy of belief and perhaps even into the operative relationship between neurological and physiological responses.

Although handling serpents is strange from

the viewpoint of mainstream Christianity, the practice from a traditional perspective is comprehensible. If you take people with their values and place them in their particular religious tradition, then, even though you may reject the specific doctrine, you can understand why they believe it. That does not mean you understand everything else that may be involved: why these people turn ultimately to God; how religion or religious practice functions in their social circumstances; why they have particular psychological responses, religious or otherwise; or how their religious and cultural traditions have evolved. But, if you are aware of their traditions personally or vicariously, you can understand their taking up serpents.

Serpent handling is not simply a socially dangerous deviant civic practice of a relatively small group of people that should be ignored, pejoratively tolerated, viewed as spectacle, or legally terminated. It is a complex traditional religious belief of a group of American Christians that should be approached respectfully and sensitively—avoiding what Nathaniel Hawthorne saw as the unforgivable sin, the violation of "the sanctity of a human heart."

Appendix A
The
Anointment

The anointment of the Holy Ghost refers to the Spirit of God descending upon, entering, possessing, filling, baptizing an individual. Sign followers generally distinguish, as does Brother Bud Gregg of Morristown, Tennessee, the anointment from the usual indwelling of the Spirit that characterizes believers and causes them to live holy lives:

> A person that has never known God, when they repent and they get baptized and they receive the Spirit of God in their life, they become a new creature according to the word of God in Christ Jesus. These people are no longer like they were, but they're changed individuals. And that is the Spirit of God that changes those people and you can see a difference. But when the Spirit of the Lord moves upon you—a lot of people calls it the anointing of God, which I call it the "anointing" a lot of times—but when the Spirit of the Lord begins to take control, take complete control of your body, he begins to move you around and he preaches through you and speaks in tongues through you, he begins to shout through you, or whatever, something else greater than a man begins to take control of a man's body and begins to do these things—that's what they call the anointing of God.

The principal scripture concerning the anointment is the description in Acts 2 of the disciples being filled with the Holy Ghost on the day of Pentecost. Other scriptures cited are: "For as many as are led by the Spirit of God, they are the sons of God" (Rom. 8:14) and "How God anointed Jesus of Nazareth with the Holy Ghost and with power: who went about doing good, and healing all that were oppressed of the devil; for God was with him" (Acts 10:38).

Everyone who experiences the anointing of the Holy Ghost describes it somewhat differently, but at the same time similarly in many ways. The experience of the anointment described by serpent handlers transcends literal translation into language, but Anna Prince's description is particularly expressive:

It's a spiritual trancelike strand of power linking humans to God; it's a burst of energy that's refreshing, always brand new; it brings on good emotions. One is elated, full of joy. You know you're right with God, totally in tune with God; everything is right with everyone on earth. It's a delicious, wonderful feeling going through your body; it's a roar of happiness; you want to laugh, jump. It's a power surge that is near to a light electrical shock and a sexual orgasm simultaneously felt, but it is not sexual or electrical, just a similar sensation. It's close to sexual without being sensual; it's loving, not making love. Love surges through the body in waves; one knows no enemies; one wants to dance in happiness or hug somebody. It's addicting—once you feel it you want to feel it again; it causes people who get hooked on the feeling to band with others who feel it in order to get a bigger and deeper high. One feels akin to God, free of guilt, pain, shame or "pull-downs" that normally plague a person. The anointed one is nearly unearthly for a few minutes. Any good feeling of self-worth and indestructibility could be felt while in this state of mind and heart. The anointing is catching; once it begins, it often runs around the room from person to person—sometimes whole buildings of people are hit at once, and everyone stands up and begins moving around the building and performing comical antics of leaping, shouting, dancing, praising God. Adults revert to uninhibited children, to uninhibited child's play—God joining his children who become as humble as little children. Most often the participant is smiling or laughing; sometimes it comes with tears and weeping, but with relief and release and answered prayer. During camp meetings where long prayer vigils are common, the sleeping faithful—even young children—often rise up in their sleep and speak in tongues, prophesy or praise God. If the urge to follow what the Spirit directs is resisted, it is called "quenching the spirit," which often brings on a feeling of remorse later. Situations can be set up to attract the Spirit and turn it on: a need to pray; someone to pray with; privacy from interruption; concert, loud, all-at-once prayer; faith that it will happen; a mind set on God; and willingness to obey God no matter what He requires.

Liston Pack explains that, just as there are different gifts of the Holy Ghost, there are different degrees and effects of the anointing:

Everybody that feels the anointing of God, I think, probably feel it somewhat different. It depends on how God deals with that individual person. Some get a tremendous physical anointing that I've heard them say, "I get numb." Some say, "I have a tingling sensation," particularly in the hands. I don't think that any two people probably get anointed just alike.

The anointing is hard, real hard to explain; and 'cause if I was to tell you that you had to feel just like me, I might tell you wrong, you see. Let every man be persuaded in his own mind, and his own conscience, and his own heart in the way that the Spirit of God would direct him, you see, or her.

Okay, to me, my anointing would come on me—I'm going to use the illustration (it's hard, I can't copy it, no way you can copy it)—but if you didn't know me, you would think I was havin' a stroke or somethin' tremendous was takin' place. Well, first of all, it would feel like my scalp would start gettin' numb. Well, next of all, my face would start, just feel like I didn't have any face. Next of all, my hands, my skin would get numb—not a numbness of bad feelin' but a numbness of

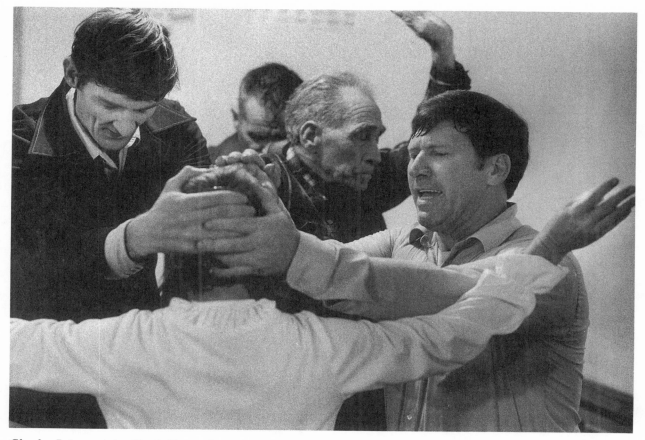

Charles Prince, right; Grady Henry, Prince's step-grandfather-in-law, with hand raised; and Jimmy Morrow follow one of the "signs" at Carson Springs: "they shall lay hands on the sick, and they shall recover," Mark 16:18. Photograph 1984 by Mike DuBose, Knoxville News-Sentinel.

joy unspeakable. Okay, then I notice my hands begin to draw; then I would almost lose complete use of my body. Then I am fully anointed. I don't care what happens. I don't care how big the serpent is or how big the devil possessed person. At my anointin', as I speak, it will bring out the demon power that's in the person or the serpent that's in the box. I don't care where it's head is; I don't care where its tail's at or the middle of it; I don't care where it's at, and I'll handle it just any way that I see fit. And that's as close to the anointing that I can explain.

In order to learn something about the physiological effects of the anointing, I proposed to Liston Pack that an electroencephalogram be made of him while he was experiencing the anointment. He agreed, and Dr. Michael Woodruff ran the EEG while the event was simultaneously recorded on videotape by Thomas Headley of the East Tennessee State University Department of Communication.

Pastor Pack said that he had prepared for the session over a period of several months by fasting occasionally, praying, and having his wife and church members fast and pray. His wife, Mary Kate, fasted for five days prior to the session; Liston, for two days. He isolated himself considerably the day before as well as the morning of the session; and he had stayed home, receiving no phone calls, keeping the curtains closed on the windows, praying, fasting, and drinking some fluids. The degree of fasting, the number of days, and length of hours were not accurately remembered by Pack; however, there was a real sense of his "sacrificing" to get ready. There was no indication that he was telling about the deprivation to make a good impression; he was simply explaining that it took considerable preparation over a lengthy period in preparing himself spiritually to receive heavy anointment under the prescribed circumstances.

The technical details of Dr. Woodruff's report are retained here for the sake of those with some specialization in the subject. His conclusions, however, are relevant to every reader interested in serpent handling.

Report

Michael L. Woodruff, Ph.D.
(Behavioral Neuroscience)
Professor, Department of Anatomy
Quillen College of Medicine,
East Tennessee State University

Electroencephalograph taken from Pastor Liston Pack 4:00 p.m. 7 Nov. 1985.

Technical considerations

Rev. Pack's EEG was recorded while he was sitting in an electrically shielded room (Faraday cage). A six channel model 6 SS Grass Electroencephalograph was used. Electrodes were placed using the international 10-20 nasion-inion system at F3, F4, P3, P4 and O1, O2 (F = frontal, with electrodes pasted on the forehead above eyes just below the scalp line; P = parietal, with electrodes pasted on lateral curvature of scalp approximately above each ear; O = occipital or posterior of the skull) and referenced to the same sided ear (A1 or A2).

Brief comment concerning normal EEG patterns in adults

When analyzed for frequencies using power spectral analysis, the normal EEG of an awake, alert adult is characterized by a range of frequencies (expressed as Hertz or Hz) beginning below 1 Hz and continuing beyond 50 Hz. This means that every EEG pattern that is observable on an ink-writing machine is a *mixture* of these frequencies. That is, while an alpha rhythm is defined as being between 8 and 13 Hz, it is, in fact, composed of a broad spectrum of frequencies. However, the slower frequencies are dominant in the alpha rhythm. The higher frequencies are dominant in the beta rhythm (14 Hz and above; although some workers in the field of EEG analysis would add an "intermediate" band of 14-18 Hz). The other two frequencies are slower than alpha. Theta is 4 to 8 Hz, while delta is 0.5 through 3 Hz.

Despite popular usage, the scalp EEG is not *brain waves*. Rather, the EEG, as recorded from the scalp, is produced by the neurons of the neocortex. The electrical activity of subcortical structures (e.g. hippocampus) may or may not be similar to the pattern recorded from the scalp.

If many neurons are generating excitatory and inhibitory potentials at the same instances in time, then they are acting in synchrony and the resulting EEG is synchronous. The delta, theta, and alpha rhythms are synchronous rhythms. The beta is a dysynchronous rhythm.

When one is alert and attentive (i.e. presumably processing, or ready to process, information), the EEG is predominately (though not exclusively) in beta, or desynchronized. As one relaxes, and especially if the eyes are closed, the EEG gradually becomes more synchronous. The synchronous waves (alpha) normally appear over the occipital (posterior) lobe first and spread forward. As the person becomes more relaxed the EEG slows; and the beginning of a "doze" will find mixtures of alpha, theta, and delta in the EEG. (Further information regarding the electrical activity of the brain and illustrations of the scalp EEG discussed above may be found in M. A. B. Brazier, *Electrical Activity of the Nervous System*, 4th ed., Baltimore: Williams, 1977.)

Rev. Pack's EEG

During the first few minutes following placement of the electrodes, Rev. Pack's EEG record was clearly one of an individual nervous in a strange environment. The EEG frequency was within the beta range, specifically between 24 and 27 Hz, from all leads. Artifact produced by saccadic eye movements was evident in the frontal leads. (Eye movement artifact is not an electrical potential produced by the brain, but rather the actual potential of the eyeball itself as it shifts in its socket. This is picked up by the frontal electrodes.) Within 3 or 4 minutes of electrode attachment, bursts of alpha lasting for 2 to 3 seconds were observable from the occipital leads (i.e., from the posterior part of the skull). This occurred with eyes open and is a normal phenomenon, but might be interpreted to indicate that Rev. Pack was becoming comfortable in the recording environment.

At onset of preparation for anointment Rev.

Pack closed his eyes, and within 45 seconds alpha was prevalent in the occipital and parietal leads (i.e., from the posterior and roof of the skull). The amplitude (as much as 100 microvolts peak-to-peak from the occipital leads and 60 to 75 microvolts in the parietal leads) and regularity of the waves (10 or 11 Hz continuously for the approximately 3.5 minutes of "relaxed preparation") increased significantly compared to the alpha that had been appearing. Alpha continued to dominate the record and spread to the frontal lobes after several minutes. As is normally seen, even in people engaged in forms of relaxation-oriented meditation, the frontal alpha was never as robust as that recorded from the occipital leads. The alpha appearing in Rev. Pack's record was never as steady (that is, the waves tended to wax and wane in amplitude), nor as slow as those I have obtained from trained meditators (TM, Yogic, or mystical Christian) in the later stages of meditation; but the alpha was comparable to early stages of such meditation. It should be noted that the final motor patterns obtained by these trained meditators differ considerably from those exhibited by Pack, as stillness and quietude accompany their meditations. Finally, one point of some interest to me is that the alpha maintained in Rev. Pack's record, even during the periods just before anointment, began when he was moving his hands in his lap (but not lifting them) and tapping his foot. This suggests to me that these movements were generated predominately by subcortical structures.

Desynchronization of the EEG on all leads accompanied Rev. Pack's indication of the anointment state. The beta frequency was dominant at between 20 and 24 Hz in the frontal and parietal leads. The amplitude was on the order of 40 microvolts in these areas. The occipital leads showed somewhat slower frequency (18-19 Hz), higher amplitude (60 to 75 microvolts) activity than the frontal and parietal leads. Once again this is not at all abnormal, even during periods of concentration and arousal; however, the occipital frequencies after anointment were slightly faster than those exhibited by Rev. Pack during the first few minutes of the recording session before he exhibited any alpha in his record.

Conclusions

Unfortunately, the record is fraught with muscle and movement artifacts, and I cannot glean any further specific information from it. However, I feel safe in concluding several things.

1. There is absolutely nothing abnormal about the EEG in a clinical sense. I find no evidence of seizure activity, abnormal slowing, or asymmetrical rhythmic patterns. I take this to indicate that the Rev. Pack's experience of anointment is not brought on by some idiopathic neuropathological state; nor is it the result of some form of self-induced epileptic seizure.

2. Preparation for anointment obviously involves a period of time during which the individual enters an EEG state similar to that customarily involved in meditation. That Rev. Pack was able to do this readily in an environment that, given his background, must have been alien to him, as well as in the presence of "skeptical" scientists, indicates to me that he has a great deal of control over his mental state.

3. There is a sudden conversion from alpha to beta when the anointment begins. The beta pattern persists throughout the experience. Anointment, therefore, is a very active state from the

point of view of the cerebral neocortex. The EEG is that of an aroused individual—not that, for example, of a Zen monk in contemplation. The chief difference between the Reverend Pack's EEG during the first five minutes of recording and the anointment condition is that in the latter the frequency recorded from the occipital leads was higher with little evidence of alpha in the raw EEG. Putative interpretation of this EEG pattern would be that it indicates an aroused state. It is clearly within normal parameters, although the accompanying behavior indicated a person in the hold of a religious experience.

4. Taken as a unit the EEG patterns exhibited by Rev. Pack during the entire session remind me of things I have read concerning hypnosis. Persons who are good candidates for hypnosis generally have more than average alpha in their normal EEGs and tend to generate more alpha with greater ease when eyes are closed than those persons not as susceptible to hypnosis. The EEG during hypnosis, however, reflects whatever state is suggested. That is, if it is suggested to a person that he is in danger from a fire in the building (which is flame free) then the EEG is desynchronized. If, on the other hand, the suggestion is that he is peacefully contemplating the ocean, then the EEG tends to be dominated by alpha. A hypothesis stemming from this, therefore, would be that the keys to understanding Rev. Pack's physiological, or at least neurological, functioning during anointment are probably more likely to be found in the literature on hypnosis, than in the literature on meditation.

This hypothesis is not intended to negate the experience of anointment, since the idea of self-hypnosis too easily becomes equated with self-delusion. However, it is a hypothesis worthy of further consideration.

Appendix B
The
Music

Music is an integral part of the serpent-handling service. The serpents do not hear the music since they do not have the auditory mechanism for airborne sound: "The conduction of ground vibrations, through the bones of the skull to the inner ear, forms the only kind of 'hearing' in snakes and can only operate as a vibration detector" (Morris and Morris 194). The effect of the vibration of the music on the serpents is undeterminable since scientific contextual data of the influence is nonexistent; however, from observation alone, it is evident that the serpents come out of the boxes sometimes striking, sometimes not. Also, the serpents are sometimes handled on occasions when no music is employed.

Believers are aware of the proposition that the music is a determining cause for the failure of serpents to bite, and they will sometimes address the matter directly. For example, in the pulpit with serpents in hand and no music being played, Brother Bob Elkins of the Church of the Lord Jesus in Jolo, West Virginia, will tell his audience that it is not the music that prevents the serpents from biting, "it's the power of God." Dewey Chafin, also of Jolo, says that he cannot detect any difference in the activity of the serpents relative to the music. "Say, you got serpents in your hand and the music starts or stops—you can't tell any difference at all. I've got bit with music full blast or without music. I don't think music would have any effect on them at all, any way."

Music no doubt is instrumental in altered states of consciousness such as the experience of being "anointed." Serpent handlers themselves attest to the significance of the music in the service and in handling the serpents. "Getting one's mind on God," as Dewey Chafin says. "Just like the preaching; you're

Tim McCoy, swirling with tambourine, joined by talented guitarist Roy Lee "Bootie" Christian, on the left. Photograph 1988 by the author.

getting in the spirit—getting more prepared to handle snakes or laying hands on the sick or anything that you're doing for God. It's like a booster—like preaching, testifying, or praying. It helps you get into the perfect will of God."

Again there is no controlled scientific data relative to the effect of music on the serpent-handling believer, but it is clear that music is not a necessary determining factor in the anointment. Liston Pack's experience while undergoing an EEG is one example.

Because of the unquestionable significance of music in the service and the role that it can play in the handling of serpents, at least some knowledge of the nature of the music is critical. The following essay provides a perceptive overview.

Music of the Serpent-Handling Service by Scott W. Schwartz

The music of selected serpent-handling services from Tennessee, West Virginia, and Georgia is improvisatory in nature and is characterized by free melodic and textual variation. It is derived from a mixture of commercial bluegrass and country-western music that utilizes simple 12- and 16-bar blues progressions of I, IV, V, and sometimes VI chords. In many instances the improvised melodies are based upon secular recorded music that is broadcast over commercial radio and television stations and is familiar therefore both to the musicians and to other church members. These secular melodies are set to religious prose and bib-

Members of the Jolo congregation dancing together in the space between pulpit and pews where the serpent handling, poison drinking, shouting, and dancing are principally conducted. Photograph 1988 by the author.

lical texts. They commonly take the form of a church hymn performed in the style of a blues piece. (Combining secular melodies and religious texts to form a sacred composition has a long tradition. The Renaissance Mass, for example, utilized many secular melodies set to sacred texts. A case in point is Jacob Obrecht's *Missa 'Fortuna desperata.'*)

Various instruments, both amplified and acoustical, are used in performing the music. Typically, piano, organ, guitar, bass, cymbals, tambourines, and trapset are employed. In addition to the varied instrumental combinations, there is usually one lead musician, either a vocalist or an instrumentalist, who serves as a moderator for each musical piece.

Frequently, an instrumental ensemble starts the service off in the form of a jam session. The

service then often gets in full swing with the performance of a vocalist. The remaining musicians sporadically make their entrances once a "communal" key and rhythmic tempo have been intuitively agreed upon. The tonal center and tempo commonly shift several times during the first stanza of each musical selection. It is also common for the numbers to terminate abruptly, usually before the concluding cadence of the final verse.

The two most distinctive characteristics of this music are: (1) the use of blues harmonic progressions and (2) melodic repetition. The first of these characteristics is not unique to this type of music. Similar harmonic progressions can be found in a variety of popular American music, ranging from jazz to country and western. In the music of the serpent-handling service, however, the essential quality of the blues progressions is the accommodation of the melody to the extemporized song texts. (Blues progressions lend themselves to this adaptation of music to text because of the final V-I harmonic resolution.)

The second characteristic is the use of melodic repetition with extemporized texts. Performance of a single piece will frequently continue repetitiously for fifteen to twenty minutes. The length and style of these *melodic* repetitions are controlled principally by the *textual* improvisation. Whereas many of the songs have a prescribed number of stanzas in the singers' "fake books" or "lead sheets," there is no apparent limit regarding the number and length of stanzas employed during any single performance. As a result, songs performed by the same group of musicians for different serpent-handling services are never the same.

In conjunction with these two dominant features, there is an integral social relationship between the musicians and the other participants in the service. At the peak of the religious service there seems to be no eye contact between the musicians. They, like the serpent-handling participants, seem to become self-involved in their performance. Each individual musician appears to be more concerned in creating a personal performance than in a group ensemble.

The individuality among the instrumentalists is characterized by flexible rhythmic tempos, varying bombastic dynamic levels, and loud, seemingly incoherent, instrumental accompaniments that often obscure the song texts. (This particular lack of intelligibility in the texts is not to be confused with speaking in tongues, another phenomenon associated with the service.) At times the combination of individual expressions appears almost chaotic. Each instrumentalist, singer, and serpent handler appears completely self-involved—they would say "led by the Spirit." Toward the conclusion of a musical piece, however, the instrumentalists seem to restore control over the event; the "lead" musician often plays a significant role in this restoration.

The music of the serpent-handling service is not melodically or harmonically complex. It is characterized by monophonic melodies built around simple blues progressions. But this outward simplicity obscures its intricate internal function.

In order to understand better the music within a service, one should examine it not simply as a separate entity but as a part of the total performance context. From this approach, the music may be viewed as more than providing a vital musicological phenomenon and complementing altered states of consciousness. It may be seen, in its complex combination of individual and group expressions, as a symbol of the entire serpent-handling service.

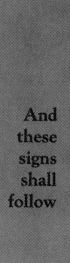

And these signs shall follow

Appendix C
The Life of George Hensley

George Hensley is such an important figure in the history of serpent handling that it is important to bring together as much data relative to him as possible. His personal story is integrated with other important events relative to serpent handling in chapters 2 and 3, but his life is so convoluted that it is difficult to keep the events in order. The following chronology provides a useful overview.

Parents

Susan Jane Hensley (1850-1919) buried in Ooltewah, Tennessee; Emanual Hensley (1850-1929), died in Knoxville, Tennessee (second wife named Sue).

Siblings

List provided by a nephew from the memory of family members: Mary, Trisa, Delia Mae, Bell, Avalina Jane (m. Brown), Hedrick, Henry, Vick (m. Lawson), Be(r)nett, Bertha (m.Weaver), George

List in the 1880 U.S. Census, 9th District (Watterson) of Hawkins County: Mary (12), Lutitia (10), Delia (8), Belle (7), Lena (4), Headrick (1)

Chronology

1880(?)

2 May   George Went Hensley born; examination for ordination implies 1880 as year of birth, as does marriage certificate of George and Inez Hutcheson, as do various newspaper accounts; the Bible of his wife Amanda states 1881; his son James Roscoe's birth certificate implies 1881; his son Loyal's birth certificate implies 1882. Loyal's birth certificate indicates that George was born in West

*George Hensley with second wife, Irene. Photograph
c. 1927 courtesy of La Creta Simmons.*

Virginia; his daughter Jean's says Scott
County, Virginia; James Roscoe's in
Tennessee. (No record of his birth
found in the vital records of Tennessee,
Virginia, or West Virginia.) According
to a newspaper account, "He said he did
not know how to read or write and
could not spell the name of his birth-
place in Tennessee" (Abbott 1). Place
of birth is likely the Watterson community outside Rogersville, Hawkins
County, in northeast Tennessee.

c. 1890

Moved, probably to Loudon County,
Tennessee.

1899

Reports of the initiation of handling
serpents:

(1) "George W. Hensley, 70 years old,
started the snake rites when he was 14"
("Snake Kills Cultist" 12); the year
1899 is computed on Hensley's age as
cited here (though erroneously) at his
death in 1955. Based on his probable
birthday, the date at age 14 would be
1894. (George may have first witnessed
the handling of serpents as a boy before
he moved to Ooltewah.)

(2) "His followers said Hensley, 56
years ago [apparently prior to the reported event of his death (1955) rather
than prior to the date of the newspaper
article], picked up a rattler in
Tennessee's Grasshopper Valley and it
didn't bite him" (Kimsey 9D).

1900

Membership in Baptist church terminated (Examination Certificate, questions 53-54).

Report of initiation of handling serpents: "The Rev. O. M. Lassiter, an
associate of Rev. Hensley in the Holiness Church, told newsmen Hensley . . .
had been bitten at least 400 times by
poisonous snakes during the past 55
years" ("Snakebitten Preacher" 3).

1901

5 May   Married Amanda Wininger at Lenoir
City (Loudon County), Tennessee;
lived soon thereafter in Ooltewah,
Tennessee.

1903

6 June   Daughter Bessie Jane born, died 24 July.

1904

9 June   Daughter Mae Marie (m. Hixon) born.

c. 1905

Inferred date of initiating serpent handling from local newspaper account of his death in 1955 reporting that he "told listeners he had been handling snakes for 50 years" ("Rattlesnake Bite Kills" 1).

1907

14 June   Daughter Katie Pearl born.

1908

Owl Holler Church of God dedicated by Homer Tomlinson; George's conversion (Examination Certificate, question 26).

1909

Initially took up a serpent at Rainbow Rock on White Oak Mountain near Ooltewah, according to reports and tradition.

20 Dec.   Daughter Rosa Frances (m. Harden) born.

1910

Started preaching (Examination Certificate, question 67); abstained from tobacco (question 44); resorted to Bible for healing (question 70); baptized with the Holy Ghost (question 29); spoke in tongues (question 30).

Initiation of practice according to 1938 report: "G. W. Hensley . . . says he started the snake handling rite 28 years ago in Sale Creek, Tennessee [near Birchwood and Grasshopper Church of God" ("Rattlesnake," *Post* 101).

1912

Became a member of the Church of God (Examination Certificate, question 68).

1913

Baptized by Church of God (Examination Certificate, question 32). (He may have been baptized earlier by the Baptists, but it is very likely at this time that, from the influence of fellow Church of God members or solely from personal conviction, he felt that he should be rebaptized.)

28 Sept.   Son Jessie Franklin born.

Year in which Hensley began to take up serpents according to inference from newspaper reports in 1936: "'I've been handling serpents for 23 years,' he said" ("Preacher Juggles Snake" 1); "Hensley said in his 23 years of snake-handling demonstrations he had seen a number of persons bitten but none had died" (Abbott 1).

1914

Report of having held a meeting along with his wife Amanda (who makes the report) for thirteen days at "Evansville" and later one at Dayton, Tennessee, with another husband-and-wife team. Divine healing mentioned, but no serpent handling (*Evangel* 4 Apr.: 7).

Reports from *Evangel* and Cleveland/Chattanooga papers of Hensley's involvement in handling serpents in Cleveland and Ooltewah, Tennessee:

Aug. Report of "conducting [with M. S. Haynes and others] a revival at the tabernacle in Cleveland, Tenn. It began the last Sunday in Aug. and is still continuing with increasing interest. . . . Twice during the meeting. [*sic*] Serpents have been handled by the Saints" (*Evangel*, 12 Sept.: 2). A later report in the *Evangel* of the revival at the tabernacle in South Cleveland: "Among those who were used under the power of God in taking up these serpents were Geo. Hensley and wife, M. S. Haynes and wife, T. L. McLain, and W. S. Gentry. Many others did it with great grace and apparent sublimity" (19 Sept.: 3). Newspaper report of "tent" meetings in South Cleveland for ten days with serpent handling, but no names mentioned ("'Holy Rollers' Handle Snakes" 12).

15 Sept. Report of the South Cleveland Tabernacle, where serpents had been handled previously, and of two men who had been bitten: "The meeting tonight was held in a barn-like affair with a sawdust floor, known as the 'taberneckle.' It is located in South Cleveland, and the 'Holy Rollers' are said to have erected it with their own funds." No mention of Hensley, but the article concludes: "The 'Church of God' and its snakes are going to move along to Ooltewah next week" ("Proselyting" 3).

17 Sept. Reference to serpent handling in the South Cleveland Tabernacle and "these saints of God in Bradley County," but no mention of Hensley ("Snakes in Demand" 1).

18 Sept. Report regarding "tent meetings" in South Cleveland with snakes, but no mention of Hensley ("Continue to Play with Poisonous Snakes" 5).

20 Sept. Hensley leads a tent meeting in Ooltewah; serpent handled by fifteen or twenty; he "announces that . . . he will walk the waters of the Tennessee river" ("Reptile in the Meetin'" 3).

22 Sept. Reported living in Owl Hollow and as saying "that if the devil tempts him to walk the river, the Lord will give him power to do it so that unbelievers may believe" ("All Depends on the Devil" 9).

23 Sept. Hensley holds meetings in Ooltewah, one each day, to continue for another month ("He Can Handle Snakes" 3).

26 Sept. Hensley reported as denying that he said he would walk on the Tennessee River ("Holy Rollers Anoint" 2).

4 Oct. Report of Hensley's meeting in Ooltewah, attended by A. J. Tomlinson, where "Two large rattlesnakes have been taken up under the power of God" (*Evangel* 4 Oct. 1914: 6).

1915

21 Aug. Report of Hensley's and N. P. Mulkey's having "closed the meeting out on the mountain," where "the rattlesnake" was

James Roscoe Hensley, a son by George's first marriage, now in retirement from his ministry in the Church of God (Cleveland). Photograph 1990 by the author.

handled, and of their presently holding a meeting in Soddy, Tennessee, "Geo. Hensley, in charge" (*Evangel* 21 Aug. 1915: 3).

29 Sept.   Son James Roscoe born in Harrison, Tennessee.

30 Oct.   Report of Hensley's closing a meeting the last of September in Dividing Ridge, Tennessee, where eighty-two of the eighty-three members had the Holy Ghost and about forty handled a rattler (*Evangel* 30 Oct. 1915: 4).

25 Dec.   Conference held by Hensley with local church (Dividing Ridge, Tennessee) and their recommendation for his ministry (Examination Certificate, questions 3, 94, 95); "Date of Credentials" in ministers ledger of the Church of God ("Evangelists H" 338); first Evangelist's Certificate (renewed in 1919). (Apparently it was a common practice to begin preaching without any formal credentials. One may infer that, after becoming a member of the Church of God and continuing to preach, Hensley applied for this level, the Evangelist's Certificate.)

1916

Held revival in Harrison, Tennessee, where it was reported that thirty or more received the Holy Ghost (*Evangel* 5 Feb.: 2).

1917

Examination Certificate by Church of God (The form is filled out in a crude handwriting and not always on the line provided; it would appear he signed it himself, "Mr. george hensly [*sic*]." He gives his home address as Birchwood, Tennessee, and his church membership as Dividing Ridge; he indicates that he had no "fair education," that he had property to cover his debt of twenty-five dollars, and that he is applying for ordination (perhaps a different level from Evangelist).

1918

Became first pastor of East Cleveland Church of God (officially organized on 13 Jan. 1918).

13 Apr.   A report from Birchwood, Tennessee, thanking God for sending Hensley to preach holiness (*Evangel* 13 Apr. 1983: 2).

8 Aug.   Daughter Esther Lee born.

1922

20 Jan.   Letter to A. J. Tomlinson from East

Above: Two sons of the first two of George Hensley's four marriages, Roscoe (Amanda's son, on the left) and Loyal (Irene's son, on the right). Photograph courtesy of J. R. Hensley.

Left: Faith Lillian, George and Irene Hensley's daughter, born 1928. Photograph courtesy of J. R. Hensley.

Chattanooga, apparently the East Chattanooga Church of God, responding to inquiry regarding Hensley's membership: "I have examined the records but did not find his name only as pastor at one time. The records here show that they have been very improperly kept. . . ."

8 (6?) Feb. Letter (unsigned copy, initialed "W MC/MP") to M. W. Letsinger, who was the Tennessee overseer at the time, stating that the writer (W MC/MP) was "in receipt of a letter from J. P. Hughes stating that the matter is arranged satisfactorly [sic] with the church, therefore, it will be alright to give them [the enclosed license] to him [George Hensley]. Please address him c/o Bertha Weaver, Waldbridge, Ohio." (Hughes was the third pastor of the East Cleveland Church of God; therefore the letter of 20 Jan. to Tomlinson was apparently from Hughes.) George may have already left the Birchwood area (although his final separation from Amanda did not occur until August) to stay with his sister Bertha Weaver—possibly before he had begun his period of backsliding. The enclosed license might have been a renewal or one of a higher level.

8 Aug. Separated from Amanda (as listed in her Bible).

Emma Jean Potts, George and Irene Hensley's daughter. Photograph courtesy of J. R. Hensley.

At some time during the years 1921-24, when M. W. Litsinger was overseer of Tennessee, turned in his license—probably in late 1922 or early 1923; reason stated on the form, entitled Revocation of Ministry, Church of God: "Resigned—has much trouble in the home."

1923

15 Mar. Son William Hilman born to Amanda.

27 Mar. Found guilty of selling liquor, $100 fine and court costs plus four months in jail; escapes from work detail in Silverdale, Tennessee. Hides out in Ooltewah.

Date unknown
Goes to Ohio perhaps to stay with his sister Bertha in Walbridge.

1926

9 Nov. Divorced from Amanda; Bill of Divorce granted to Amanda from George, who "abandoned claimant."

1927

6 Mar. Marries Irene Klunzinger in Alliance, Ohio.

1928

3 Mar. Daughter Faith born in Washingtonville, Ohio; George listed as 45 and Irene as 23 on birth certificate. (These ages would make his birth 1882 and hers 1904.)

1929

23 Oct. Son Loyal born in Malvern, Ohio.

c. 1931-32

Held meeting handling serpents at sister Bertha's church in Walbridge, according to George's niece Grace Cook.

1932

4 June Daughter Vinette born. George is pastor of East Pineville Church of God (Kane, "Snake Handlers of Southern Appalachia" 60).

1935

10 July Daughter Emma Jean born in Pennington Gap, Virginia.

Summer Newspaper reports: "Rev. Hensley conducted snake handling demonstrations" in St. Charles, Virginia ("No Law Against Handling Snakes" 1).

18 Aug. Hensley identified in newspaper as a "holiness evangelist of St. Charles [Virginia]" ("Snake Head Torn Off" 1) and reported in Ramsey, Virginia, leading 500 followers who cause "a near riot on

the highway" ("Wave Rattler in Frenzy" 17).

1936

Hensley reported to have "established the weird cult among the miners and farmers of southwestern Virginia on the Tennessee border," apparently including the church in Stone Creek, Virginia. ("They Shall Take Up Serpents," *Newsweek* 88).

Mar.   ". . . initiated an extended series of revival meetings in central Florida" (Kane, "Snake Handlers of Southern Appalachia" 61, 280).

1 Mar.   Reported as preaching and handling a rattlesnake in Tampa, Florida ("Pastor Here Whirls Snake" 1, 12).

8 Mar.   Reported outside of Tampa in Bloomingdale at a county church and being bitten; "said he was going next into Georgia but would return to Tampa soon" ("Preacher Juggles Snake" 8).

11 Mar.   Reported to have visited during the previous week, along with "some of his disciples," a man who canned rattlesnakes near Arcadia, Florida ("Snake Expert Warns People" 7).

3 May   Conducted a revival in Bartow, Florida, where Alfred Weaver was bitten and died the following day. Newspaper reports: "Hensley has been here for several weeks. He came here after giving snake-handling demonstrations in the Benjamin field fight arena at Tampa and at Bloomingdale. Since he has been

here his ceremony has been filmed by movie news reel cameramen. After the inquest he said he would discontinue his meeting here" (Abbott 6).

6 May   Conducted funeral services for Weaver and by report "said he planned to go to west Florida. He did not say when he would leave" ("County Buries Snake Victim" 7).

1936-37

Lived in Pineville, Kentucky, with Irene and family (minus Loyal).

1938

Summer   ". . . charged with breach of the peace in handling snakes" along with two other men at the Pine Mountain Church of God, Harlan County, Kentucky; reported as railroad conductor and pastor of East Pineville Church of God near Harlan, Kentucky (Kerman, "Rattlesnake Religion," *Post* 10-11).

1939

9 Sept.   Preaching and handling serpents during revival at McGhee Street Church of God (McGhee and Richards streets) in Knoxville, Tennessee ("'Deadly' Snakes Passed Around" A9).

11 Sept.   Continuing preaching at McGhee Street and reported as "touring churches in the South demonstrating his faith" ("The Reverend George Hensley of Pineville, Ky." 3).

24 Sept.   Preached his "farewell service" at McGhee Street, returned "to his home in Pineville, Ky.," but expected back on

the 26th "to conduct revival services for the rest of the week at John Sevier [on Rutledge Pike]" ("Snake Custodian" 12).

1940

Still living in Pineville when son Loyal rejoins family.

1941

7 Dec.   Residing in Duff, Tennessee (north of LaFollette), on a farm he had bought.

1942

Sold farm and moved to Evansville, Indiana; separated from Irene but reconciled and moved back to Pineville.

1943

Separated from Irene and family, who move in with Esther Lee in Chattanooga; George returned to Birchwood area, probably residing at least part of the time on sister Jane's farm in Ooltewah and with daughter Rosa.

1944

Son Roscoe hears him preach in a cottage meeting.

Spring   Irene dies at 39.

21 Aug.   Reported "of Harlan County, Ky." ("They Shall Take Up Serpents," *Newsweek* 88).

1945

20 July   Reported as having "assisted in founding the Dolly [*sic*] Pond Church of God a month ago" ("Demonstration of Faith" 1).

8 Sept.   Lewis Ford, who died 3 September of serpent bite, buried across the Dolly Pond Road from the church with an estimated 2,500 people attending funeral (Pennington, "Ford, Rattler's Victim" 1).

23 Sept. Arrested in Chattanooga along with Tom Harden while holding services; each fined $50 for disorderly conduct; Hensley reported as "of Brightsville, Tenn.," and "a member of a snake-handling cult" there (Corliss, "2 'Faith-Healing' Ministers" 1).

1946

23 Sept. Married Inez Riggs (m. Hutcheson) in Rossville (Walker County), Georgia, by a justice of the peace (George was 66, Inez 51); moved with her and her four children to Inez's farm in Soddy, Tennessee; separated in less than a year. (She had been present on 13 July when Joe C. Jackson was bitten during service at Clyde Leffew's house in Daisy, Tennessee, but Hensley name is not mentioned in report as present (Corliss, "Snake Bite During Church Rites" 1).

1947

7 Mar.   Tennessee Code 39-2208 signed, prohibiting the handling of poisonous snakes "in such a manner as to endanger the life or health of any person."

10 Aug.   Tom Harden, six other men, and five women arrested at Dolley Pond Church of God with Signs Following for handling serpents. George is not among

those indicted on 11 September, but it is reported that he would be a defense witness ("Snake Handlers of Georgia, Kentucky" 1) and he is photographed with Tom Harden and others at the trial (Smartt 1).

24 Oct.   Reported as 67 years old, a resident of Route 3, Chattanooga, handling serpents during tent services conducted for the past 30 days by the Undivided Church of God; arrested along with Reece Ramsey, 63, Cecil Denkins, 21, and Berlin Barbee, 23 ("Man Bitten Here in Snake Service" 3).

13 Dec.   Reported as assistant pastor of South Chattanooga Church of God, which was established in a heated tent ("Snake Cult Opens Church" 3).

c. 1949

Described as preaching in a tent meeting in East Chattanooga where serpents were handled; description cites 1909 as the year when Hensley initially took up serpents, apparently from information derived firsthand (Robertson 169-71).

c. 1952

Married Sally Moore (m. Norman) sometime relatively soon after Harve Norman, Sally's husband, died in 1951; moved to Georgia (he is reported later as being of Albany).

1955

24 July, Sunday

Bit by serpent near Altha (northern part of Calhoun County), Florida, 4:15 P.M.; died the following morning at 6:45 according to newspaper report ("Rattlesnake Bite Kills 75-Year-Old Cult Head" 2).

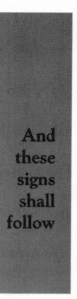

And these signs shall follow

Appendix D
Some
Questions

Almost everyone has heard about religious serpent handling, but few have ever had the opportunity to witness it. Whenever the subject comes up, it of course raises numerous questions. Usually the questions are the same, and although I do not claim to have all the answers, I have tried to answer the most common questions.

The Serpents

Is anyone other than the participants endangered by the serpents?

Normally the serpents are handled in an area inside in the building at the front away from the nonparticipants. Often the pastor or one of the other leaders is watchful when the serpents are out of the boxes so that they do not get loose or that someone does not unnecessarily get hurt. Pastor Liston Pack at Carson Springs, Tennessee, for example, will pick up serpents that are dropped or abandoned and put them back in the boxes. Barbara Elkins at Jolo, West Virginia, will watch some of the handlers intensely, particularly the females and younger ones, and will sometimes take serpents from them, apparently when she feels something is not right. When serpents are handled outdoors, a restricted area is designated—for example a platform, a tent, or sometimes space marked off by bales of hay. Precautions, however, are not always taken by and for the handlers. Sometimes serpents will be draped around someone's neck or placed in someone's hands and on a few occasions—less frequently nowadays—even thrown, unrequested, to another person.

Inscribed snake box at Jolo. Photograph 1991 by Bill Snead.

How deadly are snake bites?

The bite of the serpents commonly handled in services can be fatal, more likely if the snake is a rattlesnake than a copperhead or cottonmouth. If the bite receives proper medical treatment, the probability of death is slight.

In an authoritative study of serpent venom, F. E. Russell finds that the seriousness of snake-venom poisoning depends upon several factors relative to the snake and the person bitten. Relative to the serpent are such matters as species, size, degree of fear or anger motivating the bite, length of time and amount of venom injected, pathogens present in the snake's mouth, and the condition of its fangs and glands. Concerns regarding the person bitten are age, size, nature of bite (including location, depth, number), and medical treatment received ("The Clinical Problem" 987). Some eight thousand individuals in the United States are bitten each year by venomous snakes, and fewer than a dozen die from the bite, the majority fatalities being untreated or undertreated children or religious serpent handlers (985).

One may infer from these statistics that venomous bites received by serpent handlers would not normally be lethal if they received proper treatment; no inference can be drawn from this data relative to the comparative effects of venomous bites received by serpent handlers and those by other untreated adults. Skeptics sometimes conclude from similar statistics that adherents are not involved in great danger. Even discarding the deaths by serpent bite, a quick look at some of the photographs of "bad" bites—showing black, distended flesh or atrophied hands and missing fingers—is enough to convince anyone of the imminent harm. In regard to inherent danger, serpent handlers seem to be "damned if there is and damned if there isn't."

Serpent handlers themselves sometimes almost

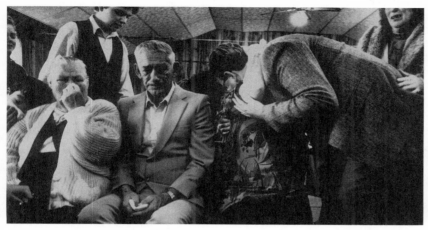

Mrs. Ray Johnson being comforted at funeral of her husband, who died of serpent bite (Lue and Ershel Blankenship, Ray's mother and stepfather, beside her). Photograph 1991 by Bill Snead.

disregard a bite. Lydia Elkins Hollins, whose mother died from a serpent bite in a religious service, wrote to me: "How's everything going? Everyone here seems to be fine—exception of me being copperhead bit—I got bit 10-13-85 [the previous week]—and my finger is still pretty bad—that's why the writing is so sloppy in this note—I'm left handed and it got me on the middle finger close to the fingernail—How's the weather there? It's damp & cool here. . . ."

Can serpents control the amounts of venom they release?

According to F. E. Russell, "Snakes rarely, if ever, eject the full contents of their glands. The amount of venom injected in the process of obtaining food appears to be related to the size of the prey. In the case of bites on humans, or in situations where the snake strikes in quick defense, the amount of venom may vary from 0-90% of the gland content" ("The Clinical Problem" 985).

Do bitten individuals build up an immunity to the venom?

It would seem from clinical studies that repeated bites of rattlesnakes, copperheads, and water mocca-

sins do not produce immunity. Whereas it is theoretically possible that humans could produce a permanent immunity, increased doses of venom at frequent intervals would probably be necessary. Any protective level of immunity seems to dissipate rapidly, and the short period of incubation for venom (2 to 15 minutes in contrast to 14 to 21 days for infectious diseases) is not conducive to the production of antibodies (Parrish and Pollard 284-85). Rather than producing immunity, repeated bites may in fact produce in some persons an "allergy to snake venoms which may make subsequent bites more dangerous" (285).

How many serpent handlers have died from serpent bites?

Precise data are not available because of the nature of the independence of the churches involved, the illegality of the practice in many cases, the lack of early statistics, and the difficulty of collecting widespread newspaper reports. Steven Kane reportedly documents 69 deaths through April 1990 (White B4). Added to that list would be Jimmy Ray Williams, Jr., who died on 13 July 1991, 18 years after the death of his father by strychnine; and Ray Johnson, who died 2 December 1991.

*Do they milk the serpents of the venom
before handling them?*

Absolutely not. Handling serpents for sign-follow-ing believers has no meaning if it is not potentially dangerous. Not only do they not tamper with them in any way, it is a common practice to handle any serpents brought to them by others.

*Does the body temperature of the
anointed individual placate the serpent
and retard its biting?*

Probably not, but nobody knows for certain. Scientific documentation of human body tempera-ture during anointment and of the effect of any difference that it might have on the serpent is nonexistent. Rattlesnakes and other pit-vipers have organs on the sides of their heads to locate prey; these organs are extremely sensitive to "detecting differences of fractions of a degree centigrade in the environment" (Morris and Morris 195). This sensitivity to temperature would enhance aware-ness of the presence of warm-blooded objects, but it does not seem to explain the low number of bites. The handlers are not always anointed; some handle serpents by faith rather than in any trance-like state. There are other conditions in which be-lievers are exposed where body temperature would not be a vital factor, e.g., reaching for a serpent, having serpents draped around their bodies or thrown to them. Since serpents are "particularly sen-sitive to tactile stimuli" (Morris and Morris 196), one might speculate on the effect of various stimuli—e.g., being held, stroked, petted, twirled, wrapped, caught, stepped upon, and dropped.

*Why are serpent handlers not bitten
more often than they are?*

The percentage of times they handle serpents with impunity is very high, although there is no statis-tical data comparing bites of handlers who are be-lievers and those who are not. There may be many factors at work determining whether handlers are bitten. One authority alludes to suggestions by other writers—"Hypnotism, neurogenic reflexes, and catalepsy"—but adds: "I feel their importance is minimal. . . . One might consider the possibility that snakes can detect fright in a person, either by proprioception [reception by the snake's brain of stimuli produced within the serpent relative to its body] or by olfaction. If this were possible, one might speculate that snakes could detect changes associated with fear or fright or, conversely, in people who were handling them" (Russell, *Snake Venom Poisoning* 529-30).

Weston La Barre, in noting a discussion of members of the Duke University Department of Parapsychology with one serpent handler, states: "The handling of snakes with impunity is obvi-ously a potential instance of the 'PK phenom-enon,' psychokinesis, or 'the power of mind over matter'" ("The Snake-Handling Cult" 332). Lisa Alther makes reference to this conclusion in an interview with Pastor Liston Pack and adds: "It strikes me that they're basically saying the same thing you are: that there's a force available—PK to them, the power of the Lord to you—to those who know how to use it" ("They Shall Take Up Serpents" 35).

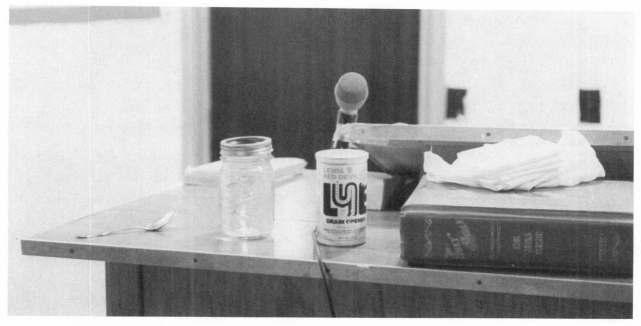

One of the various substances drunk in accordance with the scripture, "if they drink any deadly thing, it shall not hurt them," Mark 16:18. Photograph 1983 by the author.

The Poison

*Do they actually drink strychnine
and other poisons?*

Unquestionably. Proof of the validity of the claim of drinking "the deadly thing" is evident in the reports of fatalities such as that of Jimmy Williams and Buford Pack by strychnine poisoning at the Carson Springs Holiness Church of God in Jesus Name in April 1973. In the November preceding these deaths, Williams had taken carbon tetrachloride during a religious service, and lye mixed with water was also consumed at the Carson Springs church. Two jars of liquid from which Charles Prince drank at another Carson Springs service in 1983 were willingly submitted by Prince, who, along with the pastor, was glad to have its lethality documented. The toxicologist's report revealed a strychnine concentration of 249.7 and 399.6 micrograms per mil-

liliter. A lethal dose of these samples in comparison with recorded data would probably be 6 to 7 ounces and 4 to 5 ounces, respectively, although poisoning in humans has been reported with one fourth that amount (Slater 524). Based on a videotape of the jars prior to the service, approximately 1.5 to 3 ounces of the liquids were consumed (perhaps on the margin of a lethal dose) with no apparent ill results. In 1985 Prince died following a religious service during which he drank poison; the autopsy report stated: *"PROXIMATE CAUSE OF DEATH*: Rattlesnake venom reaction and/or strychnine ingestion."

What are the effects of strychnine poisoning?

Strychnine acts as a stimulant to the spine and produces convulsions. A human absorbs strychnine quickly when it is consumed orally and, with sufficient doses, undergoes a convulsion usually

164 • Serpent-Handling Believers

within fifteen to forty-five minutes (though it may be delayed for several hours) which lasts from one to two minutes. "The patient is fully conscious and suffers exquisite pain from the muscle cramps. . . . Further convulsions may occur, particularly after tactile or auditory stimulation. Death . . . usually occurs after two to five convulsions" (Slater 524).

Does one build up an immunity to strychnine?

Apparently not. Strychnine is seemingly disposed of by the body rather quickly: "Animal experiments have shown that strychnine is disposed of at the rate of about one convulsive dose per hour, but with considerable species and sex differences" (Slater 524). In certain animals, 20 percent of the convulsive dose was injected every fifteen minutes for three hours without causing convulsions, and 50 percent of the convulsive dose was administered daily for long periods without either accumulation or tolerance (524). One might infer that a lethal dose consumed by a person in small portions over a period of hours would not be fatal, but such an inference would be highly speculative since it is not based on human data.

How many have died by drinking "the deadly thing"?

The first record seems to be of V. A. Bishop who, during a revival at Trinity, Texas, in 1921, drank "seven grains of strychnine or arsenic . . . in an ounce of water" (*Evangel* 7 May 1921: 1). There are some half-dozen cases reported, but as in deaths by serpent bites, they are difficult to document because of a number of circumstances. For example, Charles Prince's death, as previously cited, is attributed to a combination of serpent venom and/ or strychnine. There are no comparative results of poison ingestion by sign followers and non-"anointed" persons.

The Fire

Are there naturalistic explanations for believers not being burned by fire or heat?

There are a number of documented incidents of individuals' contacting fire and not being burned, the "fire walk" being the best-known. The London Council for Psychical Investigation undertook in 1935 and 1936 to examine two series of fire walks held under controlled conditions at Surrey, England. In the first series of tests the surface temperature of the fire pit was 430 degrees Celsius (806 degrees Fahrenheit), the interior temperature 1400 C (2552 F); in the second series, the surface temperature was over 500 degrees C (932 degrees F). Two individuals walked, claiming faith as the reason for being unharmed. The official report concluded: "fire walking is a gymnastic feat operating on this principle: a limited number of quick and even steps on a poor conductor of heat does not result in burning of the flesh" (Feinberg 75). There were other reports published by individual scientists "in general agreeing that fire walking can be explained in terms of certain physical facts, but they did not agree on precisely what those physical facts were" (74). Other explanations include the psychological and the religious. One account of fire walking in Ceylon reported eighty persons walking a twenty-by-six-foot pit, twelve of whom were hospitalized for burns and one of whom died. "These people, the devout believer will tell you, lacked either faith or preparation" (76).

A number of other studies analyze the effect of hypnosis relative to burns. From these, Steven

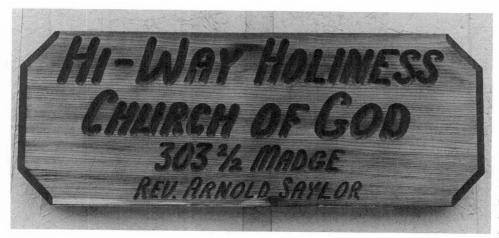

Sign on the outside of church building constructed by Pastor Saylor and his four sons, adjoining pastor's home. Photograph 1989 by Fred Brown.

Kane concludes: "Seeing that the beliefs of subjects in hypnotic trance can influence their neural activity in such a way as to augment or prevent damage in reaction to noxious stimuli—and even to produce damage in the complete absence of such stimulation—I think it not unreasonable to suggest that the entranced fire handlers' belief in their own invulnerability mobilizes the same protective nervous system process" ("Holiness Ritual Fire Handling" 382). Of course, even a clinical description (much less an explanation) of the effects of handling fire is limited without controlled testing. Available clinical studies are not adequate to explain the phenomenal reports of believers who have the "gift of fire" (see Berthold Schwarz).

The Present and Future State

How many serpent handlers are there?

Any accounting is difficult due to the autonomy of the churches and the divisions in doctrine; then, too, some congregations are rather secretive. Serpent handlers themselves do not know all the preachers and churches even in their own region. Certain groups know each other and travel long distances to attend each other's services, homecomings, and revivals. Kingston, Georgia, members travel to Jolo, West Virginia; Jolo and Sneedville, Tennessee, members go to Kentucky; the pastor of Carson Springs, Tennessee (who does not know the group in Sneedville), has gone north to Indiana, Ohio, and Michigan, as well as all over the South; leaders of the church in Fort Wayne, Indiana, go back home to Straight Creek, Kentucky. But serpent handlers do not have a clear perspective of the total body of sign followers. In 1987 Steven Kane estimated some two thousand members of "Holiness snake-handling churches in the South and Midwest" ("Appalachian Snake Handlers" 118); Mary Lee Daugherty reportedly estimated in 1983 "about 1,000 members of serpent-handling sects in West Virginia" alone (Watterlond 51). Out of these church members, a reasonable estimate might be several hundred actual handlers, but there is a considerable ebb and flow in individuals as well as churches that practice serpent handling.

Perry Bettis, serpent handler and native of the area where serpent handling emerged in Tennessee, who handled serpents for over forty years before his death by natural causes in 1991. Photograph 1989 by the author.

Are serpents handled by believers presently in the Grasshopper Valley area, where the practice may have begun?

Preacher Perry Bettis was a follower of the signs for some thirty years until his death on 11 December 1991. He handled serpents even in states where it is illegal. But for several years (c. 1984-85) he did not handle serpents in services held on his property in Birchwood, Tennessee, at the Church of Jesus Christ With Signs Following—except once or twice a year—or anywhere else in the Grasshopper Valley area. The reason he gave for the absence of handling in the valley is the lack of belief. He said that, if people believed as they once did, serpents would still be handled regularly in spite of the rigid law enforcement. He is the last person to be bitten by a serpent in a religious service in the Dolly Pond area. The bite—the only one he ever received—occurred around 1985 and caused two fingers on his right hand to become numb.

Are African Americans involved?

Yes. The first pastor of the Jolo church, Bishop W. L. Dickerson, was African American. He handled serpents, and there are a few African Americans who attend other serpent-handling churches and who do handle serpents. Kenneth Ambrose found among the serpent-handling churches he studied that there was a strong belief, supported by their actions as well as their sermons, in people of all races being accepted into their congregations; furthermore, this attitude was stronger than that indicated in an earlier study of religious beliefs in Southern Appalachia not restricted to serpent handlers ("Survey of the Snake-Handling Cult of West Virginia" 94).

Are children involved in handling serpents?

Bud Gregg of Morristown, Tennessee, is probably representative of sign followers when he says:

A child joining in the dancing at the Hi-Way Holiness Church of God, Fort Wayne, Indiana.
Photograph 1989 by Fred Brown.

We don't let children handle serpents here at the House of Prayer in Jesus Name. In fact, my children, my own children, I would encourage them not to be hasty in moving. I believe a man or a woman or a young man or woman ought to really be established in the faith, in mind, in heart, in soul—get all the foolishness out of their life— before they begin to take part in the signs of the Gospel. The youngest person we've got here, I would guess would be about twenty-five years old. So they are pretty well, they know what they're doing, they've sort of established in the thing, and they know what the serpent bite can do, what the law is, and they also know who God is, and they'd rather obey God than man.

There is always the question of the "age of accountability," or how old children should be before they are considered fully responsible to obey the gospel, including the admonition to "follow the signs." The response of believers to that question varies. If minors are saved and receive the gift of the Holy Spirit, then it is a serious problem for sign followers to deny them participation in the signs—and some are not denied. For example, Arnold Saylor of Fort Wayne, Indiana, an adult son of a sign follower, has handled serpents since he was nine years old. There are quite a few early reports as well as recent ones of children handling serpents.

Clyde Ricker, at a service at the Holiness Church of God near Lebanon, Virginia, is reported as offering an explanation. "When children—such as the nine-year-old girl—handle snakes, Ricker says it is not because the child has been anointed as such, but because an anointed adult has been directed to hand the reptile to the child" (Howard Taylor C1).

Serpent handling by mothers with babies in their arms or by others near babies is also reported: "In front of a young mother who sat holding a baby in her lap, he [one of the handlers] paused and gleefully held the reptile extended before the baby's eyes. As he laughed and the mother smiled, the baby gravely reached out and touched the snake" (Kerman, "Rattlesnake Religion," *Eve's* 97).

Among handlers, there seems now to be more concern regarding the endangerment of children, and the common procedure is that only responsible, consenting adults are allowed in close contact with the serpents.

Is the practice presently in decline?

Apparently so. According to personal testimony of handlers, their numbers are not nearly as great as they once were, even twenty years ago. Comparison is difficult since past accounts of numbers are scantier than present ones; and often news reports have been of incredulous spectators, e.g., three thousand spectators at Stone Creek, Virginia, at the memorial service of John Hensley ("They Shall Take Up Serpents," *Newsweek* 88), and twenty-five hundred at Lewis Ford's funeral in Tennessee (Pennington, "Ford, Rattler's Victim" 1). Also, reports of serpent-handling congregations, past and present, do not usually distinguish between church members and those who actually handle the serpents. In some of the congregations there is no noticeable decrease in activity, as in Jolo, West Virginia; but even there speculation arises about the sustained vitality after the three or four principal handlers are gone. Currently, there are more oral reports of churches where serpents are no longer handled than of those where the practice has been taken up.

Will the practice persist?

Probably for some time. It would seem that serpent handling will decrease as the communities are increasingly influenced by secularism and as serpent-handling preachers and churches are affected by an academic approach to scriptural exegesis and more liberal religious and cultural views. The validity of this hypothesis is substantiated by the exclusion of serpent handling through some of these influences within the Church of God, where serpent handling was once active. As Mickey Crews observes: "Like other new religious groups, this Holiness-Pentecostal sect developed some eccentric practices in its early years. These created an unfavorable public image. . . . As the Church of God began its rise into mainstream conservative evangelicalism, the organization discarded many of these unusual practices" (91).

A valuable insight into a different response of contemporary Pentecostals, particularly younger ones, is provided by a student's paper in one of Dr. Harold Hunter's religion classes at the Church of God School of Theology:

> What do we as pentecostals "make of all this?" I think many probably feel that these persons are ignorant and "don't really know any better." Some are too scared to think about it, and others probably feel they waste their time if they think about it. As for me, I am not exactly sure how to resolve the issue. Whereas many wouldn't address it as an (peripheral) issue, I feel that we as pentecostals need to deal with it. Many pentecostals have seen or heard about people hugging pot-bellied stoves or handling red hot coals and more or less view it in a positive light—as a providential act of protection. Is snake handling any different? Souls have repented as a result of both. (Stansky 9)

Even though for at least twenty years there have been indications of change in the religious views of younger members of serpent-handling churches (Ambrose, "Survey of the Snake-Handling Cult of West Virginia" 95), new recruits to the practice include young people from outside as well as within the fold.

The formal education level of these churches and especially of their preachers will be critical. At present that level is generally low. Some of the old-time preachers are illiterate, although it should be noted that they are not commonly ignorant or inarticulate. The younger members reflect increased state educational regulations, and some have attended college. The general lack of formal education, however, is particularly evident in matters of language, textual exegesis, and translation. If serpent handlers were trained in these areas, they would doubtless take different approaches to interpreting scripture. For example, in the key text, Mark 16:18, besides having a clearer understanding of the problem of its textual authenticity, they would be aware of the implications of the original Greek language and of exegetical comparison. Instead of summarily reading "They shall take up serpents" as meaning "inevitable" or "compulsory" actions to be taken by believers, they might evaluate other interpretations, such as the one by George B. Horton. He indicates that the English translation "They shall take up" is derived from one Greek word that

> appears 102 times in the New Testament and is variously translated "take up, remove, take away, destroy, put away, do away with, kill." . . . There is only one instance in the New Testament in which the exact verb form of the Greek work [sic] *airo* is

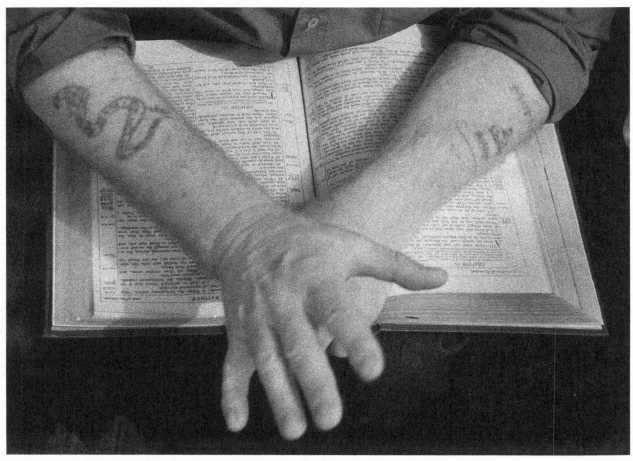

Liston Pack's arms across his Bible. Photograph by Mike DuBose.

used. In that passage (John 11:48), the identical word is translated "take away." A reading of the passage reveals the conditional structure that is intended. It is readily seen that the entire passage in Mark 16 is also conditional and is a promise of protection rather than a command to perform. (Cross 20)

What are some of the factors reinforcing the survival of the practice?

One factor, as Steven Kane suggests, is kinship: "In a number of families snake handling has been carried on for three generations or more. Ties of kinship have been a factor of crucial importance in both the diffusion and the persistence of the snake-handling faith" ("Snake Handlers" 699).

There are also factors at work within the services that reinforce the survival. These "mechanisms" or means of building commitment, as set forth by Kenneth Ambrose, involve "sacrifices ranging from minor ones of dress to the ultimate sacrifice of life," investment such as time (twelve to fifteen hours per week in church and great distances traveled), separation from and renunciation of the "outside world as evil and wicked," communion and attachment with the members of the church, especially in practicing the signs, and "moral" com-

Manifesting Luke 10:19: "Behold, I give unto you power to tread on serpents and scorpions, and over all the power of the enemy: and nothing shall by any means hurt you." Photograph of Charles Prince 1983 at Carson Springs.

mitment. Moral commitment is manifested in (1) the values of the church determining the norms of behavior for the individual and being expressed in confessions and mutual criticisms, (2) sanctions of the group for deviant behavior (for example, through prayers and the differentiation of levels of spirituality), and (3) transcendence "seen in the awe of the ritual, the power and authority of the leaders within the group, the conversion experiences, and the tests of faith" ("A Serpent-Handling Church" 58-59, 90-92). All of these factors inherent in the serpent-handling services—besides fulfilling the needs of the individuals—build commitment to the church, which is vital to the survival of its practices.

The Key Scriptures

Why do serpent handlers literally follow Mark 16:17-18 and not other scriptures?

From their point of view, they do follow all the scriptures literally; whether they actually do is open to debate. Serpent handler Byron Crawford told one newsman: "If Jesus said, 'They shall wrestle grizzly bears,' I would wrestle a grizzly bear; I'd go catch me one and try to wrestle me a grizzly bear if Jesus said to" ("ABC News").

What scriptures other than Mark 16 refer to serpent handling?

Exod. 4:3-4 And he said, Cast it on the ground. And he cast it on the ground, and it became a serpent; and Moses fled from before it. And the Lord said unto

"Boots" Parker handles fire at the Dolley Pond Church behind the rope that separated spectators from participants. Photograph c. 1945 by J. C. Collins, identification by Flora Bettis.

Moses, Put forth thine hand, and take it by the tail. And he put forth his hand, and caught it, and it became a rod in his hand.

Job 26:13 By his spirit he hath garnished the heavens; his hand hath formed the crooked serpent.

Eccles. 10:8 He that diggeth a pit shall fall into it; and whoso breaketh an hedge, a serpent shall bite him.

Luke 10:19 Behold, I give unto you power to tread on serpents and scorpions, and over all the power of the enemy: and nothing shall by any means hurt you.

John 20:30-31 And many other signs truly did Jesus in the presence of his disciples, which are not written in this book; But these are written, that ye might believe that Jesus is the Christ, the Son of God; and that believing ye might have life through his name.

Acts 2:43 And fear came upon every soul: and many wonders and signs were done by the apostles.

Acts 5:12 And by the hands of the apostles were many signs and wonders wrought among the people.

Acts 28:3-5 But when Paul had gathered a bundle of sticks, and laid them on the fire, there came a viper out of the heat, and fastened on his hand. And when the barbarians saw the venomous beast hang on his hand, they said among themselves, No doubt this man is a murderer, whom, though he hath escaped the sea, yet vengeance suffereth not to live. And he shook off the beast into the fire, and felt no harm.

1 Cor. 10:9 Neither let us tempt Christ, as some of them also tempted, and were destroyed of serpents.

What scriptures mention handling fire?

Isa. 43:2 . . . when thou walkest through the fire, thou shalt not be burned; neither shall the flame kindle upon thee.

Dan. 3:20-27 And he commanded the most mighty men that were in his army to bind Shadrach, Meshach, and Abednego, and to cast them into the burning fiery furnace. . . . And the princes, governors, and captains, and the king's counsellers, being gathered together, saw these men, upon whose bodies the fire had no power, nor was an hair of their head singed, neither were their coats changed, nor the smell of fire had passed on them.

Heb. 11:33-34 Who through faith . . . Quenched the violence of fire.

1 Pet. 1:7 That the trial of your faith, being much more precious than of gold that perisheth, though it be tried with fire, might be found unto praise and honour and glory at the appearing of Jesus Christ.

What is the scripture for the nine spiritual gifts?

1 Cor. 12:8-10 For to one is given by the Spirit the word of wisdom; to another the word of knowledge by the same Spirit; To another faith by the same Spirit; to another the gifts of healing by the same Spirit; To another the working of miracles; to another prophecy; to another discerning of spirits; to another divers kinds of tongues; to another the interpretation of tongues.

The Customs

How restrictive is the ascetic life-style of serpent handlers?

Some think that growing long sideburns and even wearing ties are inappropriate because these and similar acts of personal conduct indicate pride and worldliness. This extremely conservative attitude toward personal appearance and conduct is characteristic of other Pentecostal Holiness people, but it has many variables. One female serpent handler does not wear jewelry but feels a watch is justified by its being "necessary." On the other hand, there are congregations where for some members (and in other cases for many) the personal appearance is little or no different from what one would find in any number of rural churches—suits for men, conventional heels and dresses and coiffures for women. Some serpent handlers have televisions and watch commercial programs or allow their children to watch cartoons; some watch only carefully selected programs; others have camcorders and watch only tapes of religious services, mostly serpent-handling ones such as homecomings and revivals. Some serpent handlers use tobacco, drink caffeine and—in at least one case—alcoholic beverages, referring to the text, "whatsoever thing from without entereth into the man, it cannot defile him; . . . That which cometh out of the man, that defileth the man" (Mark 7:18, 20).

The attitudes toward material things also vary, but there seems to be a distinction made between "worldliness" and "materialism," the former leading to fleshly sins or personal exaltation, the latter not necessarily being evil. For example, the parking lots—in some cases filled with late-model non-economy cars, vans, RVs, and trucks—are not dissimilar to those of other local churches. One serpent handler in Georgia, a wealthy contractor who drives a Cadillac, as does his wife, preaches that the Lord makes prosperous those who give to His work. On one occasion this preacher quoted as biblical substantiation: "The Lord is my Shep-

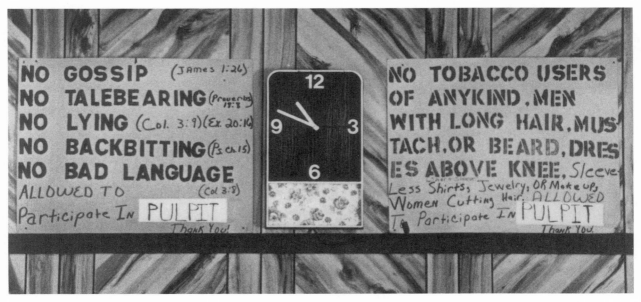

Pulpit restrictions at the Church of the Lord Jesus, Jolo. Photograph 1985 by Mike DuBose.

herd and I shall not want." As additional proof he offered an illustration: "There's a sister here today walked out one day to give somebody twenty dollars. She had twenty dollars in one hand. She said before she passed that twenty, somebody had given her a hundred. She had a hundred in the other hand—give that twenty away and a hundred in the other hand. Tell me, you can't outgive God. You can't outgive God." The preacher included a personal experience just two days before of picking up a man from the side of the road who had not eaten in days and taking him to get something to eat before seeing that the man had a ride to his destination in Alabama. Continuing his story, he related how he then drove on home, where he was met by two men who owed him some money, "only 37,000 dollars," and they wrote him a check for the money, a check he had in his pocket at the time. He concluded, "You got to be good to God, and God'll be good to you."

In regard to the general austerity of Holiness people, Anton Boisen observes: "It is important to recognize that the doctrine of holiness, which is common to all these groups, is primarily a matter of religious experience. These people are commonly austere in their piety. They forbid card-playing, dancing, theatre-going and the like, but they are not interested in virtue for its own sake. . . . Their austerity is either just a means toward obtaining and keeping that experience or else an expression of their faith in the potency of the experience" (187). For the most part, it seems that handlers are more interested in living godly, pure lives than in self-denial of physical comforts.

What are the scriptures cited relating to restrictions in dress?

Deut. 22:5 The woman shall not wear that which pertaineth unto a man, neither shall a man put on a woman's garment: for all that do so are abomination unto the Lord thy God.

Deut. 22:11 Thou shalt not wear a garment of divers sorts, as of woollen and linen together.

1 Cor. 3:16-17 Know ye not that ye are the temple of God, and that the Spirit of God dwelleth in you? If any man defile the temple of God, him shall God destroy; for the temple of God is holy, which temple ye are.

1 Cor. 6:19 What? know ye not that your body is the temple of the Holy Ghost which is in you, which ye have of God, and ye are not your own?

1 Cor. 11:5, 7, 14-15 But every woman that prayeth or prophesieth with her head uncovered dishonoureth her head: for that is even all one as if she were shaven. . . . For a man indeed ought not to cover his head, forasmuch as he is the image and glory of God: but the woman is the glory of the man. . . . Doth not even nature itself teach you, that, if a man have long hair, it is a shame unto him? But if a woman have long hair, it is a glory to her: for her hair is given her for a covering.

1 Tim. 2:9-10 In like manner also, that women adorn themselves in modest apparel, with shamefacedness and sobriety; not with broided hair, or gold, or pearls, or costly array; But (which becometh women professing godliness) with good works.

Is there a biblical basis for the custom of greeting with a kiss?

This practice of greeting, sometimes on the mouth, is based on biblical statements, such as "Greet one another with an holy kiss" (2 Cor. 13:12). This custom is not restricted to serpent-handling churches. Generally individuals do not kiss members of the opposite sex, but in congregations where members do, such as the one at Scrabble Creek, Kentucky, the concept is to kiss one another as members of the family of God in purity and in the Spirit without lust (Holliday 40). One minister preaches: "'If you feel any evil over greeting some woman any more than you would some man, the devil is in you somewhere'" (Dickinson and Benziger 141).

Do the services contain a degree of exhibitionism, showmanship, and publicity seeking?

Not only charlatans but people who follow a divine mission may love public performance. Regardless of the degree of showmanship manifested by various handlers, however, one does not get to know them and think that the ritual is simply a performance. The response of serpent handlers toward publicity varies greatly. Some welcome media exposure, if it is fair. They feel that the Second Coming of Christ will not occur until the gospel is preached to all the world and that the mass media provide the quickest way to accomplish this goal. Some pastors welcome outsiders and even invite them to testify. Some do not want anyone coming to the service with a notepad, camera, or tape recorder—in part because of their having had bad experiences previously with the press and in part because of not wanting the spirit of the meeting disturbed.

Serpent handlers are also aware of the ego problems that the presence of the media can bring out in individuals, and they are forthright in discussing the matter. Pastor Liston Pack says about one of the Homecomings at Carson Springs: "I saw lots of phony shoutin' before the mike on the camera that I don't think should have been done. I'm not the judge, but the Holy Ghost or the Spirit of God can detect the right spirit, and it seemed like some people liked to put on just a little extra motion due to they were on camera." Although the influence of outside agents is not an ethical consideration of most people, it has grave moral implications. How much do the media and spectators adversely affect the serpent handlers; do they in a sense corrupt them, infect them with pride, turn their heads? When someone dies from being bitten or drinking

Some of the thirty to forty persons, mostly young families, attending this service of the Hi-Way Holiness Church of God. Photograph 1989 by Fred Brown.

poison, the question of the effect of outsiders becomes even more serious. How guilty of complicity are journalists, television programmers, video and film makers, writers, academics, and spectators?

What about antics such as running around during the services, standing up on chairs, etc.—is all that for show?

Many of these activities are rhetorical styles reminiscent of revivalists early in this century and even more so in the nineteenth century. These styles would appear in some cases to be survivals of oral tradition. Along with other stylized mannerisms, such as certain movements of different parts of the body (e.g., head, arms, torso, and feet), they might

well be studied as traditional: learned by demonstration, accepted by a particular group, and sustained over a period of time. They are not traditions unique to serpent handlers, however.

Are not the services really a form of entertainment?

The austerity of Holiness conduct restricts a number of social activities. As folklorist Ellen Stekert points out: "Gatherings where songs were sung, dances performed, tales were told, and jokes and riddles were related, were often gatherings where social behavior was such as to offend the moral code of the new religion"; yet the services provided an acceptable context in which many of these earlier rejected traditions could continue (320). The

Tim McCoy dancing with visitor Willard Vance from Kentucky during services at Jolo. Photograph 1991 by Bill Snead.

social significance of the church service was certainly more important when it was one of a very few public activities available. Ola White, for example, remembers as a girl going to the Dolley Pond services when it was "packed in there till there wasn't even room to put another one, outside and inside and everywhere." She says people were even sitting on the ceiling joists, but she adds: "You got to look at it this away. They's just a house here and there then, and that was the main thing was a-goin' on in this community." Presently, when there are multiple social and entertainment opportunities, including movie rentals and television, there is less of a social vacuum, but serpent-handling services do continue.

It may very well be that the spontaneity of the service is more rewarding to the congregations than the handling itself, as suggested by one study: "one would expect the serpent handler to value his church and its religious services (which assign such an important role to spontaneous expression in testimony, singing, and dancing) as more generally providing a variety of opportunities for pleasurable, exciting, and significant emotional experiences" than "the occasional enactment of the serpent-handling ritual by a few members" (Tellegen 241).

Can't these services be seen simply as an activity in which people participate in order to purge themselves emotionally, to experience a catharsis of feelings, tensions, and stresses?

Certainly the services provide emotional release.

Bruce Helton,
pastor from
Evarts, Kentucky,
at a meeting in
Baxter.
Photograph 1983
by Mike DuBose.

As Charles Braden observes, a vital part of the attraction of groups such as these is that they provide a release that "many people need by temperament and do not find in the rather formal liturgical services of the 'regular' churches." Part of the release comes through the music, "which eases at least for a time the inner strains to which men and women are subject. Whether this is the best way of liberating tensions may be a matter of debate. That it does liberate them can scarcely be disputed." Another benefit of the emotional experience may be that it is a unifying force: "by reason of sharing together in the emotional experiences common to the group the members are knit into a closer, more personal fellowship than that usually found in the 'regular' churches" ("Churches of the Dispossessed" 109-10).

Is the custom of following
the signs basically fatalistic?

There is certainly the belief that all things are controlled by the power of God (Matt. 28:18). Handlers believe that their prayers will be answered (Mark 11:24), but they accept that God's ways are not man's ways (Isa. 55:8), and they pray that God's will be done (Matt. 6:10), assured that "all things work together for good to them that love God" (Rom. 8:28). They are not fatalists; they fervently pray to God, believing that they can effect change, but they reconcile themselves to God's will.

Aren't their customs, after all is said
and done, basically aberrant behavior?

If the term *aberrant* is used to mean that the practice departs significantly from mainstream contemporary American religious ritual, then the answer would be yes. But it is not aberrant behavior if viewed within the context of American religious history. As anthropologist James Birckhead states: "to place serpent-handling into its larger theological contexts . . . it is not viewed as isolated, aberrant, or bizarre, but rather as an outgrowth of a long-standing religious emphasis" ("Toward the Creation of a Community of Saints" 32).

And these signs shall follow

References

Unless otherwise attributed, all quotations in the text are to interviews conducted by the author. Tapes of these interviews and other materials not in the bibliography to which reference is made are available in the Thomas G. Burton Collection in the Archives of Appalachia at East Tennessee State University.

Archives

The Archives of Appalachia at East Tennessee State University hold a significant collection of research materials on religious serpent handling. Primary sources include some one hundred audio tapes and fifty video tapes. Audio tapes are on reel-to-reel or cassette format; video tapes are on VHS or 3/4" U-Matic format. These tapes document church services and homecomings as well as ministers' and other church members' views on serpent handling and related phenomena. Among the churches documented are those in Georgia, Indiana, Kentucky, North Carolina, Tennessee, Virginia, and West Virginia. The tapes are contained in the Broadside Television Collection, Thomas G. Burton Collection, Burton-Headley Collection, Burton-Manning Collection, and Charles Gunter, Jr., Collection.

Secondary sources such as books, dissertations, and vertical-file materials (mainly copies of articles from magazines, journals, and newspapers) are included in the archives. The archives also hold black-and-white and color photographic negatives and prints taken during church services and homecomings. These prints are contained in the Thomas Burton Collection, the J. B. Collins Photographs, and the Kenneth Murray Photographs.

The following list ranges from scholarly studies to fiction and tabloid journalism, reflecting the wide and varied reactions to this practice. Items listed with "Burton Collection" are in the Archives of Appalachia.

Printed Sources

Abbott, Bill. "Man Bitten by Preacher's Snake Dies." *Tampa Morning Tribune* 5 May 1936: 1, 6.

Abell, Troy. *Better Felt Than Said.* Waco, Tex.: Markham Press, 1982.

———. "The Holiness-Pentecostal Experience in Southern Appalachia." Diss. Purdue Univ., 1974. UMI DDJ75-17142.

"Aid Refused on Snake Bite." Newspaper article, n.d. Burton Collection.

"Ain't It the Truth." *Louisville Courier-Journal* 26 Oct. 1947, magazine sec.: 4.

"Alabama Judge Fines 3 for Snake Handling." *Chattanooga Times* 26 July 1955: 3, 11.

Aldridge, Larry. "Sunday's Scene at Snakehandling Service." *Greeneville* (Tenn.) *Sun* 4 July 1973: 16.

———. "Venomous Testimony." *Knoxville Journal* 7 July 1980: 1.

"All Depends on the Devil." *Daily Times* (Chattanooga) 23 Sept. 1914: 9.

Alland, Alexander. "Possession in a Revivalist Negro Church." *Journal for the Scientific Study of Religion* 1 (1962): 204-13.

Allen, Zack. "Snakehandler Dies From Rattler Bite." *Asheville Times* 19 Aug. 1985: 1.

Alther, Lisa. *Kinflicks.* New York: Random, 1976. 369-74.

———. "They Shall Take Up Serpents." *New York Times Magazine* 6 June 1976: 18-35.

Ambrose, Kenneth Paul. "A Serpent-Handling Church in a Midwestern City." Diss., Ohio State Univ., 1978. UMI 7902066.

———. "Survey of the Snake-Handling Cult of West Virginia." Master's thesis, Marshall Univ., 1970.

"Americana." *Time* 10 Mar. 1947: 22-23.

Anderson, Lee. "County Group Fined $50 Each For Offenses." *Chattanooga News-Free Press* 11 Feb. 1948: 1.

Anderson, Robert M. *Vision of the Disinherited.* New York: Oxford Univ. Press, 1979.

"Any Deadly Thing." *Time* 8 Sept. 1947: 28.

"Appalachians Worship Like Brazilians" *The Daily Times* (Knoxville) 28 Oct. 1985: 11.

Ardery, Julia S., ed. *Welcome the Traveler Home: Jim Garland's Story of the Kentucky Mountains.* Lexington: Univ. Press of Kentucky, 1983.

Armer, Cathy. "The Law Puts The Bite On Snake Handlers: One Snake Is Killed; Others Are Confiscated." *The Mountaineer* (Waynesville, N.C.) 8 July 1985: 1+.

"Arrington Home, 'Tired and Weak.'" *Asheville Citizen* 13 Aug. 1985, sec. 2: 9.

"Arthur Brisbane Says Death of Rev. Andersen Caused by Ignorance of the Universe." *Post* (Big Stone Gap, Va.) 8 Oct. 1936: 1.

Bach, Marcus. *Strange Sects and Curious Cults.* New York: Dodd, 1962.

Bacon, A. M., and E. C. Parsons. "Folk-Lore from Elizabeth City Country, Va." *Journal of American Folklore* 35 (1922): 250-327.

Ball, Richard A. "The Southern Appalachian Folk Structure as a Tension Reducing Way of Life." Photiadis and Schwarzweller. 69-80.

Barber, Theodore X. "The Concept of Hypnosis." *Journal of Psychology* 45 (1958): 115-31.

———. "The Effects of 'Hypnosis' on Pain: A Critical Review of Experimental and Clinical Findings." *Psychosomatic Medicine* 25 (1963): 303-33.

———. "Hypnotizability, Suggestability, and Critical Review of Research Findings." *Psychological Reports* 14 (1964): 299-320.

Barbour, Roger W. "Reptiles of Big Black Mountain, Harlan County, Kentucky." *Copeia* 30 June 1950: 100-107.

Bartelman, Frank. *Azusa Street*. Plainfield, N.J.: Logas International, 1980.

———. *What Really Happened at Azusa Street*. Northridge, Calif.: Voice Christian Publication House, 1962.

Bauman, Richard. "Snake Handling: Should It Be Banned?" *Liberty* 70 (1975): 2-5.

Bean, Betty. "Acceptance, Anger Mark Funeral." *Knoxville Journal* 17 July 1991: A1, 14.

———. "Church Mum on Snakebite Death." *Knoxville Journal* 16 July 1991: A1.

———. "Man Dies of Snakebite in Church." *Knoxville Journal* 15 July 1991: A1, 7.

———. "Police in Dark about Snakebite Details." *Knoxville Journal* 16 July 1991: A7.

———. "Snake Handling Isn't Concern, Sheriff Says." *Knoxville Journal* 18 July 1991: A3.

Bellah, Robert N. "Christianity and Symbolic Realism." *Journal for the Scientific Study of Religion* 9 (1970): 89-115.

Berger, Joe. "Praise the Lord." *Weekly World News* 22 May 1990: 46-47.

Best, Billy. "From Existence to Essence: An Appalachian Studies Curriculum." Diss. Univ. of Massachusetts, 1973. UMI DDJ74-08578.

Bible, Estic B. *The Recollections of Estic B. Bible*. Collection of Newport, Tenn., newspaper articles, 1972-75. Privately published by Jane Bible Henley and Elizabeth Bible Wiley, n.d. Burton Collection.

Birckhead, Roy James. "A Critique of Weston LaBarre's *They Shall Take Up Serpents: Psychology of the Southern Snake-Handling Cult*." Paper, 1970.

———. "A Dissonance Approach to Appalachian Serpent-Handling Cults." Paper, 1971.

———. "God's Not Dead, He is Still Alive: A Study of Reality in a Southern Appalachian Serpent-Handling Church." Paper presented to American Anthropological Association, Mexico City, Nov. 1974.

———. "'Holy, Holy, Holy'—The Context and Structure of Religious Action in a Southern Appalachian Pentecostal-Holiness Church 'With Signs Following.'" Working proposal, 1972.

———. "'Power' and Everyday Life in a Southern Appalachian Serpent-Handling 'Community.'" Paper read at Southern Anthropological Society Meeting, Atlanta, 1976.

———. "Rules and Regulations in a Southern Appalachian Serpent-Handling Church." Paper presented to American Anthropological Association, Dec. 1975.

———. "Sign and Symbol in a Southern Appalachian Serpent-Handling Church." Paper presented to American Anthropological Association, Dec. 1975.

———. "Toward the Creation of a Community of Saints." Diss. Univ. of Alberta, 1976.

"Bite Fatal for Snake-Handling Pastor." *Chattanooga Times* 6 Apr. 1974: 1.

"Bitten By 11 Snakes." *Cincinnati Enquirer* 18 Aug. 1931.

Bloch-Hoell, Nils. *The Pentecostal Movement: Its Origins, Development, and Distinctive Character*. New York: Humanities Press, 1964.

Boisen, Anton T. "Economic Distress and Religious Experience: A Study of the Holy Rollers." *Psychiatry* 2 (1939): 185-94.

Book of Minutes: A Compiled History of the Work of the General Assemblies of the Church of God. Cleveland, Tenn.: Church of God Publishing House, 1922.

Boquet, P. "Immunological Properties of Snake Venoms." *Snake Venoms*. Ed. Chen-Yuan Lee. New York: Springer-Verlag, 1979. 751-824.

Bourgignon, Erika. "Dreams and Altered States of Consciousness in Anthropological Research." *Psychological Anthropology*. Homewood, Ill.: Dorsey Press, 1979. 616-17.

———. *Religion, Altered States of Consciousness, and Social Change*. Columbus: Ohio State Univ. Press, 1973.

"Boy Badly Bitten During Snake Rite." *Chattanooga Times* 19 Aug. 1946: 7.

Boyatzis, F. "Drinking as a Manifestation of Power Concerns." Paper presented at Ninth International Congress on Anthropological and Ethnological Sciences, Aug. 1973.

Braden, Charles S. "Churches of the Dispossessed." *Christian Century* 26 Jan. 1944: 108-10.

———. *These Also Believe: A Study of Modern American Cults and Minority Religious Movements*. New York: Macmillan, 1956.

———. "Why Are the Cults Growing?" *Christian Century* 26 Jan. 1944: 45-48.

Bradford, Jeff. "Signs of Belief, Signs of Death." *ETSU Today* (Johnson City, Tenn.) Dec. 1984: 7-8.

"Bradley Paper Seeks to 'Ban' Snake Handling." *Chattanooga News-Free Press* 4 Sept. 1946: 5.

Brewer, Earl. "Religion and the Churches." *The Southern Appalachian Region: A Survey*. Ed. Thomas R. Ford. Lexington: Univ. Press of Kentucky, 1962. 201-18.

Brown, Fred. "Cleric Died Needlessly, Sister Says." *Knoxville News-Sentinel* 8 Sept. 1985: B1, 3.

———. "Crackdown on Snake-handling Vowed by Sheriff." *Knoxville News-Sentinel* 17 July 1991: A3.

———. "Family Buries Snake-Handling Minister Who 'Went Too Far.'" *Knoxville News-Sentinel* 25 Aug. 1985: A9.

———. "In the Hands of the Lord . . . " *Knoxville News-Sentinel* 10 Dec. 1984: B1, 7.

———. "Sheriff Confiscates Snakes Used in Religious Service." *Knoxville News-Sentinel* 8 July 1985: B1.

———. "Snakebite Victim Took Strychnine, Refused Aid." *Knoxville News-Sentinel* 20 Aug. 1985: A1, 5.

———. "Testing the Faith." *Knoxville News-Sentinel* 25 Aug. 1985: A1, 9.

"Bunn Declares He Will Preach From Court House Steps." *Durham Morning Herald* 10 Nov. 1947, sec. 1: 1-2.

"Bunn Is Arrested; Faces Trial Today." *Durham Morning Herald* 6 Nov. 1947, sec. 1: 1.

"Bunn, Massey Are Guilty Of Handling Snakes." *Durham Morning Herald* 20 Nov. 1947, sec. 2: 1.

"Bunn Obtains Continuance Of 'Snake-handling' Case." *Durham Morning Herald* 7 Nov.1947, sec. 2: 1.

Callahan, North. *Smoky Mountain Country*. New York: Little, 1952.

Callaway, Jim. "Snakes Handled Again in Defiance of Law; Rev. Hall Says Courts Can't Stop Beliefs." *Chattanooga News-Free Press* 19 June 1954: 15.

Campbell, John C. *The Southern Highlander and His Homeland*. Lexington: Univ. Press of Kentucky, 1969.

Campbell, Joseph. *The Hero With a Thousand Faces*. New York: Pantheon, 1968.

Campbell, Will. *Glad River*. New York: Holt, 1982.

———. "Which is the Real Evil: Snake Handling or the Establishment Church? A Study of the Appalachian Folk Religion." *Southern Voices* 1 (1974): 41+.

Carden, Gwen. "The Gospel of Death." *Globe* 26 July 1983.

Carden, Karen W., and Robert W. Pelton. *The Persecuted Prophets*. South Brunswick, N.J.: A. S. Barnes, 1979.

Carlson, A. "Tongues of Fire Revisited." Unpublished papers, Univ. of Calif., Berkeley.

Carter, Michael and Kenneth Ambrose. "Appalachian Serpent-Handlers in the Urban Midwest: A Test of the Satisfaction Hypothesis." Paper presented at 5th Annual Appalachian Studies Conference. Abstract in *Critical Essays in Appalachian Life and Culture*. Ed. Rick Simon. Boone, N.C.: Appalachian Consortium Press, 1982. 109.

Caudill, Harry. *Night Comes to the Cumberlands*. Boston: Little, 1963.

Cave, Sidney. *Redemption, Hindu and Christian*. Freeport, N.Y.: Books for Libraries Press, 1969.

Chaffee, G. E. "The Isolated Religious Sect as an Object for Social Research." *American Journal of Sociology* 35 (1929-30): 618-30.

Chapman, Loring, Helen Goodell, and Harold Wolff. "Increased Inflammatory Reaction Induced by Central Nervous System Activity." *Transactions of the Association of American Physicians* 72 (1959): 84-110.

"Charges Dismissed Against Ministers." *Chattanooga Times* 16 Oct. 1945: 3.

Chason, R. H. "Christianity, Man and Methods." *Pentecostal Holiness Advocate* 13 Sept. 1917: 13.

Chaze, William. "Religious Snake Handling Flourishes in Appalachia." *Times-News* (Hendersonville, N.C.) 26 Feb. 1973: 9.

————. "Snake-Handling Flourishes Anew in South." *Johnson City* (Tenn.) *Press-Chronicle* 30 Dec. 1972: 14.

————. "Snake-Handling Still Practiced in South." *Chattanooga News-Free Press* 24 Dec. 1972: 9.

Cheney, Brainard. *Strangers in This World.* East Tennessee State Univ., Johnson City, Archives of Appalachia. Original manuscript at Vanderbilt Univ.

"Church Fights Law Against Snakes." *Louisville Courier-Journal* 9 Apr. 1940, sec. 2: 1.

The Church of God Evangel (Cleveland, Tenn.), 1914-89. Originally *The Evening Light and Church of God Evangel.*

"Church Undeterred by Snakebite Death." *Johnson City* (Tenn.) *Press-Chronicle* 15 Feb. 1986: 7.

"Church Resists Probe into Snakebite Death." *Knoxville News-Sentinel* 16 July 1991: A4.

"City Council Rules Against Snake-Handling." *Durham Morning Herald* 21 Oct. 1947, sec. 1: 1,3.

"City Man Dies of Snake Bite." *Chattanooga Times* 25 Oct. 1976: 1.

Clark, Doug. "Snake Handlers Should Be Left Alone, Says Columnist." *The Mountaineer* (Waynesville, N.C.). 14 Aug. 1985: 5A. Rpt. from 6 Aug. 1985 *High Point* (N.C.) *Enterprise.*

Clark, Elmer T. "Charismatic or Pentescostal Sects." *The Small Sects of America.* Mass.: Peter Smith, 1981. 85-132.

Clark, Joseph D. "Folk Medicine in Colonial North Carolina as Found in Dr. John Brickell's *Natural History.*" *North Carolina* 17 (1969): 100-110.

Clarke, Kenneth. "Snake Handling and Plato: Identifying Academic Folklore." *Kentucky Folklore Record* 21 (1975): 100-104.

Clements, William M. "Review Essay: Snake-Handlers on Film." *Journal of American Folklore* 90 (1977): 502-6.

Cobb, Alice. "Sect Religion and Social Change in an Isolated Rural Community of Southern Appalachia—With Case Study, Fruit of the Land." Diss. Boston Univ., 1965. UMI 65-11566.

Cohn, Werner. "Personality and Pentecostal Groups—A Research Note." Paper, Univ. of British Columbia.

Coles, Robert. "God and the Rural Poor." Ergood and Kuhre. 326-27.

————. *Migrants, Sharecroppers, Mountaineers.* Boston: Little, 1971.

Collins, John L. *Primitive Religion.* Totowa, N.J.: Littlefield, 1978.

Collins, J. B. "'Snake Handling' Not New." *Chattanooga News-Free Press* 2 July 1973: 1.

————. *Tennessee Snake Handlers.* Chattanooga: Chattanooga News-Free Press,1947.

"Colonel Bunn Gets Term In Jail Here; Fails To Pay Fine." *Durham Morning Herald* 24 May 1949, sec. 2: 1.

Conn, Charles W. *Like A Mighty Army Moves the Church of God.* Cleveland, Tenn.: Church of God Publishing, 1977.

"Continue to Play with Poisonous Snakes." *Chattanooga News* 18 Sept. 1914: 5.

"Copperhead Quickly Seized in Scramble with Cultists." *Richmond Times-Dispatch* 6 Aug. 1945: 10.

Corliss, Alex. "Snake Bite During Church Rites Proves Fatal to Daisy Worshipper." *Chattanooga Times* 15 July 1946: 1, 2.

————. "2 'Faith-Healing' Ministers Held for Handling Snake in City Limits." *Chattanooga Times* 24 Sept. 1945: 1.

"County Buries Snake Victim; Shows Banned." *Tampa Morning Tribune* 6 May 1936: 7.

"Court Upholds State's Ban on Snake Worship." *Chattanooga News-Free Press* 11 Dec. 1948: 1+.

Crabtree, Lou V. P. "Little Jesus." *Sweet Hollow.* Baton Rouge: Louisiana State Univ. Press, 1984.

————. "Salvation." Unpublished manuscript. Burton Collection.

Crane, Charles. "Demonstration of Faith With Gyrations Held in Dolly Pond Church." *Chattanooga News-Free Press* 20 July 1945: 1-2.

Crapps, Robert W. "Religion of the Plain Folk of the Southern United States." *Perspectives in Religious Studies* 4 (Spring 1977): 37-53.

Crasilneck, Harold B., et al. "Use of Hypnosis in the Management of Patients with Burns." *Journal of the American Medical Association* 158 (1955): 103-6.

Creason, Joe. "Leaders Claim Kentucky Has 1,000 Cult Members." *Louisville Courier-Journal* 26 Oct. 1947, magazine sec.: 6-9.

Crews, Harry. *Feast of Snakes*. New York: Ballantine, 1976.

Crews, Mickey. *The Church of God: A Social History*. Knoxville: Univ. of Tennessee Press, 1990.

Cross, James A., et al. "Signs Following Believers." *The Church of God Evangel*. 79 (June 1989): 17-23.

Culp, James D. Letter (reply to 9 Sept. 1986 editorial). *Kingsport Times-News* 19 Sept. 1986: A8.

"Cult Snakes: Why Cultists Prefer Copperheads to Rattlers." *Scientific American* Oct. 1940: 215.

"Cultist Dies of Snake Bite." *New York Times* 17 July 1951: 30.

"Cultist Dies of Snakebite." *Chattanooga News-Free Press* 14 June 1954: 1+.

"Cultist Dies of Snakebite: Believed Dolly Pond Leader." *Chattanooga Times* 25 July 1955: 3.

Cutten, George B. *Speaking With Tongues*. New Haven: Yale Univ. Press, 1927.

Cyclopedic Index of Assembly Minutes (1906-1949) of the Church of God. Comp. M. A. Tomlinson, et al. Cleveland, Tenn.: White Wing Publishing House, 1950.

"Dade Sheriff Says Will Use His Powers to Halt Snake Handling." *Chattanooga News-Free Press* 14 Aug. 1954: 1.

Daugherty, Mary Lee. *Saga of the Serpent Handlers*. Unpublished manuscript. Appalachian Ministries Educational Resource Center, Berea College, Berea, Ky.

————. "Serpent-Handling as Sacrament." *Theology Today* Oct. 1976: 232-43. Rpt. in Photiadis, *Religion in Appalachia*, 103-111.

Davenport, Frederick Morgan. *Primitive Traits in Religious Revivals*. New York: Macmillan, 1917.

Davis, Byron. "Bass May Continue Handling Snakes." *Chattanooga News-Free Press* 17 July 1973: 5.

Davis, Lee. "Copperhead Bites Two Women at Knox Revival; One Faints and Returns, One Goes to Hospital." *Knoxville News-Sentinel* 17 Sept. 1939, home ed., 1.

Davis, Wade. *The Serpent and the Rainbow*. New York: Warner, 1985.

"Deadly Bite." *Greeneville* (Tenn.)*Sun* 19 Aug. 1985: 1, 6.

"'Deadly' Snakes Passed Around in Revival Meet at Church Here." *Knoxville News-Sentinel* 10 Sept. 1939, home ed., A9.

"Deaths and Funerals" (Garland Ray Johnson.) *Welch* (W.Va.) *Daily News* 4 Dec. 1991.: 2.

"DeKalb Church Burns." Newspaper article, 12 June 1954. Burton Collection.

"DeKalb Probing Death of Woman Caused by Snake Bite at Church." *Chattanooga News-Free Press* 23 Feb. 1971: 1.

Derlach, Luther P. and Virginia H. Hine. "The Charismatic Revival: Processes of Recruitment, Conversion, and Behavioral Change in a Modern Religious Movement." Paper. Univ. of Minnesota.

Desmet, Kate. "Deadly Snakes Help Flock Keep Faith." *Detroit News* 20 July 1986: A3.

Diamond, Stanley. "The Rule of Law Versus Custom." *Social Research* 38 (1971): 42-72.

Dickinson, Eleanor. Dickinson Collection of Revival Artifacts. Smithsonian Institution.

———. Dickinson Study Collection of Revival Artifacts, Books, and Tapes. Tennessee State Museum, Nashville.

———. Personal Collection of Revival Art and Artifacts. San Francisco.

———. Religious Art and Artifacts. Collection. Graham Museum, Wheaton College, Ill.

———. *Revival!* New York: Harper, 1974.

———. Revival Drawings. In the collections of the Library of Congress, National Collection of Fine Arts, Smithsonian Institution, Tennessee State Museum, Knoxville Museum of Art, Oakland Museum, and Corcoran Gallery of Art.

———. "Revival Study Sites" (map including 85 serpent-handling churches), *Revival*, Tennessee State Museum Catalogue, Nashville, 1981-82. 18-19.

Dickinson, Eleanor, and Barbara Benzinger. *That Old Time Religion*. New York: Harper, 1975.

Dillow, Joseph. *Speaking in Tongues*. Grand Rapids, Mich.: Zondervan Press, 1975.

"Dolly Pond Sect Quiet Under New State Law." *Chattanooga News-Free Press* 31 Mar. 1947: 1.

"Dolly Ponders Quit Handling Snakes: Trustee 'Doesn't Have Faith Enough.'" *Chattanooga Times* Aug. 1948. Clipping file of Chattanooga-Hamilton County Bicentennial Library.

Dorgan, Howard. *Giving Glory to God in Appalachia*. Knoxville: Univ. of Tennessee Press, 1987. 89-90.

Douthat, Strat. "'They Shall Take Up Serpents': Minister of Snake-Handling Sect Recalls His Son's Death." *Los Angeles Times* 16 June 1974: A1, 2, 4.

Dunlap, Benjamin. "Keepers of the Faith." *New Republic* 22 Nov. 1975: 19.

Durasoff, Steve. *Bright Wind of the Spirit: Pentecostalism Today*. Englewood Cliffs, N.J.: Prentice, 1972.

Dykes, Jim. "Judge OKs Poison, But Bans Snakes." *Knoxville News-Sentinel* 22 Apr. 1973: A1-2.

Eastridge, Karen. "Professors Document Lives of Religious Snake-Handlers." *East Tennessean* (East Tennessee State Univ.) 9 Mar. 1984: 2.

Eaves, Thomas F., Sr. "Snakes, Poison and Deadly Results." *Tennessee Valley Christian* (Scottsboro, Ala.) June 1992: 1.

Edstrom, Ed. "Snake-Tossing Preachers Offer to Let Hearers Pick 'Em Up; Find No Takers." *Louisville Courier-Journal* 15 Sept. 1939, sec. 3: 12.

"11 Snake Cultists Jailed; Refused to Pay $57 Fines." *Louisville Courier-Journal* 8 Sept. 1940: 1.

Elifson, Kirk W. and Peggy S. Tripp. "Development and Analysis of Serpent Handling Ritual." Paper presented at Association for the Sociology of Religion Meeting, San Francisco, 1975.

———. "The Practice of Serpent Handling as a Religious Ritual." Paper presented at Oct. 1975 meeting of Society for the Scientific Study of Religion, Milwaukee. Abstract in *Book of Abstracts*. Ed. Thomas Pilarzyk. Milwaukee: Plankinton House, 24-26 Oct. 1975: 3.

———. "Ultimate Faith: The Religion of Serpent Handlers." Manuscript, 1976.

Ellis, James Benton. *Blazing the Gospel Trail*. Cleveland, Tenn.: Church of God Publishing House, 1941.

Ergood, Bruce, and Bruce E. Kuhre, eds. *Appalachia: Social Context Past and Present*. 2d ed. Dubuque, Iowa: Kendall-Hunt, 1983.

Estep, Bill. "Woman Dies of Snakebite Received at Harlan Church." *Lexington Herald-Leader* 14 Feb. 1986: 1.

———, and Todd Pack. "Pastor's Death Won't End Snake-Handling at Church." *Lexington Herald-Leader* 31 Jan. 1989: A1, 4.

Estep, Granville. *A Mountain Preacher*. Cleveland, Tenn.: White Wing Publishing House and Press, 1986.

"Evangelists H." Ministers ledger at Hal Bernard Dixon, Jr., Pentecostal Research Center, Cleveland, Tenn. 338.

Examination Certificate. George Hensley file. Church of God Headquarters, Cleveland, Tenn.

"'Faith' Failed." *Tampa Morning Tribune* 6 May 1936: 8.

"Faith Healers Meet Begins Here Tonight." *Durham Morning Herald* 15 Oct. 1948, sec. 1: 1-2.

"'Faith' Service Snake-Bite Fatal." *New York Times* 5 May 1936: 25.

Farley, G. M., with Robert W. Pelton. *Satan Unmasked.* Tuscaloosa, Ala.: Portals, 1979.

Farley, Yvonne Snyder. "Holiness People." Ergood and Kuhre. 329-33.

Farmer, William Reuben. *The Last Twelve Verses of Mark.* London: Cambridge Univ. Press, 1974.

Farris, John. *Wildwood.* New York: Tom Doherty Associates, 1986.

"Fatal Snake Bite Inspires Local Ban." *Polk County Democrat* (Bartow, Fla.) 8 May 1936: 1.

Feinberg, Leonard. "Fire Walking in Ceylon." *Atlantic Monthly* 5.203 (1959): 73-76.

"Film Looks at Snake Handling." *Knoxville Journal* 27 Sept. 1984: B8.

"Fine Refused by Snake Handlers; Will Work Off 53 Day Sentence." *Chattanooga Times* 25 Sept. 1945: 3, 11.

"5 Held on Charge of Snake Handling." *Chattanooga Times* 14 June 1948: 3.

"5 Men Fined $50 Each For Handling Reptiles." *Chattanooga Times* 15 June 1948: 4.

Flagg, Fannie. *Fried Green Tomatoes at the Whistle Stop Cafe.* New York: Random, 1987.

Flowers, Ronald B. "Freedom of Religion Versus Civil Authority in Matters of Health." *The Annals of the American Academy of Political and Social Science* 446 (Nov. 1979): 149-62.

Flugel, J. C. "Polyphallic Symbolism and the Castration Complex." *International Journal of Psychoanalysis* 5(1924): 155-96.

Foster, K. Neill. *Help! I Believe in Tongues.* Minneapolis: Bethany Fellowship, 1975.

"Four Handle Snake During Worship." Newspaper article. Burton Collection.

Frodsham, Stanley H. *With Signs Following.* Rev. ed. Springfield, Mo.: Gospel Publishing House, 1946.

"Funeral Held for Snake Bite Victim." *Citizen Tribune* (Morristown, Tenn.) 17 July 1991: A1, 5.

"Gary Long of Romulus Discusses Pentecostal Snake-Handling Church." *Detroit News* 20 July 1989: A3.

Gaster, Theodore H. *Myths, Legends, and Custom in the Old Testament.* New York: Harper, 1969.

Gay, Volney P. "Death Anxiety in Modern and Pre-Modern Ritual." *American Imago* 37.3 (1987): 180-214.

Gerlach, Luther P., and Virgina H. Hine. "Five Factors Crucial to the Growth and Spread of a Modern Religious Movement." *Journal for the Scientific Study of Religion* 7 (1968): 23-40.

Gerrard, Nathan L. "Churches of the Stationary Poor in Southern Appalachia." Photiadis and Schwarzweller. 99-114.

———. "The Serpent Handling Religions of West Virginia." *Poor Americans: How the Poor White Live.* Ed. Marc Pilisuk and Phyllis Pilisuk. Chicago: Aldine Publishing Co., 1971. 65-76.

———. "The Serpent-Handling Religions of West Virginia." *Trans-Action* 5 (1968): 22-28.

———, and Louise B. Gerrard. "Scrabble Creek Folk: Part I, Mental Health." Report for the Wenner-Green Foundation, 1966.

———. "Scrabble Creek Folk: Mental Health, Part II." Unpublished report, Dept. of Sociology, Morris Harvey College, Charleston, W.Va., 1966. Also compiled for the National Institute of Mental Health, Public Health Service, 1966.

Gibson, E. P. "The American Indian and the Fire Walk." *Journal of American Social Psychical Response* 46 (1952): 49.

Gill, Jerry H. *The Possibility of Religious Knowledge.* Grand Rapids, Mich.: Eerdmans, 1971.

Gilliland, Tom. "Woman, 40, Critically Bitten in Snake Rites." *Chattanooga News-Free Press* 19 June 1962: 1+.

Gillin, J. L. "A Contribution to the Society of Sects." *American Journal of Sociology* 16 (1910-11): 236-52.

Gilmore, Susan K. "Personality Differences Between High and Low Dogmatism Groups of Pentecostal Believers." *Journal for the Scientific Study of Religion* 8 (1969): 161-64.

"Girl Bitten by Snake in Church Ready to Handle Serpents Again." *Chattanooga Times* 17 June 1954: 9.

"Girl, 14, is Bitten by Snake at Cult." *Chattanooga Times* 23 Aug. 1948: 3.

Golden, Dick. "Snake-Handlers Are Like Jitterbugs, Psychologist Says." *Knoxville News-Sentinel* 20 Sept. 1939, home ed., 1.

Golden, Richard. "'Snake-Handling' Woman Bitten Because of Lack of Faith, She Declares." *Knoxville News-Sentinel* 19 Sept. 1939, home ed., 1.

Goller, Elaine Cloud. "Snake-Handlers Testing Faith Less Frequently." *Johnson City* (Tenn.) *Press-Chronicle* 7 Oct. 1984: 34.

Goodman, Felicitas D. "Altered Mental State vs. 'Style of Discourse': Reply to Samarin." *Journal for the Scientific Study of Religion* 11 (1972): 297-99.

———. *How About Demons? Possession and Exorcism in the Modern World.* Bloomington: Indiana Univ. Press, 1988.

———. "Phonetic Analysis of Glossolalia in Four Cultural Settings." *Journal for the Scientific Study of Religion* 8.2 (1969): 227-39.

———. *Speaking in Tongues: A Cross-Cultural Study of Glossolalia.* Chicago: Univ. of Chicago Press, 1972.

Graber, Robert B. "Commentary Anabaptism: Repression or Release." *Journal of Psychological Anthropology* 3 (Winter 1980): 31-32.

"Graham Says Snake Handlers Wrong." *Chattanooga Times* 26 Apr. 1973: 33.

Grebe, Maria Ester. "Relationships Between Music Practice and Cultural Context: The Kultrun and its Symbolism." *World Music* 3 (1978): 84-106.

Grodsky, Lawrence. "The Saints and the Serpents." *Hustler* July 1990: 82-89.

Grogan, David and Chris Phillips. "Courting Death, Appalachia's Old-Time Religionists Praise the Lord and Pass the Snakes." *People* 1 May 1989: 79-82.

Hadfield, Arthur J. "The Influence of Suggestion on Body Temperature." *Lancet* 2 (1920): 68-69.

———. "The Influence of Suggestion on Inflammatory Conditions." *Lancet* 2 (1917): 678-79.

"Handling Deadly Snakes Tests Churchgoers' Faith." *Peoria Journal Star* 16 June 1974: A10.

"Harlan Holiness Church Disciple Bitten By Snake During Ritual." *Louisville Courier-Journal* 25 May 1939: 2.

Harrison, Michael L. "Sources of Recruitment to Catholic Pentecostalism." *Journal for the Scientific Study of Religion* 13 (1974): 49-64.

Haught, James A. "Game Expert, Doctors View Snake-Handling." *Charleston Gazette* 25 June 1961: 14.

Hawley, F. "The Keresan Holy Rollers: An Adaptation to American Individualism." *Social Forces* 26 (1948): 272-80.

"He Can Handle Snakes But Will He Walk the River?" *Daily Times* (Chattanooga) 24 Sept. 1914: 3.

"He Followed Bible and Got Snake Bite." *Bristol* (Tenn.) *Herald Courier* 18 June 1971: 9.

"'He Was a Believer.'" *Greeneville* (Tenn.) *Sun* 20 Aug. 1985: 1, 7.

"High Court Lets Stand Ban on Snake Handling." *Chattanooga News-Free Press* 8 Mar. 1976: 1.

"High Court Reverses Snake Death Verdict, Upholds Conviction in Child Beating Case." *Richmond Times-Dispatch* 14 Oct. 1947: 2.

Hilgard, Ernest R. *Hypnotic Susceptibility.* New York: Harcourt, 1965.

Hilgard, Josephine R. *Personality and Hypnosis.* Chicago: Univ. of Chicago Press, 1970.

Hill, Jackson. "Music and Mysticism: A Summary Overview." *Studia Mystica* 4 (Winter 1979): 42-51.

Hine, Virginia. "Pentecostal Glossolalia: Toward a Functional Interpretation." *Journal for the Scientific Study of Religion* 8 (1969): 211-26.

Hinton, Elmer. "Justice in a Hurry." *Nashville Tennessean Magazine* 6 Sept. 1959: 10+.

Hoekema, Anthony A. *What About Tongue Speaking?* Grand Rapids, Mich.: Eerdmans, 1966.

Hoffer, Eric. *The True Believer: Thoughts on the Nature of Mass Movements.* New York: Harper, 1951.

"Holiness Church Services Omitted Snake Handling." *Johnson City* (Tenn.) *Press-Chronicle* 3 Aug. 1973: 8.

"Holiness Faith Healers." *Life* 3 July 1944: 59-62.

"Holiness Preacher's Boast Fails with Rattlesnake." *New York Times* 10 Aug. 1934: 4.

Holliday, Robert Kelvin. *Tests of Faith*. Oak Hill, W.Va.: Fayette Tribune, 1966.

Holt, John B. "Holiness Religion: Cultural Shock and Social Reorganization." *American Sociological Review* 5 (1940): 740-47.

"Holy Rollers Anoint One of Their Patients." *Sunday Times* (Chattanooga) 27 Sept. 1914: 2.

"'Holy Rollers' Handle Snakes with Impunity." *Chattanooga News* 10 Sept. 1914: 12.

Hooker, Elizabeth. *Religion in the Highlands*. New York: Home Missions Council, 1933.

Hopkins, E. Washburn. "Fire Walking." *Encyclopedia of Religion and Ethics* 6 (1913): 30-31.

Hudson, Charles. "The Structure of a Fundamentalist Christian-Belief System." *Religion and the Solid South*. Ed. Samuel Hill, Jr., et al. Nashville: Abingdon, 1972.

Hughes, Richard T. "Restorationist Christianity." *Encyclopedia of Southern Culture*. Ed. Charles Reagan Wilson and William Ferris. Chapel Hill: Univ. of North Carolina Press, 1989. 1303-6.

Humphrey, Richard. "Religion in Appalachia: Implications for Social Work Practice." *Journal of Humanics* (East Tennessee State Univ.) Dec. 1980: 4-18.

Hundley, Tom. "Serpent Handlers Test the Power of Their Lord." *Chicago Tribune* 11 Sept. 1988, sec. 1: 16, 18.

"Hundreds Demonstrate Faith in Jesus with Fire, Serpents." *Johnson City* (Tenn.) *Press-Chronicle* 2 July 1973: 1.

Hunter, Harold D. "Serpent Handling." *Dictionary of Pentecostal and Charismatic Movements*. Ed. Stanley M. Burgess and Gary B. McGee. Grand Rapids, Mich.: Zondervan, 1988. 777-78.

———. *Spirit-Baptism: A Pentecostal Alternative*. New York: Univ. Press of America, 1983.

Hurley, Bob. "A Snake Handler's Death: The Church Tells Its Side of the Story." *Greeneville* (Tenn.) *Sun* 26 Aug. 1985: 11.

———. "They Buried Jim Ray Williams, But the Snake Mystery Lives On." *Greeneville* (Tenn.) *Sun* 17 July 1991: A3.

Hurst, Arthur F. *The Psychology of the Special Senses and Their Functional Disorders*. London: Oxford Univ. Press, 1920.

Hyorth, Alphie. "Snakehandler May Move Services; Arrington Still Hospitalized." *Asheville Citizen* 7 Aug. 1985, sec. 2: 13.

Hyorth, Tracy D. "Arrington Says He Grabbed Snake as 'Instant Reflex.'" *Asheville Citizen* 15 Aug. 1985: 1-2.

———. "Snakes Used By Worshippers Found Poisonous." *Asheville Citizen*. n.d.: 1. Burton Collection.

"'I May Take Up Serpents, But I'm Not A Snake-Handler.'" *Johnson City* (Tenn.) *Press-Chronicle* 10 June 1973: 33.

"It's In the Book." *Kingsport Times-News* 15 Aug. 1971: B1, 10.

Jackson, Anthony. "Sound and Ritual." *Man* 3 (1968): 293-99.

James, Edwin Oliver. *The Beginnings of Religion; An Introduction and Scientific Study*. Westport, Conn.: Greenwood Press, 1973.

James, William. *The Varieties of Religious Experience: A Study in Human Nature*. New York: Modern Library, 1929.

Jaquith, James R. "Toward a Typology of Formal Communicative Behaviors: Glossolalia." *Anthropological Linguistics* 9.8 (1967): 1-8.

"Jobless Coal Miner Demonstrates His Faith By Handling Snakes." *Houston Chronicle*, n.d. Burton Collection.

Jones, Charles Edwin. *A Guide to the Study of the Holiness Movement*. ATLA Bibliography Series, no. 1. Metuchen, N.J.: Scarecrow, 1974.

Kane, Steven M. "Appalachian Snake Handlers." *Perspectives on the American South*. Ed. James C. Cobb and Charles R. Wilson. Vol. 4. New York: Gordon and Breach, 1987. 115-27.

———. "Aspects of the Holy Ghost Religion: The Snake-Handling Sect of the American Southeast." Master's thesis, Univ. of North Carolina, 1973. UMI DD J7918559.

———. "Holiness Fire Handling in Southern Appalachia: A Psychophysiological Analysis." Photiadis, *Religion in Appalachia*, 113-24.

———. "Holiness Ritual Fire Handling: Ethnographic and Psychophysiological Considerations." *Ethos* 10 (1982): 369-84.

———. "Holy Ghost People: The Snake-Handlers of Southern Appalachia." *Appalachia Journal* 4 (Spring 1974): 255-62.

———. "Ritual Possession in a Southern Appalachian Religious Sect." *Journal of American Folklore* 87 (Oct.-Dec. 1974): 293-302.

———. "Snake Handlers." *Encyclopedia of Religion in the South*. Ed. Samuel H. Hill. Macon, Ga.: Mercer Univ. Press, 1984. 698-99. Rpt. in *Encyclopedia of Southern Culture*. Ed. Charles Reagan Wilson and William Ferris. Chapel Hill: Univ. of North Carolina Press, 1989. 1330.

———. "Snake Handlers of Southern Appalachia." Diss. Princeton Univ., 1979. UMI 7918559.

Kauffman, Betsy. "Church Members Says Snake Victim's Kin Lacked Faith." *Knoxville News-Sentinel* 22 Nov. 1988: 1.

Kelley, Dean M., ed. "The Uneasy Boundary: Church and State." *Annals of the American Academy of Political and Social Science* 446. Ed. Richard D. Lambert. Philadelphia: AAPSS, 1979.

"Kentucky Header of Cult Featured." *Chattanooga News-Free Press* n.d.: 1+. Burton Collection.

"Kentucky Man Dies as Result of Church Snake-handling Ritual." *Johnson City* (Tenn.) *Press-Chronicle* 30 Aug. 1983: 18.

"Kentucky Man Killed by Rattler in Rite of Snake-Handling Cult." *New York Times* 30 Oct. 1973: 27.

Kephart, Horace. *Our Southern Highlanders*. New York: Macmillan, 1922.

Kerman, K. "Rattlesnake Religion." *Eve's Stepchildren*. Ed. Lealon Jones. Caldwell: Caxton Printers, 1942. 93-102. Rpt. in *The American Imagination at Work*. Ed. Ben C. Clough. New York: Knopf, 1947. 156.

———. "Rattlesnake Religion." *St. Louis Post-Dispatch* 11 Sept. 1938: 10-11.

"Kidd: Fatality Sparked Proposal To Bar Snake Handling in Church." Interview with Senator Culver Kidd (Milledgeville, Ga.). Burton Collection.

Kildahl, John P. *The Psychology of Speaking in Tongues*. New York: Harper, 1972.

Kimbrough, David L. "Park Saylor and the Eastern Kentucky Snake-Handlers." Diss., Indiana Univ., 1992.

Kimsey, Don. "The Jaws of Death." *Atlanta Journal* 8 Jan. 1973: D9.

King, J. H. "History of the Fire-Baptized Holiness Church." *Pentecostal Holiness Advocate* 1921.

Kinsolving, Lester. "Tongues Speakers Star Performers." *Johnson City* (Tenn.) *Press-Chronicle* 8 June 1973: 8.

Kiss, Tony. "Haywood Sheriff Bitten By Rattlesnake During Cult's Religious Service." *Asheville Citizen* 5 Aug. 1985: 1-2.

Klauber, Laurence. *Rattlesnakes: Their Habits, Life Histories, and Influence on Mankind*. 2d ed. 2 vols. Los Angeles: Univ. of California Press, 1973.

Klinger, Rafe. "Rattler Makes Believer Out of Snake Cultist." *Weekly World News* 25 Mar. 1986: 2.

Kobler, John. "America's Strangest Religion." *Saturday Evening Post* 28 Sept. 1957: 25-30.

La Barre, Weston. *The Ghost Dance: Origins of Religion*. Garden City: Doubleday, 1964.

———. "The Snake-Handling Cult of the American Southeast." *Explorations in Cultural Anthropology*. Ed. Ward H. Goodenough. New York: McGraw, 1964. 309-33.

———. *They Shall Take Up Serpents*. Minneapolis: Univ. of Minnesota Press, 1962. Rpt. New York: Schocken Books, 1969.

———. (LeBarre [sic]). "Transference Cures in Religious Cults and Social Groups." *Journal of Psychoanalysis in Groups* 1 (1962): 66-75.

Lake, Clancy and Harry Cook. "Snake Handling Rites to Continue in DeKalb Area." *The Birmingham News* 31 May 1953: 1, 12.

Lang, Andrew. "The Fire-Walk." *Modern Mythology.* New York: Longmans, 1897.

Lapsley, J. N., and J. M. Simpson. "Speaking in Tongues: Infantile Babble or Song of the Self?" *Pastoral Psychology* Sept. 1964: 16-24.

———. "Speaking in Tongues: Token of Group Acceptance and Divine Approval." *Pastoral Psychology* May 1964: 48-55.

"Laws Don't Bother Area 'Snake Man.'" *Bristol* (Tenn.) *Herald-Courier* 10 July 1977: B3.

"Lay Preacher Says Victim Refused Help." 14 June 1954. Burton Collection.

"Leave Snake-handlers Alone, Readers Say." *Asheville Citizen* 16 Aug. 1985: 4.

Leavenworth, Don. "Sheriff Jack Arrington Bitten: Snake Handling Services May Be Discontinued." *High Point* (N.C.) *Enterprise* 8 Aug. 1985: 1+.

Lee, C. Y., and S. Y. Lee. "Cardiovascular Effects of Snake Venoms." *Snake Venoms.* Ed. Chen-Yuan Lee. New York: Springer-Verlag, 1979. 547-90.

Lee, Christina. "Efficacy Expectations and Outcome Expectations as Predictors of Performance in a Snake-Handling Task." *Cognitive Therapy and Research* 8.5 (1984): 509-16.

Letter to A. J. Tomlinson, 30 Jan. 1922. George Hensley file, Church of God Headquarters, Cleveland, Tenn.

Letter to M. W. Letsinger, 8 (6?) Feb. 1922. George Hensley file, Church of God Headquarters, Cleveland, Tenn.

Linney, Romulus. *"The Sorrows of Frederick"* and *"Holy Ghost."* New York: Harcourt, 1966.

"Local Man Struck by Snake in Church Rushed to Hospital." *Chattanooga News-Free Press* 2 July 1973: 1.

"Local Minister Says He'll Present Self at Court Tomorrow." *Durham Herald* 22 May 1949, sec. 1: 8.

"Local Prison Camp Heads Use 'Nazi' Tactics, Bunn Claims." *Durham Morning Herald* 5 Nov. 1948, sec. 2: 1.

Looff, David. *Appalachia's Children.* Lexington: Univ. Press of Kentucky, 1971.

"Lord Willing, Snakes Will Be Handled." *Johnson City* (Tenn.) *Press-Chronicle* 28 June 1973: 1.

"The Lord's Bidding." *Newsweek* 23 Apr. 1973: 23.

Lougee, George E. Jr. "Bunn And Massey Found Guilty Of Handling Poisonous Snakes." *Durham Morning Herald* 27 Mar. 1948. sec. 1: 1-2.

———. "Durham Police Seize Five Snakes as Faith Healers' Meet Opens." *Durham Morning Herald* 16 Oct. 1948, sec. 1: 1-2.

Lucas, F. H. *The Symptoms of Acute Poisoning.* New York: Macmillan, 1953.

MacCaughelty, Tom. "Faith Healers Hold Pair of Sessions on Last Day of Convention in City." *Durham Morning Herald* 18 Oct. 1948, sec. 2: 1.

———. "Officers Take Fondler, Snake in Raid Here." *Durham Morning Herald* 17 Oct. 1948, final ed.: 1-2.

McClellan, Stephanie. "'They Shall Take Up Serpents': Spotlight on Snake-Handling Deaths Gives Misleading Picture of Sects." *Kingsport Times-News* 21 July 1991: B1-2.

McDavid, J., Jr. "Personality and Situational Determinants of Conformity." *Journal of Abnormal Social Psychology* 58 (1959): 241-46.

"McGhee Street Church of God." *Knoxville News-Sentinel* 11 Sept. 1939: 3.

McJunkin, Cathy. "Sheriff Breaks Silence; Still Quiet About Snakebite." *Asheville Citizen-Times* 11 Aug. 1985: 1.

Maguire, Marsha. "Confirming the Word." *Quarterly Journal of the Library of Congress* 38 (1981): 166-79.

Malefijt, de Waal Annemarie. *Religion and Culture.* New York: Macmillan, 1968.

"Man Bitten by Snake at Church Service is 'Fair.'"
12 July 1973. Burton Collection.

"Man Bitten Here in Snake Service." *Chattanooga
Times* 24 Oct. 1947: 3.

"Man Dies From Snake Bite at W. Virginia Church
Ritual." *Chattanooga News-Free Press* 25 Aug.
1982: A4.

"Man 'Healed' from the Bite of Copperhead." *Chattanooga Times* 11 Mar. 1977: 19.

Marett, Robert Ranulph. *Psychology and Folklore*.
Detroit: Gale, 1974.

"Mark 16: 9-20 Examined." *Pentecostal Holiness
Advocate* 22 Aug. 1918: 8-9.

"Mark 16: 9-20 Reviewed." *Pentecostal Holiness
Advocate* 29 Aug. 1918: 8-11.

Marlette, Doug. "Kudzu." Comic strip, n.d. (" . . .
Yessir, that town was so backwards . . . even the
Episcopalians handled snakes!")

Martin, Ira. *Glossolalia in the Apostolic Church*. Berea,
Ky.: Berea College Press, 1960.

Mason, Mike. "Man Dies of Snakebite Following
Church Service." *Greeneville* (Tenn.)*Sun* 15 July
1991: A9.

———. "Police Get Little Help After Snake Bite
Death." *Greeneville* (Tenn.)*Sun* 16 July 1991: 7.

Mathews, Garret. "Lifting Up Their Snakes to the
Lord." *Houston Chronicle* 18 June 1983: 3, 5.

Mathison, R. R. *Faiths, Cults, and Sects of America:
From Atheism to Zen*. Indianapolis: Bobbs, 1960.

"A Matter of Faith." *Time* 10 Sept. 1973: 76.

May, L. Carlyle. "A Survey of Glossolalia and Related
Phenomena in Non-Christian Religions." *American Anthropologist* 58 (1956): 75-96.

Mead, Frank S. *Handbook of Denominations in the
United States*. 4th ed. New York: Abingdon, 1965.

"Member of Snake-handling Religious Sect Dies from
Bite." Newspaper article, n.d. Burton Collection.

Messer, Dewey. "'Snakehandlers Of God' Hold
Open Air Service." Newspaper article, n.d.
Burton Collection.

Miller, William. "Salvation Cocktail." *Habersham
Review* 1, no.1 (1991): 71-77.

Miller, William Marion. "The Snake Dilemma."
Journal of American Folklore 53 (1940): 217-18.

"Minister Answers to 'Higher Law.'" *Johnson City*
(Tenn.) *Press-Chronicle* 15 Aug. 1985: 12.

Minton, Sherman A. *Giant Reptiles*. New York:
Scribner's, 1973.

———, and Madge R. Minton. *Venomous Reptiles*.
New York: Scribner's, 1969.

"'Miracle' Heals Bitten Snake Handler." *Johnson City*
(Tenn.) *Press-Chronicle* 10 Mar. 1977: 28.

"Mistrial Ends Snake Cultist Hearing Here." *Chattanooga
News-Free Press* 13 Nov. 1947, city ed.: 1.

Mitchell, Carolyn. "Affirmation of Faith." *Chattanooga
Times* 16 Oct. 1977: D9.

Moore, J. Kenneth. "Ethnic Hymnody Series: Socio-
Economic Double Entendre in the Songs of the
Snake-Handlers." *Hymn* 37.2 (1986): 30-36.

———. "The Music of the Snake Handlers of Southern West Virgina." Master's thesis, New York City
Univ., 1976.

Moritz, A. R., and F. C. Henriques. "The Relative
Importance of Time and Surface Temperature in
the Causation of Cutaneous Burns." *American
Journal of Pathology* 23 (1947): 695-720.

Morris, Ramona, and Desmond Morris. *Men and
Snakes*. New York: McGraw, 1965.

Morrow, Jimmy. "77 Years—The History of Serpent-
Handling Churches (1929-1985)." Manuscript.

Moss, Gary. "Arrington Gives Account of Snake Bite
Incident." *The Mountaineer* (Waynesville, N.C.)
14 Aug. 1985: A1+.

———. "Many Local Ministers Say Snake Handlers
'Tempt God.'" *The Mountaineer* (Waynesville,
N.C.) 12 Aug. 1985: 1+.

———. "Sheriff Bitten While Trying to Interrupt
Snake Handlers." *The Mountaineer* (Waynesville,
N.C.) 5 Aug. 1985: A1-2.

———. "Snake Handler: Once Bashful Charles Prince Uses Media to Spread the Gospel." *The Mountaineer* (Waynesville, N.C.), n.d. Burton Collection.

Mullis, H. Thomas. "Psychological Aspects of Snake Handling in the Southern United States." Paper presented to Popular Culture Association, New Orleans, Mar. 1988.

Munger, G. Frank. "'Serpent Handlers' Worship God . . . To Their Own Conscience." *Daily Beacon* (Univ. of Tennessee, Knoxville) 30 Apr. 1973: 2-3.

Munn, Robert. *Appalachian Bibliography.* 2 vols. Morgantown: West Virginia Univ. Library, 1967-.

"Murl Bass, Snakehandler, Said Resting Comfortably." *Johnson City* (Tenn.) *Press Chronicle* 4 July 1973: 9.

Murray, Kenneth. *Down to Earth—People of Appalachia.* Boone, N.C.: Appalachia Consortium Press, 1974.

Nadel, S. P. *Nupe Religion.* London: Kegen Paul, 1954.

"National Affair." *Time* 8 Sept. 1947: 25.

Neal, G. Dale. "Sheriff's Condition Stable." *Asheville Citizen* 6 Aug. 1985.

Needham, Rodney. "Percussion and Transition." *Man* 3 (1968): 606-14.

Neher, Andrew. "A Physiological Explanation of Unusual Behavior in Ceremonies Involving Drums." *Human Biology* 34 (1962): 151-60.

Nichol, John. *The Pentecostals.* Plainfield, N.J.: Logos International, 1966.

"Nine Face Charges in Snake Bite Death." *Louisville Courier-Journal* 28 Aug. 1940, sec. 2: 1.

"No Law Against Handling Snakes." *Post* (Big Stone Gap, Va.) 8 Oct. 1936: 1.

"No Real Sense Arguing with Snake Handlers." *Knoxville Journal* 18 July 1991: A16.

Noble, W. J. "Beware of the Church of God." *Pentecostal Holiness Advocate* 11 Oct. 1917: 2-3.

(Norwood, Anna Prince.) "Chained by Fear." *True Story* May 1957: 56-61+.

Oberst, Nancy. "Snake Bite Victim Buried." *Newport Plain Talk* 17 July 1991: A1, 2.

Oesterly, William Oscar. *The Sacred Dance: A Study in Comparative Folklore.* Brooklyn: Dance Horizons, 1968.

Ogden, Warner. "Two Snake Handlers Die After Taking Strychnine." *Knoxville News-Sentinel* 9 Apr. 1973: 1.

Oliver, James A. *Snakes in Facts and Fiction.* New York: Macmillan, 1958.

"Opinion: Insurance Shouldn't Cover Snake Handling." *Kingsport Times-News* 9 Sept. 1986: A6.

"Paralyzing Prayers." *Time* 17 Sept. 1945: 23-24.

Park, Robert E. *On Social Control and Collective Behavior.* Chicago: Univ. of Chicago Press, 1967.

Parrish, Henry M., and C. B. Pollard. "Effects of Repeated Poisonous Snakebites in Man." *The American Journal of Medical Sciences* 237 (1959): 277-86.

"Pastor Here Whirls Snake, It Escapes, People Flee." *Tampa Morning Tribune* 2 Mar. 1936: 1, 12.

Pattison, E. Mansell. "Behavioral Science Research on the Nature of Glossolalia." *Journal of the American Scientific Affiliation* (Sept. 1968): 73-86.

———. "Speaking in Tongues and About Tongues." *Christian Standard* 15 Feb. 1964.

Peck, John. "85-Year-Old Preacher Has 34 Snake Bites on His Career Record." *Johnson City* (Tenn.) *Press-Chronicle* 9 Nov. 1984: 11.

Pelton, Robert W., and Karen W. Carden. *In My Name Shall They Cast Out Devils.* South Brunswick, N.J.: A. S. Barnes, 1976.

———. *Snake Handlers: God Fearers? or Fanatics?* Nashville: Thomas Nelson, 1974.

Pennington, Charles. "Ford, Rattler's Victim, Buried; Flock Handles Snakes in Ritual." *Chattanooga Times* 9 Sept. 1945: 1.

———. "Snake-Handling 'Preacher' Dies of Rattler's Bite in Ceremony." *Chattanooga Times* 5 Sept. 1945: 1.

———. "Snakes Figured in Pagan Religions But Only Lately in Christian Rites." *Chattanooga Times* 16 Sept. 1945: 21.

"Pentecostal Churches." *Britannica Year Book.* 1977.

Pentecostal Holiness Advocate. Article on Mark 16: 17, 18. May 10, 1917: 12-13. Serpent Handling clipping file in Chattanooga-Hamilton County Bicentennial Library.

Phillips, Chris. "God Tells Me To Handle Snakes, So I've Got To." *Woman's World* 27 Mar. 1990: 26-27.

Photiadis, John D., ed. *Religion in Appalachia*. Morgantown: West Virginia Univ. Press, 1978.

Photiadis, J., and H. K. Schwarzweller. *Change in Rural Appalachia*. Philadelphia: Univ. of Pennsylvania Press, 1970.

Photiadis, J. and R. B. Maurer. *Religion in an Appalachian State*. Morgantown: West Virginia Univ. Press, 1974.

Plagenz, George R. "Handling a 'Little Snake, Big Devil.'" *Johnson City* (Tenn.) *Press-Chronicle* 19 Sept. 1985: 9.

Polanski, N., R. Lippitt, and F. Redl. "An Investigation of Behavioral Contagion in Groups." *Human Relations* 3(1950): 319-48.

"Police Confiscate Snake Handled By Cult Leader." *Durham Morning Herald* 2 Nov. 1947, sec. 1: 1, 10.

"Police Raid Virginia Snake Sect And Kill 4 of Their 8 Rattlers." *New York Times* 30 July 1945: 21.

"Police Visit Snake-Handling Service, But Make No Arrests." *Durham Morning Herald* 26 Oct. 1947, sec. 1: 1.

Pratt, James B. *The Religious Consciousness*. New York: Harper, 1920.

Pratt, Scott. "Evangelist Dies After Snake Bite." *Johnson City* (Tenn.) *Press-Chronicle* 20 Aug. 1985: 1-2.

———. "Evangelist Dies: Bitten By Rattler." *Johnson City* (Tenn.) *Press-Chronicle* 19 Aug. 1985: 1.

———. "Prince's Relative Still Willing to 'Take Up Serpents.'" *Johnson City* (Tenn.) *Press-Chronicle* 20 Aug. 1985: 8.

———. "Relatives to Continue Snake Handling." *Johnson City* (Tenn.) *Press-Chronicle* 21 Aug. 1985: 5.

"Preacher and Snakes go to Briceville for More Services." *Knoxville News-Sentinel* 24 Sept. 1939: B11.

"Preacher Arrested in Snake-Handling." *Chattanooga News-Free Press* 17 June 1954: 1+.

"Preacher Charged with Forcing Wife To Put Hand in Snake Box." *Elizabethton* (Tenn.) *Star* 9 Oct. 1991: 10.

"Preacher Dies of Three Snake-Bites." *Bristol* (Tenn.) *Herald Courier* 1 Oct. 1936: 3.

"Preacher Faces Assault Charge." *Johnson City* (Tenn.) *Press* 9 Oct. 1991: 11.

"Preacher Fined $50 for Handling Snakes." *Louisville Courier-Journal* 4 Sept. 1940, sec. 2: 8.

"Preacher Juggles Snake Again, Says It Bit Him." *Tampa Morning Tribune* 9 Mar. 1936: 1, 8.

"A Preacher's Date with Death." *Edmonton* (Alberta) *Journal* 15 June 1974: 20.

Preece, Harold and Celia Kraft. *Dew on Jordan*. New York: Dutton, 1946.

Price, Ed. "Video Becomes 'Social Documentary.'" *Johnson City* (Tenn.) *Press-Chronicle* 17 Nov. 1985, Features, Opinion section: 1.

"Prince Autopsy Completed, No Results Yet Released." *Greeneville* (Tenn.)*Sun.* 21 Aug. 1985: 1.

"Prince Didn't Expect to Die, Relative Says." *Johnson City* (Tenn.) *Press-Chronicle* 21 Aug. 1985: 1.

"Prince Had Trust in Faith." *Asheville Times* 20 Aug. 1985: A10.

"Prince: His Faith Never Faltered." *Greeneville* (Tenn.)*Sun* 20 Aug. 1985: 1, 7.

"Proselyting with Snakes." *Daily Times* (Chattanooga) 16 Sept. 1914: 3.

Pruyser, Paul W. *A Dynamic Psychology of Religion*. New York: Harper, 1968.

Quigley, Linda. "Tent Revivalists: Signs, Wonders, and Miracles." *The Tennessean* (Nashville) 28 Feb. 1988: F1.

Ranaghan, Kevin Mathers. "Rites of Initiation in Representative Pentecostal Churches in the United States 1901-1972" Diss. Univ. of Notre Dame, 1974. UMI DD J74-19055.

"Rattler Bites Woman; Non-Believers Blamed." *Chattanooga Times* 25 Aug. 1948: 12.

"Rattler May Bite Father Here But Law Plans to Protect Boy." *Nashville Tennessean* 1 Sept. 1934: 1.

"Rattlesnake Bite Kills 75-Year-Old Cult Head." *Pensacola News* 25 July 1955: 1-2.

"Recovery Expected of Snakebitten Man." Newspaper article, July 1973. Burton Collection.

"Religion and Snakes." Editorial. *Herald* (Cleveland, Tenn.) 24 Sept. 1914: 7.

"Reptile in the Meetin'." *Daily Times* (Chattanooga) 21 Sept. 1914: 3.

"The Reverend George Hensley of Pineville, Ky., Who Is Touring Churches in the South Demonstrating His Faith." *Knoxville News-Sentinel* 11 Sept. 1939, home ed., 3. Photo.

Revocation of Ministry. George Hensley file, Church of God Headquarters, Cleveland, Tenn.

"Right with the Lord?" *Peoria Journal Star* 11 Mar. 1973: A11.

Risley, Eleanor de la Vergne. *The Road to Wildcat*. Boston: Little, 1930.

"Rites Without Snakes Held for Cult Member." *Chattanooga Times* 5 Sept. 1946: 13.

Robertson, Archie. *That Old-Time Religion*. Boston: Houghton, 1950.

Robinson, Henry. "He Handles Snakes to Test Faith in God." *Asheville Citizen & Times* 12 July 1985: 3.

Rosenberg, Bruce. *Can These Bones Live? The Art of the American Folk Preacher*. 1970. Chicago: Univ. of Illinois Press, 1988.

Ross, Charlotte T., ed. *Bibliography of Southern Appalachia*. Boone, N.C.: Appalachian Consortium, 1976.

Rouse, L. G. "Marvelous Miracles and Incidents in My Life." N.p., n.d. Pentecostal Research Center, Cleveland, Tenn.

Rousselle, Robert. "Comparative Psychohistory: Snake-Handling in Hellenistic Greece and the American South." *Journal of Psychohistory* 11 (Spring 1984): 477-89.

Rowe, Dewey. *Serpent Handling as a Cultural Phenomenon in Southern Appalachia*. New York: Carlton Press, 1986. Rpt. of thesis, Dept. of Geography and Geology, East Tennessee State Univ., 1982.

Russell, Findlay E. "The Clinical Problem of Crotalid Snake Venom Poisoning." *Snake Venoms*. Ed. Chen-Yuan Lee. New York: Springer-Verlag, 1979. 978-96.

———.*Snake Venom Poisoning*. Philadelphia: Lippincott, 1980.

Samarin, William J. "The Linguisticality of Glossolalia." *Hartford Quarterly* 8.4: 49-75.

———. "Sociolinguistic vs. Neurophysical Explanations for Glossolalia: Comment on Goodman's Paper." *Journal for the Scientific Study of Religion* 11 (1972): 293-96.

———. *Tongues of Men and Angels*. New York: Macmillan, 1972.

Sargent, William. *Battle for the Mind*. New York: Doubleday, 1975.

———. "Some Cultural Group Abreactive Techniques and Their Relation to Modern Treatment." *Proceedings of the Royal Society of Medicine* 42 (May 1949): 367-74.

Schwartz, Scott W. "Fire Handling in Appalachia: Myth, Magic or Just Good Old-Fashioned Folklore?" Paper presented to 15th Annual Meeting of Appalachian Studies Conference, Asheville, N.C., 21 Mar. 1992.

———. "Sacred Fire Handlers: Music's Symbolic and Functional Relationship to the Appalachian Serpent-Handling Service." Paper presented to 14th Annual Meeting of Appalachian Studies Conference, Berea, Ky., 23 Mar. 1991.

Schwarz, Berthold E. "Ordeal by Serpents, Fire, and Strychnine." *Psychiatric Quarterly* 34 (1960): 405-29. Rpt. in *Appalachian Images in Folk and Popular Culture*. Ed. W. K. McNeil. Ann Arbor: UMI Research Press, 1989.

Scott, Bob. "Sister: Prince's Forgotten Prayers Led to Death." *Asheville Citizen* 30 Aug. 1985: 1-2.

———. "Snake Handler Buried." *Asheville Citizen* 23 Aug. 1985: 1, 7.

———. "Snake Handler Struck By Rattler; Dies From Bite." *Asheville Citizen* 20 Aug. 1985: 1-2.

———. "Snake Handlers, Lawmen Clash: Deputies Seize Boxes of Poisonous Snakes." *Asheville Citizen* 1985: 1, 9. Burton Collection.

———. "Snake Handlers Say They'll Move on to States Where Handling is Legal." *Asheville Citizen* 5 Aug. 1985: 3.

———. "Topton Woman Gives Insider's View of Snake-Handling Practices." *Asheville Citizen-Times* 22 July 1991: Al, 3.

———. "Worshippers Take Up Snakes in the Name of the Lord." *Asheville Citizen-Times* 7 July 1985: A1, 5.

Scott, Donald F. "Ordeal by Fire." *The Psychology of Fire.* New York: Scribner, 1974. 67-75.

"Second Snake Taken From Colonel Bunn." *Durham Morning Herald* 9 Nov. 1947, sec. 1: 1.

"Seizure Of Snakes Fails To Stop Cult Meetings." *Durham Morning Herald* 3 Nov. 1947, sec. 1: 3.

"Sermon on Snakes and Religion." *Chattanooga News* 28 Sept. 1914: 3.

"Serpent-Handling Preacher Here, Bitten by Deadly Snake, Refuses Medical Attention, Says 'Faith Will Heal' Him of Poisonous Venom." *Knoxville News-Sentinel* 3 July 1940: 1.

"Sheriff Released From the Hospital." *The Mountaineer* (Waynesville, N.C.) 12 Aug. 1985: 1+.

"Signs Following Believers." *White Wing Messenger* (Church of God of Prophesy, Cleveland, Tenn.). 24 Nov. 1945: 2, 4.

Simpkins, O. Norman. *An Informal, Incomplete Introduction to Appalachian Culture.* Huntington, W.Va.: Marshall Univ. Press, 1971.

Sims, Patsy. "Acts of Faith: The Charmed Lives of Snake Handlers." *TDC* (publication of Discovery Channel) May 1991: 34-41.

———. *Can Somebody Shout Amen?* New York: St. Martins, 1988.

Slater, Irwin H. "Strychnine, Picnotoxin, Pentylenetetrazol, and Miscellaneous Drugs." *Drill's Pharmacology in Medicine.* Ed. Joseph R. DiPalma. 4th ed. New York: McGraw, 1971. 517-32.

Smartt, Vaughn. "Snake Cult Jury Split 6-6; Mistrial of 12 is Expected." *Chattanooga Daily Times* 13 Nov. 1947: 1-2.

Smith, Charles R. *Tongues in Biblical Perspective.* 2d ed. Winona Lake, Ind.: BMH Books, 1973.

Smith, Dave. "Snake Sermon." *Cumberland Station.* Chicago: Univ. of Illinois Press, 1976. 13.

"Snake At Service Bites 3 Cultists." *New York Times* 6 Aug. 1940: 21.

"Snake Bite Case Ends in Mistrial." *The Birmingham News* 14 Sept. 1961: n.p.

"Snake Bite Faith Test Called Mockery of God." *New York Times* 13 Aug. 1934: 30.

"Snake Bite Fatal to Dolly Pond Preacher During Rite in Georgia." *Chattanooga News-Free Press* 13 Aug. 1954: 1.

"Snake Bite Is Fatal to Cultist; Another Struck Down by Rattler." *Chattanooga Times* 27 Aug. 1946: 9.

"Snake Bite Kills Church Member." *Johnson City* (Tenn.) *Press Chronicle* 31 Jan. 1989: 13.

"Snake Bite Kills Sect Member." *New York Times* 31 Aug. 1955: 27.

"Snake Bites Man And Dies." *New York Times* 23 July 1945: 21.

"Snake Bites Sheriff at Religious Service." *Knoxville News-Sentinel* 5 Aug. 1985: A6.

"Snake Cult Case Called Mistrial." *Chattanooga Times* 14 Nov. 1947: 3.

"Snake Cult Facing Legislative Prohibition in State." *Louisville Courier-Journal* 5 Mar. 1940, sec. 2: 1.

"Snake Cult Opens Church on Sunday." *Chattanooga Times* 13 Dec. 1947: 3.

"Snake Cult Preacher Arrested; Refuses, Then Consents to Bond." *Chattanooga Times* 18 June 1954: 22.

"Snake Cultist Hearing Passed Till Tomorrow." *Chattanooga Times* 24 Aug. 1948: 3.

"Snake Custodian, Chided by Pastor at Farewell Demonstration, Thrusts Copperhead Down Throat." *Knoxville News-Sentinel* 25 Sept. 1939, home ed., 12.

"Snake Defiers Jailed." *New York Times* 1 Aug. 1940: 18.

"Snake Expert Warns People Preacher's Rattlers Poisonous." *Tampa Morning Tribune* 11 Mar. 1936: 7.

"Snake Handler Answers to 'Highest Law.'" *Maryville-Alcoa Daily Times* 12 Aug. 1985: 1.

"Snake Handler Bitten at Church Service." *Knoxville News-Sentinel* 17 June 1971: 41.

"Snake Handler Church Burned, Sheriff Hunts Arson Suspects." *Chattanooga News-Free Press* 12 July 1954: 1.

"Snake Handler Didn't Pray Before Handling Rattler, Sister Says." *News and Observer* (Raleigh) 31 Aug. 1985: A17.

"Snake Handler Dies of Bite, As His Father-in-law Did." *New York Times* 23 Oct. 1974: 48.

"Snake Handler Dies of Snakebite in Church." *Johnson City* (Tenn.) *Press* 16 July 1991: 10.

"Snake Handler Gets Suspended Sentence." *Knoxville News-Sentinel* 4 Sept. 1985: B5.

"Snake Handler Says 'Higher Law' Makes Him Handle Reptiles." *Johnson City* (Tenn.) *Press-Chronicle* 14 Aug. 1985: 14.

"Snake Handler Still Hospitalized." *Kingsport Times-News* 23 Nov. 1988: B3.

"Snake Handlers Back: One Believer Bitten." *Kingsport Times-News* 18 June 1971: 1.

"Snake Handler's Church is Burned." *Chattanooga Times* 13 July 1954: 9.

"Snake Handlers Fined $150 Each; One Appeals." *The Birmingham News* 10 May 1956: 55.

"Snake Handlers of Georgia, Kentucky to Attend Trial Here; Snakes Barred." *Chattanooga Times* 12 Nov. 1947: 1-2.

"Snake Handlers Undaunted." *Asheville Citizen* 10 Sept. 1985: 1.

"Snake Handling." *Christian Century* 102 (1985): 857.

"Snake Handling: A Discussion of the Death of a Preacher Who Was Bitten." *Knoxville News-Sentinel* 8 Sept. 1985: E4.

"Snake Handling: A Ritual as Old as the Hills." *Johnson City* (Tenn.) *Press-Chronicle* 22 July 1973: 44.

"Snake Handling at Church Continues." *Knoxville News-Sentinel* 18 Sept. 1939, home ed., 11.

"Snake Handling Evangelist Dead from Rattler Bite." *Daily Times* (Greeneville, Tenn.) 20 Aug. 1985: 15.

"Snake Handling Fading." *Kingsport Times-News* 29 July 1990: A7.

"Snake Handling Film in Kingsport." *Johnson City* (Tenn.) *Press-Chronicle* 2 Nov. 1973: 2.

"Snake Handling: Man Says N.C. Law Keeps Him From Practicing Religion." Newspaper article, n.d. Burton Collection.

"Snake Handling Preachers May Be Returned to Jail." Newspaper article, n.d. Burton Collection.

"Snake Head Torn Off to Climax Sunday Meeting at Ramsey." *Coalfield Progress* (Norton, Va.) 22 Aug. 1935: 1.

"Snake Kills Cultist." *New York Times* 26 July 1955: 12.

"Snake Ordinance Upheld: Bunn Says He Will Take Issue to Federal Court." *Durham Morning Herald* 8 Jan. 1949: 3.

"Snake Power." *Time*. 1 Nov. 1968: 86.

"'Snake' Preachers Released on Bond." *Chattanooga Times* 28 Sept. 1945: 10.

"Snake Proves Faithless." *Cincinnati Enquirer* 16 Aug. 1931.

"Snake Rites Get Protest." *Chattanooga News-Free Press* 14 Aug. 1959: 1.

"Snake Sect Prays for Jail Doors to Open." *Louisville Courier-Journal* 10 Sept. 1940: 7.

"Snake Services Bring Comments." *Asheville Citizen-Times* 1 Sept. 1985: D3.

"Snake Tests Barred to Preacher's Son." *New York Times* 2 Sept. 1934, sec. 2: 1.

"Snake Trials of Five Here Continued Until Oct. 28; Large Group in Court." *Durham Morning Herald* 20 Oct. 1948, sec. 2: 1.

"Snake-Bite Preacher Gets a Call to Akron; Says Serpent Was Sent to Open World to Him." *New York Times* 19 Aug. 1934: 9.

"Snakebite Victim at Church is Dead." *Chattanooga Times* 10 Aug. 1948: 3.

"Snake-Bitten Child Remains Untreated." *New York Times* 3 Aug. 1940: 28.

"Snakebitten Man Still on Critical List." Newspaper article, n.d. July 1973. Burton Collection.

"Snakebitten Preacher Dies; Listed as Suicide for Shunning Medicine." *Chattanooga Times* 26 July 1955: 3, 11.

"Snakehandler Case Opens as Statute Case." *Chattanooga News-Free Press* 12 Nov. 1947: 5.

"Snakehandler Declines Offer [of Geisha Girl bathhouse]." Newspaper article, n.d. Burton Collection.

"Snake-Handlers Meet Again; Bunn Says Law 'Crazy Idea.'" *Durham Morning Herald* 27 Oct. 1947, sec. 1: 1-2.

"Snakehandler's Relative Says 'It Was A Horrible Death.'" *Greeneville* (Tenn.)*Sun* 20 Aug. 1985: 1, 7.

"Snake-Handling Ban." *Church and State* 29.5 (1976): 22 (110).

"Snake-Handling Cultists Resemble Other Groups." *Science News Letter* 17 Aug. 1949: 103.

"Snake-Handling Preacher Convicted." *Atlanta Journal-Constitution* 13 Feb. 1992: A3.

"Snakehandling Preachers Pay Fines, Freed." Newspaper article, n.d. Burton Collection.

"Snake-Handling Religious Rites." *Awake!* (publication of Jehovah's Witnesses) 8 Nov. 1962: 5-8.

"Snake-Handling Ruling Stirs Encroachment Cry." *Bristol* (Tenn.) *Herald-Courier* 21 Sept. 1975: A10.

"Snake-Handling Sect Asks Court for Protection." *Louisville Courier-Journal* 22 Aug. 1940, sec. 1: 11.

"Snake Handling Sect Prays For Jail Doors to Fall." *Louisville Courier-Journal* 9 Sept. 1940, sec. 1: 2.

"Snake-Handling Trial Postponed to Oct. 20." *Chattanooga Times* 12 Oct. 1947: 3.

"Snake-Rite Leaders Fast." *New York Times* 4 Aug. 1940: 31.

"Snakes Banned at Small Church." *Johnson City* (Tenn.) *Press-Chronicle* 22 Apr. 1973: 3.

"Snakes Handled at Burials of Strychnine Victims." *Newport* (Tenn.) *Plain Talk* 13 Apr. 1973: 1, 3.

"Snakes in Demand: Church of God Adopts New Stunts to Prove Presence 'The Power.'" *Cleveland* (Tenn.) *Herald* 17 Sept. 1914: 1.

"Snakes Kill Preacher." *New York Times* 1 Oct. 1936: 15.

"Snakes Part of Church's Faith" (Powells Crossroads, Ala. AP). Newspaper article, n.d. Burton Collection.

"Snakes Passed During Revival: Handlers Active Again in South Carolina." *Chattanooga News-Free Press* 8 July 1953: 25.

Snead, Bill. "For Heaven's Snakes." *Washington Post* 15 Sept. 1991: F1, 4.

———. "The Last Temptation of Brother Ray." *Washington Post* 15 Dec. 1991: F1, 10.

Soesbee, Gilbert. "Cocke Co. Native Dies of Snake Bite." *Newport* (Tenn.) *Plain Talk* 15 July 1991: 1.

Stagg, Frank. *Glossolalia*. Nashville: Abingdon, 1967.

Stansky, Rod. "The Historical and Theological Development of Snake Handling." Unpublished paper, 1984. Burton Collection.

Stanton, Al, and Gray Gabel. "Refuses Aid Despite Pain—Ft. Payne Handler Bitten by Snake." *The Birmingham News* 30 Apr. 1956: 1, 10.

Stark, Rodney. "A Taxonomy of Religious Experience." *Journal for the Scientific Study of Religion* 5 (1965): 97-116.

Stekert, Ellen. "The Snake-Handling Sect of Harlan County, Kentucky: Its Influence of Folk Tradition." *Southern Folklore Quarterly* 27 (1963): 316-22.

Sternfield, Jonathan. *Firewalk: The Psychology of Physical Immunity*. Great Barrington, Mass.: Burkshire House, 1990.

Stone, W.F. "States Power to Require an Individual to Protect Himself." *Washington and Lee Law Review* 26(1969): 112-19.

Stuart, Jesse. *Daughter of the Legend.* New York: McGraw, 1965.

Sturtevant, William. "Categories, Percussion, and Physiology." *Man* 3 (1968): 133-34.

Summer, William Graham. *Folkways.* New York: Mentor, 1960.

"Supreme Court Actions." *New York Times* 9 Mar. 1976: 19.

"Supreme Court Refuses to Hear Appeal of Bunn." *Durham Morning Herald* 5 Apr. 1949: 1.

"Supreme Court Refuses to Review Decision Against Snake Handling." *Chattanooga Times* 9 Mar. 1976: 1.

"Surgery Lowers Swelling in Snakebitten Man's Arm." *Chattanooga News-Free Press* 3 July 1973: 1.

Sweet, William Warren. *Religion in the Development of American Culture.* New York: Scribner's, 1952.

Synan, Vinson. *The Holiness-Pentecostal Movement in the United States.* Grand Rapids, Mich.: Eerdmans, 1971.

"Take Sect's Snakes Alive." *New York Times* 6 Aug. 1945: 17.

"Taking Up Rattlesnakes in the Name of Jesus." *Native Stone* (Asheville, N.C.) 5 July 1973: 1-5.

Taulieb, Paul. "Snake Church." *US* 18 July 1983: 34-36.

Taylor, A. W. "Snake-Handling Cults Flourish." *Christian Century* 64 (Oct. 1947): 1308.

Taylor, Howard. "Beware the Snake." *Bristol* (Tenn.) *Herald Courier* 6 Jan. 1974: C1, 4.

Tellegen, Auke, et al. "Personality Characteristics of a Serpent-Handling Religious Cult." *MMPI— Research Developments and Clinical Applications.* Ed. James M. Butcher. New York: McGraw, 1969. 221-42.

"Ten Cultists Ruled Guilty." *Chattanooga Times* 12 Feb. 1948: 1.

"Tennessee Preacher, Virginia Woman Die of Snake Bites in Rites of Religious Sect." *New York Times* 5 Sept. 1945: 25.

"Tennessee Snake Handlers Seized." *New York Times* 24 Sept. 1945: 10.

"Tester Had 'Call' To Let Snake Bite." *New York Times* 13 Aug. 1934: 30.

"Testing of Faith Kills Two." *Johnson City* (Tenn.) *Press-Chronicle* 10 Apr. 1973: 9.

" . . . They Shall Take Up Serpents." *Knoxville News-Sentinel* 10 Dec. 1984: A1.

"They Shall Take Up Serpents." *Newsweek* 21 Aug. 1944: 88-89.

"They Shall Take Up Serpents . . . " *St. Louis Post-Dispatch* 18 Mar. 1973: 32, 37-39.

"3rd Snake Cultist Dies in Cleveland." *Chattanooga Times* 3 Sept. 1946: 15.

Thomas, Jean. *Blue Ridge Country.* New York: Duell, 1942.

Thompson, Escar. "Court Tells Preacher to Stop Handling Snakes in Church." *Chattanooga News-Free Press* 22 Apr. 1972: A4.

"Three Accused—Snake Handlers Trial is Slated Here on May 9." *The Birmingham News* 1 May 1956: 23.

Tomlinson, A. J. *A. J. Tomlinson, God's Anointed Prophet of Wisdom: Choice Writings of A. J. Tomlinson in Times of His Greatest Anointings.* 2d ed. Cleveland, Tenn.: White Wing Publishing House, 1970.

———. *Historical Annual Addresses.* Cleveland, Tenn.: White Wing Publishing House, 1970.

Tomlinson, Homer. *Amazing Fulfillments of Prophecy.* Cleveland, Tenn.: White Wing Publishing House, 1934.

———, ed. *Diary of A. J. Tomlinson.* Queen's Village, N.Y.: Church of God, World Headquarters, 1949-55.

———. *Journal of Happenings: The Diary of A. J. Tomlinson, March 7, 1901-November 3, 1923.* Typed copy in Tomlinson College Library, Cleveland, Tenn.

———. *The Shout of a King*. New York: Church of God, U.S.A. Headquarters, 1968.

Travis, Fred. "Bradley Baffled by Snake Problem." *Chattanooga Times* 28 Aug. 1946: 9.

"Trenton Snake Handler is Dead, Bitten During Ft. Payne Service." *Chattanooga Times* 15 June 1954: 9.

"Trial of Five North Alabama Snake Handlers Postponed for Decision of Appeals Court." *Chattanooga News-Free Press* 16 Sept. 1954: 2.

Tripp, Peggy S. and Kirk W. Elifson. "Death By Serpent Bite Among a Religious Sect: A Sociological Interpretation." Paper presented at Annual Proceedings of American Sociological Association, New York, 1976.

———. "Deviant Beliefs and Persecution: The Case of Serpent Handlers." Paper presented to American Sociological Association, 1977.

"2 Die After Drinking Strychnine During Services at Holiness Church." *Cocke County* (Tenn.) *Banner* 9 Apr. 1973: 1.

"Two Holiness Church Members Dead After Taking Strychnine." *Newport* (Tenn.) *Plain Talk* 9 Apr. 1973: 1, 3.

"Two Snake Handlers Receive $50 Fines and Costs Each in Court." *Durham Morning Herald* 19 Oct. 1948, sec. 2: 1.

Valentine, Charles A. *Culture and Poverty: Critique and Counter Proposals*. Chicago: Univ. of Chicago Press, 1968.

Van Hoorebeke, Kala. "The Rhetorical Paradigm in the Service of the Snake Handling Cult." Master's thesis, Western Illinois Univ., 1980.

Vance, Paul. "A History of Serpent Handlers in Georgia, North Alabama, and Southeastern Tennessee." Master's thesis, Georgia State Univ., 1975.

"Vigorous Rattler Replaces Worn-Out Copper at Church." *Knoxville News-Sentinel* 27 Sept. 1939: 1.

Vines, Carla A. "3 Ministers Defy Injunction Forbidding Snake Handling." *Chattanooga News-Free Press* 21 Apr. 1973: 2.

"Virginia Snake-Handling Law To Be Tested." *Mountain Life & Work* Nov. 1968: 22.

Waddey, John. "Bible Records No Snake-handling Services." Letter. *Knoxville News-Sentinel* 16 Dec. 1984.

"Walter Henry, 51, Bitten by Rattler." *Chattanooga News-Free Press* 26 Aug. 1946: 2.

"Wanted—Poison Serpents for Church Services." *Newport* (Tenn.) *Plain Talk* Classified sec. 31 May 1972.

Warburton, T. Rennie. "Holiness Religion: An Anomaly of Sectarian Typologies." *Journal for the Scientific Study of Religion* 8.1 (1969): 130-39.

Watson, Burke. "Alley's Sympathetic Play About Snake-Handlers Has Inflamed Some Cities." *Houston Chronicle* 7 May 1983: 31.

Watterlond, Michael. "The Holy Ghost People." *Science 83*, vol. 30 (May 1983): 50-57.

"Wave Rattler in Frenzy." *New York Times* 19 Aug. 1935: 17.

Weatherford, W. D., and Earl Brewer. *Life and Religion in Southern Appalachia*. New York: Friendship Press, 1962.

Webber, Joel F. "Snake Facts and Fiction." *Texas Game and Fish* May 1951: 12-13, 30.

Weisberger, Bernard A. *They Gathered at the River: The Story of the Great Revivalists and Their Impact Upon Religion in America*. Boston: Little, 1958.

Weller, Jack E. "Salvation is not Enough." *Mountain Life and Work* 4.5 (1969): 9-13.

———. *Yesterday's People*. Lexington: Univ. of Kentucky Press, 1966.

"West Virginia a Refuge for Snake-Handling Sect." *Houston Chronicle* 23 Oct. 1983.

White, Gayle. "They Take Up Serpents with Faith 'Good Enough to Die By.'" *Atlanta Constitution* 16 Apr. 1990: B1, 4.

Wigginton, Elliot. "The People Who Take Up Serpents." *Foxfire 7*. Ed. Paul Gillespie. Garden City, New York: Anchor-Doubleday, 1982. 370-428.

Wilburn, Eliza. "Hall Says Ike May Get Case." *Chattanooga News-Free Press* 23 June 1954: 7.

———. "Preacher Dies of Snake Bite." *Chattanooga News-Free Press* 15 Aug. 1955: 1.

———. "Six Face Charges—DeKalb Religious Snake Handlers Under Indictment." *The Birmingham News* 20 July 1954: 23.

———. "Snake Handler Convicted and Fined $50 and Costs." *The Birmingham News* 16 Sept. 1954: 6.

Wilson, Bryan R. "The Pentecostal Minister: Role Conflicts and Status Contradictions." *American Journal of Sociology* 64 (1959): 494-504.

———. "The Pentecostal Movement." *Religious Sects*. New York: World Univ. Library, 1970. 66-92.

Wilson, John. "Doc Walls, Snake Provider at Church Rite, Coming Here." *Chattanooga News-Free Press* 12 July 1973: 1+.

"Woman, Bitten at Wake, Dies." *Knoxville News-Sentinel* 14 Feb. 1986.

"Woman Refuses Aid in Snakebite." *Chattanooga Times* 20 June 1962: 11.

Womeldorf, J. A. "Rattlesnake Religion." *Christian Century* 64 (Dec. 1947): 1517-18.

Wood, William W. *Cultural and Personality Aspects of the Pentecostal Holiness Religion*. The Hague: Mouton, 1965.

Yardley, Jim. "Mark of the Serpent: Southerners Cling to Deadly Practice." *Atlanta Journal-Constitution* 9 Feb. 1992: M1.

———. "Poison and the Pulpit." *Atlanta Journal-Constitution* 9 Feb. 1992: M1, 6.

Yinger, J. M.. "Religion and Social Change: Functions and Dysfunctions of Sects and Cults Among the Disprivileged." *Review of Religious Research* 4 (1962): 65-84.

———. *The Scientific Study of Religion*. New York: Macmillan, 1970.

———. *Sociology Looks at Religion*. New York: Macmillan, 1963.

Zaretsky, Irving I., and Mark P. Leone, eds. *Religious Movements in Contemporary America*. Princeton: Princeton Univ. Press, 1974.

Films, Videos, and Records

"ABC News with Peter Jennings." 15 Dec. 1986. Television program, 30 min. Segment on serpent handling in North Georgia, North Carolina, Tennessee, and West Virginia, 4 min.

Bagwell, Wendy. *Here Comes the Rattlesnakes*. Caanan Records. Waco, Texas, FS-715, n.d.

"Brother Roy Healing and Casting-Out-Devils." Madison, Tenn. By Eleanor Dickinson. 1980. Video, color, 30 min.

Cape Fear. Dir. Martin Scorsese. Universal, 1991.

"Carson Springs: A Decade Later." Prod. Thomas G. Burton and Thomas F. Headley. East Tennessee State Univ., 1983. Video, 3/4" U-Matic and VHS, 29 min.

"Chase the Devil." Channel 4 (UK). 1982. Television program. Segment on serpent handling.

Dickinson, Eleanor. *Southern Revival Services*. Library of Congress, Archive of Folk Song, Audio and Video Tape Collection #14,079+; 1968 to present.

Discovery Channel program. Yorkshire Television, 1986. Feature on the Church of the Lord Jesus, Jolo, W.Va..

Faces of Death. Prod. Rosilyn T. Scott. Video. 1979. F.O.D. Productions. 2 min. feature.

"False Gods: Snake Church." "A Current Affair," Fox Broadcasting Co. 28 June 1990. Television program. Segment, 8 min.

"Fire and Serpent Handlers." Videotaped by Wayne Barrett. East Tennessee State Univ., Archives of Appalachia. Reels 134A, 134B, 3/4" U-Matic, black-and-white, 50 min. each. Dubbed on "Cable Snake Video." Burton-Headly Collection. Series B, Tape 30. 3/4" U-Matic and VHS, black-and-white, 60 min.

"Following the Signs: A Way of Conflict." Prod. Thomas G. Burton and Thomas F. Headley. East Tennessee State Univ., 1987. Video, 3/4" U-Matic and VHS, 29 min.

"Geraldo." Tribune Entertainment. 4 Oct. 1991. Television program. Interviews with Dewey Chafin and Anna Prince.

Hearst Collection, UCLA Film and Television Archive. General newsreel footage of religious serpent handlers.

"The Holiness People of West Virginia." By Eleanor Dickinson. 1978. Video, 30 min.

"Holy Ghost People." Prod. Blair Boyd and Peter Adair. Adair Films. CRM/McGraw-Hill Films, 1968. Video, 3/4" U-Matic, black-and-white, 53 min.

"I Believe: Religion in the Tennessee Valley." WDEF-TV, Chattanooga, 1989. Video, VHS, 3 min.

The Jolo Serpent Handlers. By Karen Kramer. Karen Kramer Films, New York, 1977. Film, 16 mm, 40 min.

"Lifesense—Snakes." BBC Natural History Unit, 1991. Television program. Feature on the use of serpents in the Church of the Lord Jesus, Jolo, W.Va.

"The Lord's Supper, Footwashing, and Baptism in the Holston River." By Eleanor Dickinson. 1980. Video, color, 8 min.

"Music in the Southern Appalachian Mountains." By Eleanor Dickinson. 1978. Video, 30 min.

Night of the Hunter. With Richard Chamberlain, Diana Scarwid, and Burgess Meredith. Made for ABC-TV Production, 1991. 120 min.

Paramount newsreel. Unreleased footage from the 1950s with George Hensley's name on the index. Film Libraries, Inc., Sherman Grinberg, New York.

The People Who Take Up Serpents. By Gretchen Robinson. Independent Southern Films, Greenville, S.C., 1979. Film, 16 mm.

"Poison Pulpit." WSB-TV, Atlanta, 1991. Television program on services at the Church of the Lord Jesus, Rome, Georgia, including interviews with Carl Porter and Junior McCormick.

Program on the Church of the Lord Jesus, Jolo, W.Va. WJLA-TV, Washington. Television program, n.d.

"Real Time in West Virginia with Four Holiness People." By Eleanor Dickinson. 1978. Video, black-and-white, 35 min.

"Revival!" By Eleanor Dickinson. 1980. Video, black-and-white and color, 30+ min.

"Saga of the Serpent Handlers." WVLC-TV, Charleston, W.Va., 1981. Three television programs. Prod. with Mary Lee Daugherty by West Virginia Library Commission Video Services, Charleston.

"Sally Jessy Raphael." Multimedia Entertainment. NBC-TV. 23 Mar. 1992. Television program. Interviews with Darlene Summerford and sister-in-law Charlotte.

The Serpent and the Rainbow. Dir. Wes Craven. Universal, 1988.

"The Serpent Handlers: Jolo, West Virginia." Prod. H. Thomas Mullis and Edward D. Jervey. Bureau of Telecommunications, Radford Univ., 1988. 3/4" U-Matic.

"Six Short Tapes on Various Aspects of the Revival Movement." By Eleanor Dickinson. 1980. Video, black-and-white and color, 30+ min.

"Snake Handlers Digest." By Allen Muse and Milton McClurken. WTVF-TV, Nashville, July 1973. Television program, 15 min.

"Snakehandling O'Sheas." *Saturday Night Live.* Television program, 5 min. Satiric segment.

"Test of Faith." WWVA-TV, Bluefield, West Virgina. Three-part television series.

"They Shall Take Up Serpents." *Montage.* Series. Prod. Scott Siegler. WKYC-TV, Cleveland, Ohio. Film, 16 mm, 24 min.

They Shall Take Up Serpents. Prod. Thomas G. Burton and Jack Schrader. East Tennessee State Univ., 1973. Film, 16 mm, 19 min.

True Adventure. Prod. Bill Burrud. Television program from series. Prod. 1960-61; includes newsreel footage of handling fire by Raymond Hays. Burton Collection.

True Believers. KPIX, San Francisco, 1990. Television program. Segment on serpent handling, 6 min., 30 sec.

"What's Up America?" *Showtime*. Syndicated series. East Tennessee State Univ., Archives of Appalachia. Burton-Headley Collection. Series B, Tape 29, Accession #227. Video, 3/4" U-Matic, 12 min.

Legal References

State Codes

Florida State Codes 372.86, .88-.91, .912, .921. 1971.

Georgia State Code. 27-5-4. 1968.

Kentucky State Code. 437.060. 1940.

North Carolina State Codes. 14-416-418, 421-422. 1949; 14-419-420. 1981.

Tennessee State Code. 39-17-101. 1989.

Virginia State Code. 18.2-313. 1950, Rev. 1960 and 1975.

Court Cases

Harden v. State of Tennessee. 216 S.W. 2d 708. Supreme Court of Tennessee. 1948.

Harris v. Harris. 343 So. 2d 762. Supreme Court of Mississippi. 1972.

Hill v. State. 88 So. 2d 880. Court of Appeals of Alabama. 1956.

Kirk v. Commonwealth. 44 S.E. 2d 409. Supreme Court of Appeals of Virginia. 1947.

Lawson et al. v. Commonwealth. 164 S.W. 2d 972. Court of Appeals of Kentucky. 1942.

Sherbert v. Verner et al., Members of South Carolina Employment Security Commission, et al. 374 U.S. Appeal from the Supreme Court of South Carolina. 1963.

State of Tennessee v. Pack. Court of Appeals for Tennessee. Eastern Section. 1974.

State of Tennessee v. Pack. 527 S.W. 2d 99. Supreme Court of Tennessee. 1975.

State v. Massey et al. 51 S.E. 2d 179. Supreme Court of North Carolina. 1949.

**And
these
signs
shall
follow**

Index

Serpent-Handling Believers was designed and composed by Kay Jursik at The University of Tennessee Press on the Apple MacIntosh using Microsoft Word® and Aldus PageMaker®. Linotronic camera pages were generated by Typecase, Inc. The book is set in Goudy Oldstyle and is printed on 60# Glatfelter B-16 paper. Manufactured in the United States of America by Thomson-Shore, Inc.